D0762014

3 0700 10862 6564

Dickens Redressed

DICKENS REDRESSED

The Art of *Bleak House* and *Hard Times*

ALEXANDER WELSH

Yale University Press   New Haven and London

Printed in the United States of America.

Library of Congress Cataloging-in-Publication Data
Welsh, Alexander.
Dickens redressed : the art of Bleak house and Hard times /
Alexander Welsh.
p.   cm.
Includes bibliographical references (p.) and index.
IBSN 0-300-08203-7 (cloth : alk paper)
1. Dickens, Charles, 1812-1870. Bleak House.   2. Dickens, Charles,
1812-1870. Hard times.   3. Satire, English—History and criticism.
4. Social problems in literature.   I. Title.
PR4556 .W45   2000
823'.8—dc21   99-087254

A catalogue record for this book is
available from the British Library.

The paper in this book meets the guidelines
for permanence and durability of the Committee
on Production Guidelines for Book Longevity of
the Council on Library Resources.

10 9 8 7 6 5 4 3 2 1

For Dickens readers right and left

Contents

Acknowledgments

So many useful things have been written about Dickens and his work that it is nearly impossible to keep up with the scholarship on the subject. My indebtedness to other critics is recorded, to the best of my ability, in the notes at the end of this book. Scholars who have painstakingly edited the novels—in this case Sylvère Monod and the late George Ford—deserve special thanks. The editing of Dickens's letters by Graham Storey, Kathleen Tillotson, and others has been acclaimed by many. In my first chapter I draw upon one of my own grateful reviews, in *Modern Philology*, of their work. The argument comparing Dickens to Mill on the nature of facts and the role of art stems from an invitation by Patrick Brantlinger, on behalf of the Midwest Victorian Association and the editors of *Victorian Studies*, to speak at their conference on information a few years ago. Ruth Bernard Yeazell has again been a faithful reader of my drafts and has generously shared many thoughts about Dickens. Diane Repak and Audrey Healy, with invaluable technical assistance from Imraan Coovadia, brilliantly executed the final draft. I also thank Timothy Peltason and a second reader for the Yale University Press for their good advice. No author could ask for more helpful editors than Lara Heimert and Susan Laity.

AN INTRODUCTION

One would think that *Bleak House* and *Hard Times,* about to celebrate the sesquicentennials of their original appearances, need no introduction. The first is perhaps more frequently alluded to in news stories and opinion pages than any novel except *Don Quixote;* the second, because of its brevity and its famous schoolroom scene, is familiar to young and old. My favorite clipping from the *Bleak House* file is this oblique notice from Newt Gingrich, as reported by the *New York Times* on 5 January 1995:

> Referring to his controversial statement that children of teen-age mothers on welfare should be put in orphanages—a statement that he said had been distorted and cheapened—Mr. Gingrich said: "My father, who's here today, was a foster child who was adopted as a teen-ager. I am adopted. We have relatives who are adopted. We are not talking out of some vague, impersonal, Dickens, Bleak House, middle-class, intellectual model. We have lived the alternatives."

If I understand Gingrich, *Bleak House* is a sort of icon for the intelligentsia, from whom he wishes to dissociate himself on this occasion. Among university-educated people the novel often stands for all of Dickens, or they refer to it appreciatively because of its send-up of the system, its attack on lawyers and politicians, and its compassion for the homeless. Gingrich waves that all away as a mere fiction. At the same time, in this interview, he unconsciously resembles that great clown of *Hard Times,* the self-made Mr. Bounderby.

I am not the first to devote a book to *Bleak House,* and in her recent *Poetic Justice,* Martha C. Nussbaum gives about three chapters to *Hard Times.* Nussbaum's idea of this novel may be somewhat strained, because she wants it to be representative of novels in general, and it is untypical even for Dickens. But as a moral philosopher she has in the past used novels by Henry James and others not merely to illustrate a point here and there but to teach ethics. The subtitle of her book is "The Literary Imagination and Public Life," and she believes it would be well if we all—as individuals, communities, even governments—treated individuals with the respect for their different life stories that novels show. Nussbaum is no Gingrich; for her, fancy sometimes serves better than fact. If anything, she renders Dickens more sentimental than he is, as she amplifies what she deems to be the lessons *Hard Times* offers. The hypnotic effect of Mr. Gradgrind in the novel is such that, while reversing the direction of that gentleman's questions in M'Choakumchild's schoolroom, she adopts a similar procedure of her own:

> In my law school class, when we reached this point in the novel, before I made any observations of my own about fancy, I decided to ask my students about nursery rhymes: why did Dickens attach such importance to them? I called on a dark-haired student in the second row who had said little in the class so far, though what he said was especially thoughtful. Mr. Riley, I said, did you ever sing "Twinkle, twinkle little star?" Yes, Mr. Riley had. What did you think about when you sang that song? Do you remember how it made you feel?

Though fact and fancy have changed places, those questions would make me squirm. Nussbaum herself remarks that "asking such questions in the University of Chicago Law School might be thought to be as odd as bringing Sleary's circus into the Gradgrind schoolroom." But like Ms. Jupe in the novel, Mr. Riley rises to the occasion.

The words of the Speaker of the House of Representatives and the professor of law and ethics are obviously not calculated statements about Dickens. For that very reason they attest to the continuing impact of *Bleak House* and *Hard Times*. It may be true that most people today first encounter the novels in school or college English classes: they are, after all, difficult as well as pleasurable to read. *Hard Times* can be read by children, but I confess that for me, as perhaps for Nussbaum, it is more difficult to come to terms with than its far more weighty forerunner. The two are the first of six completed novels of Dickens's later career, the period most celebrated by academic critics. Yet much late-twentieth-century criticism would suggest that these novels are somehow complicit in the very conditions they attack, or enclosed by the language with which they are written. I have long held that literature has to be appreciated historically and that literature indeed shapes as well as responds to the broader culture of which it is a part. But the idea that novels do just what the times require or language constrains them to do is a half-truth at best. If the idea were strictly true, it would be wholly uninteresting. It ignores that Dickens—in the present instance—wrote precisely those novels that others did not write and thus shortchanges his achievement—when it doesn't place him in the pillory outright. It distorts the way novels are ordinarily perceived, as productions of a particular author hoping for as many readers and rereaders as possible. For better or worse—that is, for pleasure and instruction or disgust and bafflement—*Bleak House* and *Hard*

Times are Dickens's deliberately made stories as communicated in print.

The midpoint of the nineteenth century was the midpoint of a writing career spanning forty years, during which the author had the advantages and disadvantages of being famous from the start. *The Personal History of David Copperfield* was completed in 1850, and Dickens's father died early the following year. And undoubtedly both the fine autobiographical novel and the personal loss had their public effect: contemporaries professed to be less happy with the novels that followed. Yet *Bleak House*, the first of these novels, was the most ambitious to date and uniquely composed of two distinct narratives. For one narrative Dickens adopted the method of his *Copperfield*— and in the widest sense, the plot—but in the process redressed himself as a woman. These days we would say that the author cross-dressed as Esther Summerson, his new narrator. I prefer the idea of redressing because it preserves so many more of the root meanings of the verb, from the Latin *dirigere*, to direct. Dickens redressed and redirected himself. Personally, in fact, he was something of a dandy when it came to clothes; but he offers little or nothing about Esther's costuming in the novel. Rather, as in *Copperfield*, he redressed his protagonist's childhood, compensated for it, restored the abandoned self to love and success in life. Both first-person narratives engage in apparently uncritical wish fulfillment, in which the readership is generously invited to share.

After *The Posthumous Papers of the Pickwick Club*, his first, quixotic undertaking, almost every Dickens novel demands a modified biographical criticism, since he characteristically projected in his fiction the desires and fears and satisfactions of a single ego, the protagonist's, as if it were his own. This penchant for egocentric design, as I call it, is capable of producing an underlying psychological representation of great truth and frankness, like a revealing dream. Dickens is not at all famous as a student of character, nowhere near the company of George Eliot and Tolstoy in that respect; yet the ways in which his characters, or players in the several actions of his multiplot novels, relate to the protagonist is of great interest: David Copperfield is not without his Uriah Heep, his Agnes, and the others. Surprisingly—surprisingly because the protagonist is a woman and one-half of the narrative is initially devoted to other matters—*Bleak House* accepts nearly everything such egocentric design has to offer and puts it to new uses. *Bleak House* is *Copperfield* with an added, satiric narrative that at first dominates the novel but eventually yields to a light, and necessarily ironic, Copperfieldian maneuver. Esther Summerson's narrative quietly subsumes the other; its clever self-aggrandizement attains a modest apocalypse of its own, while the grand apocalypse awaited by the satire turns out to be a joke.

A good way to make sense of *Bleak House*, therefore, is to begin with Esther Summerson and to trace out her relationship to the other principal actors, most especially her friend Ada Clare and her mother, Lady Dedlock. The parts these two play and the sufferings they endure have far more to do with Esther's needs than with their own. The competing third-person narrative, to be sure, opens far more space to view as it lights down at will on the myriad beings, places, and institutionalized suffering of the world that surrounds the heroine. Dickens has set about redressing additional wrongs, amending the world by satirizing it in *Bleak House*. The very premise of his satire is the interconnection of the human inhabitants of London, great and small. By inventing numerous characters, setting them in motion, and letting their actions tell on one another, their author repeatedly enforces this impression of connectedness. A symbiosis between John Jarndyce and Harold Skimpole affords the most brilliant and perplexed insight of this vision: both the good man and the parasite are entranced by the systemic condition of our lives. So much, indeed, has been written by other critics on the Court of Chancery as the symbolic center of Dickens's satire that I focus here on the degradations of Tom-all-Alone's. Homelessness anywhere testifies to a kind of collective cruelty, though strange oases of kindness like George's Shooting Gallery lend perspective and allow us to think better of ourselves. In a last chapter on *Bleak House,* I explain my dissent from two influential readings by J. Hillis Miller and D. A. Miller, and there I return to the novel's divided narrative.

The satiric voice of *Bleak House* is eventually muted rather than subdued. Dickens, it seems, next goes about redressing that novel by crafting *Hard Times.* He makes amends for all that artful egocentrism by constructing a novel virtually without a hero and leaving room for little but satire. Though the most sympathetic character, Louisa Gradgrind, is again a woman, she is presented from the outside, as all the others are. The careful counterpoint of the two voices of *Bleak House* is no more to be heard. The language of *Hard Times* sometimes grates, as if Dickens were too impatient or the satire were getting the better of him. The unease may be due to his trying to cope with a more intractable social question than any he had approached thus far: the question of the just deservings of labor and capital in the new industrial age. To readers committed to either cause, the short novel must seem disappointing. But Dickens also turns toward education and the importance of the arts. He even turns upon himself, as I believe, in the sketch of Bounderby. None of these moves is wishful; the mode throughout tends to be a rather slapstick satire or else pathos. *Hard Times* may be thought of as counterapocalyptic: but the smoke and fire of Coketown are real, the author insists, even if he chooses to regard the whole place as a circus.

I began to think of the novel itself as a kind of circus after I had turned on and then switched off a 1995 BBC dramatization of *Hard Times*—a version expressly prepared for school use. The BBC played up one aspect of the novel's possible appeal to children at the expense of the other; they stressed the monstrousness of M'Choakumchild's schoolroom but not the ridiculousness. The very name of the man is funny, probably more so to a child than to an adult. Surely, I thought, the monsters in front of the class were meant to be laughed away. Yet all the clowning in *Hard Times*, which sometimes extends to the narrative manner, is difficult to assess. A clown's performance may evoke a joyful or a fearful laughter, started by empathy possibly, but released by the assured distance from the spectator. Many have supposed that Dickens, coming on strong for fancy rather than fact, was celebrating his own role as an entertainer—and indeed, the high calling of the artist. If so, he still distances the business from himself and all respectable persons by locating it in the circus. But as I also hope to show, the importance assigned to art by John Stuart Mill is not that different, though utilitarianism is supposedly under fierce attack in this novel. It may be that *Hard Times* is altogether too ambitious a work for its size. Exactly one-fourth the length of *Bleak House*, it serves well as an epilogue to that higher example of this novelist's art.

In order to say anything useful about *Bleak House* and *Hard Times*, naturally, I have often to infer something of the author's purposes. Fortunately, we know a great deal about Dickens—what kind of a man he was, whom he knew, something of what he read, nearly everything of what he wrote—and a great deal more about his times, so it is possible to think intelligently about what he was or was not up to. But I have to infer even more about his readers' possible responses, and there the evidence widely varies or is missing altogether. When I generalize about the reader of a certain passage, it does not mean that I already know what you think. It means that I am either reporting how the passage has been read or, more likely, trying to persuade you to read it the way I do.

Bleak House and Dickens

The titles of *Bleak House* and *Hard Times* told part of the story. Their harsh notes did not bode well, and Victorian reviewers rather hoped the author might serve up indefinitely the feasts of high spirits and delightful caricatures for which he was famous. In truth, most of the novels after *David Copperfield*, with their strident and sometimes baffling attacks on English society, were relatively less popular among educated readers than they are today.[1] After eight extraordinary novels and five Christmas books, the writer was conceivably too famous to please reviewers anew, whatever he might choose to write about a house or the times. At least "Bleak" and "Hard" gave fair warning.

Penned by this writer, titles of merely two syllables each were also certain to be understatements. Dickens's novels came in two sizes, depending on the mode of serialization. Novels like *Hard Times,* designed for weekly installments, could vary in length, since they typically appeared side by side with other features in an ongoing periodical. On average these are the shorter novels, whereas those published as monthly pamphlets priced at a shilling each were uniformly long: nineteen monthly numbers, including the last double number, allowed for some sixty to seventy chapters in all. The novelist became adept at matching his handwriting to the required thirty-two printed pages for each month, or almost twenty thousand words. *Bleak House,* therefore, is proportionately the shortest title in all of Dickens, with its two words of one syllable doing duty for nearly four hundred thousand words of the novel as a whole. Moreover, the dour title successfully bridged a narrative that was uniquely divided between an impersonal voice entirely in the present tense and the first-person voice of the heroine in past tense, so that the same two words necessarily applied both to the personal histories recounted in the novel and to its social project.

Dickens began in 1851 by trying out somewhat different titles, on slips of paper that are preserved with the manuscript of *Bleak House* now in the Victoria and Albert Museum. The slip bound uppermost with the manuscript proposes two titles only: "Tom-all-Alone's" and, beneath it, "The Ruined House." "Tom-all-Alone's" persists in the first position through nine slips, while changes are rung on the house, as either "Ruined" or "Solitary." On the second slip, beneath the other titles, appear "Bleak House Academy" and "The East Wind"; but "Bleak" does not appear again until the tenth and last slip, first in a longer title, "Bleak House / and the East Wind / How they both got into Chancery / and never got out," then—beneath a line drawn across the slip as if to draw up a sum—simply "Bleak House."[2] In the novel as written, "Tom-all-Alone's," the notorious slum in London, might do very nicely as a title for the social conditions initially identified with the failures of the court of Chancery; and "Bleak House," being the home of John Jarndyce and temporarily of Esther Summerson, would do very well for the personal histories unfolding there. But Dickens assimilated both titles, along with various centers of interest, public and private, and his two distinct narrative methods to a single *Bleak House*. The swift compression of the title, a poetic act in itself, reflects Dickens's confidence and daring at this time.

Bleak House, the place in the novel, is not that bleak. Mr. Jarndyce may suffer inwardly there, experiencing in the east wind the folly and suffering of humankind; but his house has become primarily a shelter and retreat, a place of order if not normalcy. Far more bleak are two other interior spaces of the novel, Sir Leicester and Lady Dedlock's Chesney Wold and the Lord Chancellor's court, both beset by depressing weather outside. Bleakest of all is the condition of the very poor in England, dying around us every day. Thus of the two words, "House" is minimal but positive, and "Bleak" is what that house must be as it reflects the housed and houseless all around. So Dickens set out to unify around this title a remarkable vision, and so for today's readers he undoubtedly succeeded. For all its scope and variety, *Bleak House* is more thoroughly pulled together—has fewer loose ends—than any other novel from his hand. His friend and biographer John Forster, who generally shared the Victorian opinion that the novels after *Copperfield* were lesser achievements, nevertheless judged *Bleak House,* "in the very important particular of construction, perhaps the best thing done by Dickens."[3]

The change from personal to impersonal titles signaled a new departure for Dickens. With a single exception—the pilgrimage of Little Nell was called *The Old Curiosity Shop,* after its mere starting place—all of the earlier novels were named for a principal character, usually the hero; and Dickens did not return to this practice until the posthumous *Mystery of Edwin Drood.* The contrast with the titles of the later novels, beginning with *Bleak House,* is especially striking as against *David Copperfield,* the autobiographical novel whose eponymous hero's initials were Charles Dickens's own in reverse. *Bleak House* thus appears to inaugurate the later period in the canon by proclaiming a fiction less egocentric than was earlier the case. If so, the turn seems well prepared for by Dickens, if never quite anticipated. Thirty-five years ago Steven Marcus argued persuasively that the novelist was still striving, in the dream visions packaged as Christmas books (1843–47), to resolve his personal feelings before he could comfortably return to the trauma of his childhood in *Copperfield* (1849–50).[4] Fifteen years ago I argued that the identity crisis, if it could be called that, derived from a disappointment more public than familial during Dickens's first visit to America, which he then projected in a hilarious survey of selfishness named *Martin Chuzzlewit* (1843–44) and a tragic study of pride named *Dombey and Son* (1846–48), before undertaking the more masterful and complacent book about a novelist with the initials D.C.[5]

Yet Dickens never quit entirely his habit and great gift of projection, even if the balance in his novels began to shift from wish fulfillment to satire. An egocentric design is still apparent in the finely self-critical redaction of *Copperfield* known as *Great Expectations,* and it returns in full form with *Our Mutual Friend,* his last completed novel, for which the eponymous title coyly omits the eponym. The novels in between are on balance more objective than subjective in construction, perhaps, yet we cannot begin to grasp the design of *Bleak House* (March 1852–September 1853) without observing which of its many characters and actions fall in with the wishes of its heroine, wishes so deeply imagined by Dickens that they can only be attributed to projection again. (The same is only a little less true of the heroes of *Little Dorrit* and *A Tale of Two Cities.*) Moreover, as I shall claim, the very purpose of objectivity in the double narrative of *Bleak House* never quite frees itself from egocentricity, unless we read *Hard Times* as the longer and grander novel's epilogue. For *Hard Times* (1 April–12 August 1854) does appear to overcome the persistent projection of the novelist or his alter ego on a large scale.

In the interval prior to the writing of *Bleak House,* the real-life novelist fended off the inevitable letdown after completing his autobiographical novel by exploiting to the full his editorial, Thespian, and social talents. A half a year before *Copperfield* was done with, in fact, Dickens had launched his own successful weekly, *Household Words.* This magazine frankly deployed

the novelist's fame ("Conducted by Charles Dickens") to pur-
vey not only fiction but human-interest features and serious
journalism on issues of the day. Its purpose, the editor wrote
to Elizabeth Gaskell, one of his first and finest contributors,
was "the raising up of those that are down, and the general improvement of our social condition."[6] To another contributor he
wrote, "All social evils, and all home affections and associations,
I am particularly anxious to deal with, well,"[7] and this expressed
dichotomy was a standard one for nineteenth-century life and
letters. In contemplating the pitch and pace of Dickens's activities in this period, one sometimes forgets the continuous effort
of managing *Household Words* and its sequel, *All the Year Round:*
soliciting, reviewing, revising or rejecting contributions, planning issues with his subeditor William Wills, reading proof—
to say nothing of writing for the magazine himself. When
the conductor was taking the needed break between novels or
deliberately staying out of London, at the seaside or on the
Continent, in order to concentrate on his novel writing, these
chores never left him. He also continued to serve, sometimes
with Wills's help, as almoner to Angela Burdett Coutts, most
notably in the home she established for reformed prostitutes in
Shepherd's Bush.

When a novel was being put to paper, Dickens disciplined
himself to write intensely in the morning. Even so, he had
to relieve his steady application to nineteen monthly installments by some changes of scene; and he required a sizable
break to struggle with the larger rhythms of intensity in imagining first one fictional world and then another. Unlike Balzac
or Thackeray, he never conceived of characters making appearances in more than one novel; hence the end of a novel was like
a death, or many deaths. Composing the end of *Copperfield* he
wrote to Forster, "I seem to be sending some part of myself into
the Shadowy World," and to Miss Coutts, "I . . . don't know

whether to laugh or cry."[8] To a number of correspondents he called this parting "a paroxysm of Copperfield." By now he had established the habit of throwing himself into amateur theatricals after completing a novel, but far from abandoning himself by this behavior, he seems to have been exercising simply a different form of control in order to forestall a letdown from writing. This time Dickens counted on managing, directing, and acting in *Not So Bad As We Seem,* written especially by Edward Bulwer-Lytton to benefit a new Guild of Literature and Art. "Coming out of a paroxysm of Copperfield, into a condition of temporary and partial consciousness, I plunge into histrionic duties," he wrote to Lavinia Jane Watson, whose home in Rockingham Castle was to serve for the play and as a model for Chesney Wold in the next novel: "So, Copperfield is to blame, and I am not, for this wandering note."[9] Though he rarely explained to such friends what he was attempting in his fiction, these expressions amply testify to the degree of concentration that was necessary and the need for release.

To a more exalted personage, the duke of Devonshire, Dickens wrote requesting a house suitable for a command performance of *Not So Bad As We Seem:* on receipt of the letter the duke wrote in his diary, "I have made a friendship with Charles Dickens. I worship him."[10] The Guild players were duly invited to use Devonshire House for their comedy; and there, on 16 May 1851, the queen and prince consort enjoyed the acting of Dickens and the others. This performance alone took some doing on the manager's part, and the company then took the play on tour: Dickens was nothing if not addicted—like his hero Copperfield—to hard work as well as good times. It is also possible to exaggerate his professionalism and his commitment to pure capitalism in the marketing of books and magazines. To the present day, patronage, a far older condition of literary production, has never deserted the art of writing altogether, and patronage was highly important to Dickens, even though he had no need to measure any tangible results from it. The Watsons, the duke, the queen, and Miss Coutts were patrons, without whom the writer would have felt himself a lesser being; his letters speak as much of this patronage, and of his own patronage of those in his sphere of influence, as they do of professionalism and marketing skills; and *Bleak House*, for all its renewed satire of privilege and tradition and its dignified captain of industry, was to be a novel more aware and more respectful of feudal England than was *Copperfield* by far. Possibly the difference reflects the presence of Queen Victoria and Prince Albert for the performance at Devonshire House. To Dickens, performing the role of Lord Wilmot in *Not So Bad As We Seem,* was given a speech extolling the "Order" of professional writers and anticipating the protection of such a queen (Bulwer-Lytton's play is set in the reign of George I):

> Oh, trust me the day shall come, when men will feel that it is not charity we owe to the ennoblers of life [writers and artists]—it is tribute! When your Order shall rise with the civilization it called into being; and shall refer its claim to just rank among freemen, to some Queen whom even a Milton might have sung, and even a Hampden have died for.[11]

Meanwhile the writing of *Bleak House* awaited the purchase and refurbishing of a new London residence, the author's. In this interval, besides the editing of *Household Words,* the home at Shepherd's Bush and other relief efforts, and the Guild and its performances, the acquiring of Tavistock House occupied Dickens. For this enterprise he relied heavily on the advice of his brother-in-law Henry Austin, an engineer who worked for the Board of Health, but needless to say had himself to cope with the workmen who were hired. It may be that the pent-up anger of the new owner is reflected in the Growlery he forthwith created for John Jarndyce in the novel. "I am three parts distracted and the fourth part wretched," he writes to Miss Coutts, "in the agonies of getting into a new house—Tavistock House, Tavistock Square. Pending which desirable consummation of my troubles, I *can not* work at my new book—having all my notions of order turned topsy-turvy. I hope when you come back you will find us settled, and me at hard work—and will approve, both the tangible house and the less substantial Edifice."[12] The "Edifice," or *Bleak House,* was his first novel to await so determinedly the construction of a new study as its place of composition. A few weeks on he complains to Richard Watson, "I am at present in such convulsions of repairing and moving, that it takes Thirty [of the contractor's] men to hold me. I am perfectly wild to get into my new Study (having a new book on my mind); and all the Trades of the civilised earth seem to be whistling in it, and intending to grow grey in it."[13] At this time Dickens seems increasingly conscious of his personal need for what he calls, in another letter on moving house, "a system of Order."[14] Little wonder that in the novel he would come down hard on Mrs. Jellyby's topsy-turvy ways or choose for his protagonist a true housekeeper, Miss Summerson, who would suit Mr. Jarndyce's domestic fancy and be rewarded with a Bleak House of her own at the end.

In all such activities Dickens exercised control, often with lively good humor in the telling, over recalcitrant material, much as one would expect of a novelist capable of so formidable a composition as *Bleak House* and, it appears, much to the discomfort and suffering of his immediate family. But there were some events, and one in particular, over which he could have no such control and of which he could not write thus freely to his friends. Dickens's father died on 31 March 1851, five months after the publication of the last number of *David Copperfield*, in which he had sat for an affectionate, utterly devastating, and justly famous portrait as Wilkins Micawber and as such been dispatched to Australia. Furthermore, John Dickens, who was sixty-five, did not die peacefully but from a drastic and futile operation, performed with only a few hours' warning. What we know of the death is mostly contained in this message from the son to his wife:

> My Dearest Kate. I have been greatly hurried and shocked today. Mr. Davy came here this morning, to say that he thought it impossible my father could live many hours. He was in that state from active disease (of the bladder) which he had mentioned to nobody, that mortification and delirium, terminating in speedy death, seemed unavoidable. Mr. Wade was called in, who instantly performed (without chloroform) the most terrible operation known in surgery, as the only chance of saving him. He bore it with astonishing fortitude, and I saw him directly afterwards—his room, a slaughter house of blood.

Dickens assured Catherine that his father was "wonderfully cheerful and strong-hearted," but the visit he paid him the following evening was the last, and within the week John Dickens died "quietly" without recognizing his son.[15] The cause, as set down in the death certificate: "Rupture of the Urethra from old standing stricture and consequent mortification of the scrotum from infiltration of urine."[16]

Dickens went on with his life that week. One can only guess how he felt about this unmentionable death of a parent. The Freudian wisdom is that sons may secretly wish to kill; but few sons, fortunately, ever have to think so precisely on the castration of a father. "My poor father" is the expression Dickens limited himself to with four or five correspondents, in conveying the sad news of the death only. To Catherine he reported "having been up, now, three whole nights—and out walking about, two." He hoped "to leave it all behind me tomorrow afternoon," when he planned to take the train with Forster and rejoin her at Malvern. "I have sometimes felt, myself, as if I could have given up, and let the whole battle ride on over me. But that has not lasted long, for God knows I have plenty to cheer me in the long run." [17] Beyond this, his letters say nothing of the passing of John Dickens, who had given the son more trouble over the years than the son had given the father. Ten days later, as Dickens finished addressing the annual dinner of the General Theatrical Fund, Forster broke the news to him that his eight-month-old daughter Dora Annie had died since he left home that evening.

Of this infant death, Dickens could be more forthcoming. He mourned for Dora Annie and did not hold back in writing of her to others. It is possible to feel that Victorians sometimes coped with their griefs by beautifully resigning themselves to infant deaths and turning such children into angels: *Bleak House* offers both the brickmakers' dead child as an emblem for pity and a putative "dead child" and "mother of the dead child"— Esther and her mother—who matter a good deal more to the novelist and his readers. Yet Dickens had special reason to feel a ghostly guilt on Dora Annie's account. Her death was also closely tied up with his feelings about his wife, who was taking the water cure at Malvern during these weeks because of a breakdown triggered by the child's illness. Dora Annie, their ninth child, had been born during the writing of *Copperfield* and was unhappily named for two make-believe persons, Dora Copperfield, the hero's first wife, and Annie Strong, the wife of Dr. Strong; and primarily Dickens thought of the child as named for Dora, the child-wife he was at that very time planning to kill off in number 17 of the novel. Now, after the real child's infant death, he confessed to friends that indeed Dora "was an ill omened name."[18]

Dickens's sons, who, beginning with the first, Charley, were named after famous writers not characters, were at least spared this particular confusion of real and imagined life. Students of the deliberately autobiographical *Copperfield* occasionally wonder if, when the novelist consigned Dora to death, he might wishfully have been setting aside his own wife; but his noisy separation from Catherine Dickens was still some years away, and there is no special evidence of their estrangement at this time. Still, the father got to name both Doras, and by the time the second was born he was committed to killing, however sadly and skillfully, the first—the child-wife of his Copperfield and replica of that hero's young mother. To write of the naming of the real child as ill-omened seems an understatement: it was more like a gratuitous act of competition with Catherine in childbearing, and its timing was appalling. Dickens left London for Broadstairs, where the rest of the family were encamped, the afternoon of the day his wife gave birth, there to write to her faithfully and to finish number 17. Four days on he hastily reported progress, but was unsure whether he could return to London in two days or three: "It depends upon Dora— I mean *my* Dora." On the following day he wrote Catherine again: "Even now, I am uncertain of my movements, for, after another splitting day, I have still Dora to kill—I mean the Copperfield Dora—and cannot make certain how long it will take to do. But if I could manage it before dinner tomorrow . . ."[19] In offering these pleasantries, the novelist could in no wise anticipate the real Dora's death eight months later, yet it would be surprising if all this superior creativity during the birth of a child did not take its toll on the real mother and father by the following spring.

Catherine Dickens was still at Malvern, improving in health, when her Dora died on 15 April 1851, and Forster brought the mother back to London. "I am not without some impression that this shock may even do her good," Dickens was able to hope.[20] On the evidence of the eventual birth of their tenth child, Edward Bulwer-Lytton Dickens (called "Plornish"), soon after the first number of *Bleak House* was in print, Mrs. Dickens was pregnant again, for the last time, by June 1851. Therefore, when we try to characterize the "later" Dickens, we should keep in mind that the novels after *Copperfield* were written by one whose fathering in the ordinary sense had come to an end. An alteration in family life may be assumed, particularly when the sexual union has centered so evidently on child-making, as in this case. We know that Dickens joked at this time about having enough children, that his new friendship with Wilkie Collins increased his acquaintance with a style of living other than the strictly monogamous, and that eventually he forced his wife to separate from him. That a change in the family role as the father turned forty should effect any change in the ambition of the writer is purely speculation. It is impossible to deny that Dickens was anything but an extraordinarily creative novelist ever since his commission to write *Pickwick*, on the strength of which he had married Catherine Hogarth in 1836. Still, the concurrence of the death of his father, the cessation of his fathering, and a still more ambitious dedication to his writing was undoubtedly significant. Fifty years later a similar concurrence of events would appear in Sigmund Freud's life history.

No reader can miss the deaths that occur in *Bleak House*. John Ruskin, notoriously, complained of these. Ruskin ticked off the various deaths in the novel by causes, as a public health officer might, and testily attributed them to the meaninglessness of life in the modern metropolis which was London.[21] I cannot recall anyone connecting this aspect of the fiction to the deaths of John Dickens and Dora Annie before Robert Newsom raised the possibility in his biographical excursion into the darker cast of *Bleak House*.[22] In one way or another many readers do respond to an air of mourning or loss in this novel, not least perhaps as that emptiness against which Esther Summerson's forced cheerfulness seeks to assert itself; the novelist's mourning could very well account for what Ruskin experienced as the meaninglessness of unrelieved death. By careful association with two articles by Dickens, one contemporary with *Bleak House* and the other nearly a decade later, both of which allude in passing to *Macbeth*, Newsom is able to give weight to the largely silent impress of John Dickens's death on the novelist's spirits at the outset of this new course of writing.[23]

Macbeth frequently echoes in Dickens's mind at the time, and not most obviously because of his father's death. The role of Macbeth was closely identified with his friend William Charles Macready, who was retiring from the theater at the height of his fame just when Dickens was redoubling his effort to command the reading public. Macready's farewell engagement at the Haymarket began 28 October 1850 with *Macbeth* and concluded 3 February 1851 with *King Lear*—a play of incalculable importance to Dickens, which his friend had restored to the English stage in 1838. The novelist, who saw Macready regularly in any case, was present for the latter performance as well as for the traditional benefit performance, of *Macbeth,* on the afternoon of 26 February, just a month before he learned of his father's mortal illness.[24] Curiously, a sentence in a letter from Dickens to Gaskell, which survives only as an extract in a bookseller's catalogue, offers grounds for associating the deeds of Macbeth with the baby boy Plornish, who followed little Dora Annie into the world soon after she went out of it. The extract inadvertently describes, not Dickens's father at all, but the infant as murder victim: "A golden baby has just arrived at Tavistock House—a perfect Californian little Duncan—his silver skin laced (internally) with his golden blood."[25]

The allusion to the western shores of the United States was not, in 1852, to well-tanned youths but to miners laden with gold, and Dickens was likely led to this regular line of joking with his fellow novelist from an uneasy comparison of his income from writing to hers. The quotation of Macbeth in the awkward moment of lying about Duncan's guards suggests murderousness all right, and possibly some grim confusion of the deaths a year before of both his father and his child. It would hardly be surprising, then, if Dickens suffered some guilt in mourning those losses, of a father who had often been a trouble to him and a child whose namesake he had set up for the kill, the one so swiftly followed by the other. Such is the implicit significance of *Macbeth* for Newsom, who broaches the subject safely enough with an indirection typical of Freud himself: "Psychoanalytically inclined critics will have little difficulty in coming up with an account of why *Macbeth* should have been so much in Dickens's thoughts at this time: *Macbeth* is, after all about regicide, but the play itself recognizes the close relationship, indeed, the psychological equivalence between that crime and parricide."[26] But it is not clear how much follows from this conventional diagnosis or Freudian knowingness and innuendo about Oedipal desires. I have often been skeptical about the degree to which Dickens can be read as a novelist specializing in unconscious guilt; and I am not persuaded that the invention of the Oedipus complex can be divorced from the peculiar pressures on male bourgeois ambition in the nineteenth century.[27] A joyous, cheerful identification of childbirth with Macbeth's victim, as in the letter to Gaskell, more likely betrays the renewed ambition of the novelist to surpass himself—and no doubt his previous profits—with the new novel that was just beginning to appear.

Shakespeare's play was indeed a study of guilt, for Macbeth is eminently capable both of killing and of knowing when killing is wrong. But the play is also a study of ambition, ambition of the despairing kind that lives for the future at the expense of the present.[28] With the success of *Copperfield* behind him, Dickens excitedly turns despair into exhilaration. His letters tell us nothing of his plans for *Bleak House*, only of his determination to clear a space for it and his eagerness to write. To no one does he seem to have hinted of his choice of a female protagonist, or more astonishingly of the uniquely divided task of storytelling for his new novel. Yet curiously, the letters of this period contain another echo of *Macbeth*. In a letter to Mary Boyle, who was to act with him as soon as he finished his autobiographical novel, Dickens wrote on 7 October 1850, "I am transported beyond the ignorant Copperfieldian present, and soar into the Rockinghamian future!"[29] They were to act at Rockingham Castle, of course, and this time he is paraphrasing Lady Macbeth's devotion to the future:

> Great Glamis! worthy Cawdor!
> Greater than both, by the all-hail hereafter!
> Thy letters have transported me beyond
> This ignorant present, and I feel now
> The future in an instant.[30]

For this kind of thinking, Duncan is merely a detail. The expression foretells but one thing of the later years of Dickens and that is renewed ambition. This meaning is glossed by a letter in French a few days earlier, to his friend Alfred D'Orsay in Paris, which also peers beyond the Copperfieldian present, with Dickens's own emphasis on the key words: "Je suis fort occupé, en ecrivant le dernier livraison de Copperfield—meilleur (j'espere et je crois) de mes livres, *à present*."[31] The novelist dared to believe that his best work was still to come, and this high ambition—call it self-knowledge—anticipates the judgment of most Dickens students today.

Deaths nonetheless shadowed *Bleak House,* even if they were less guilty deaths than those enacted by Lady Macbeth and her husband. Besides the deaths in the family before Dickens conceived of the novel, there were deaths of friends once it was under way: Richard Watson's on 24 July, D'Orsay's on 3 August 1852; and the novelist became aware that Macready's wife was dying soon after his friend stood up to MacDuff one last time. Bleak House in the novel is bleak in part because the earlier proprietor Tom Jarndyce, John Jarndyce's great-uncle, has taken his own life there in despair. The day after Esther Summerson arrives, Jarndyce introduces her to the Growlery, the study to which he regularly retreats in order to growl—to work off the anger that the suit in Chancery, or the behavior of humankind, too commonly inspires. "The Growlery is the best-used room in the house," he warns Esther, as if it might be a room to be used for composing such a novel as this. For purposes of the novel, clearly, the house's history began with Tom Jarndyce's entrapment in the Chancery suit that brought about his suicide:

> It had been called, before his time, the Peaks. He
> gave it its present name, and lived here shut up: day
> and night poring over the wicked heaps of papers
> in the suit and hoping against hope to disentangle
> it from its mystification and bring it to a close.
> In the meantime the place became dilapidated, the
> wind whistled through the cracked walls, the rain

fell through the broken roof, the weeds choked the passage to the rotting door. When I brought what remained of him home here, the brains seemed to me to have been blown out of the house too; it was so shattered and ruined. (8.87,89)[32]

This violent image certifies that Bleak House is a frame of mind, a shattered and ruined frame of mind. Jarndyce apologizes for this: "I told you this was the Growlery, my dear." Esther has to remind him that the house has been improved, made delightful in a cozy Victorian fashion, with unexpected passages and nooks and corners filled with charming things. And of course she is quite wise, as Jarndyce says, to return him to "the bright side of the picture." At the end of the novel he will present her with a replica of these improvements and the improvements she will make herself: a new Bleak House of her own, which she will have earned by her contribution to the writing and where a Mr. Woodcourt, who does not yet exist, can continue courting her forever. Meanwhile, Mr. Jarndyce cannot help darkening the bright side by mentioning that "Bleak House" has a more oblique reference to a place that has not improved at all:

> There is, in that city of London there, some property of ours, which is much at this day what Bleak House was then,—I say property of ours, meaning of the Suit's. . . . It is a street of perishing blind houses, with their eyes stoned out; without a pane of glass, without so much as a window-frame, with the bare blank shutters tumbling from their hinges and falling asunder; the iron rails peeling away in flakes of rust; the chimneys sinking in; the stone steps to every door (and every door might be Death's Door) turning stagnant green; the very

crutches on which the ruins are propped, decaying.
(8.89)

Again Jarndyce's language is violent: a house with its brains
blown out, now houses with their eyes stoned out. His words
prove to be the first description of the slum called Tom-all-
Alone's, which as we have seen provided an alternative title for
the novel since its inception. The area is thought to be called
Tom-all-Alone's because of its earlier connection with Tom
Jarndyce, since the property, we are given to understand, is in
this wretched condition because the costs of the Chancery suit
have used up the wherewithal for keeping it in repair. But no
disposition of this unimproved annex of Bleak House is given
at the end of the novel: it is as if the apocalyptic, or mock
apocalyptic, collapse of the suit releases only enough energy to
free Miss Flite's birds and provide a home for Esther.

For the large edifice called *Bleak House,* which contains all of
these properties and more, Dickens employed so many materials and fasteners, characters and relationships, that no archi-
tectural critic can positively know where to enter. The novel's
design is most obviously and strictly chronological, with each
of the two narratives keeping rough time together, and this
temporal ordering is of great use in the introduction of characters (here as in other novels). With as many as sixty men,
women, and children to account for and render memorably,
virtually every chapter in the first half of the novel introduces
more than one. Connections among the characters continue to
be made, but after the center point is reached—marked by the
spectacular though unseen combustion of Krook, the surrogate
Chancellor, in the one narrative and by the unconscious passage
of Esther's illness in the other—no important new character
appears except Vholes, who is to consume Richard Carstone,
the novel's closest approach to a conventional hero. "Make

man-eating unlawful, and you starve the Vholeses" (39.483) — though little is left of Carstone after Dickens and Summerson themselves are done with him.

In no way can the reader or critic do without Esther Summerson. Study of *Bleak House* often begins with its famous opening paragraph, with its grim city and grim invitation to the end of time. But as Dickens's procedure eventually shows, a single human consciousness can provide not only thought and feeling but continuity in time and space. Therefore I propose to reorder the materials as necessary and to study first the affective center of the novel, the protagonist and narrator Summerson. *Bleak House* moves closer than one might suspect to the previous novel told by David Copperfield. The heroine's story subsumes that of two prominent characters, Ada Clare and Lady Dedlock. Jarndyce's role is more independent but still closely bound up with that of the heroine. An adequate understanding of the plot of the novel depends on tracing the relations of these four characters before turning to the social and satirical themes represented by Tom-all-Alone's and the Court of Chancery. In no way does the heroine understand everything about Bleak House, but she can place us in a position to know more. I shall try to call her Summerson when I mean the narrator, Esther when and as she participates in the action; but this distinction is bound to blur.

2

Esther Summerson, Heroine

"The autobiographical form of *Copperfield* was in some respect continued in *Bleak House* by means of extracts from the personal relation of its heroine." In these terms John Forster admitted a certain likeness between the two novels, minimized the heroine's contribution by using the misleading word "extracts," and then proceeded to disparage the result: "a difficult enterprise, full of hazard in any case, not worth success, and certainly not successful."[1] Though the same paragraph concluded with Forster's high estimate of the novel's construction, this dim view of Esther Summerson's share of the narrative has predominated among Dickens critics until the present generation.[2] One can see right away that the biographer might have been more cautious here, since this half of *Bleak House* plus *David Copperfield* and *Great Expectations* are the only novel-length stories that Dickens composed in the first person. Judith Wilt has countered: "Dickens wrote three fictional autobiographies; in one he made himself a woman."[3] The coincidence and sequence would seem to indicate more connectedness than Forster allows, and in truth the female narrator of *Bleak House* sustains a number of habits of her immediate predecessor. As we have seen, the title of the new novel hints that readers may be in for something quite different, but the retrospective narrators' names, Copperfield and Summerson, are far less disjunctive.

One habit causes the names of the protagonists actually to converge. Both the fictitious novelist and the fictitious housekeeper adroitly preserve a sense of their various relationships in life by accepting, and incorporating in their narratives, the pet names by which others address them. Copperfield, especially, registers nuances of meaning in the ways he is addressed by the many friends and caretakers of his younger days: "Davy" by his mother and Peggotty, "Master Davy" by the Yarmouth clan, "Copperfield" in school but sometimes "Daisy" by Steerforth, "Master—I should say Mister" by Uriah Heep, "Doady" by his wife Dora, "Trotwood" by Agnes Wickfield after being renamed so by his aunt Betsey Trotwood. Esther Summerson is scarcely less accommodating: though to the world she is Miss Summerson, and Esther to her close friends, she is fond of the pet names bestowed by her "guardian" John Jarndyce, which typically have an aura of nursery tale or housekeeping about them. Esther no more reflects, after she learns her mother's identity, that her real name cannot be "Summerson" than David seems moved one way or the other by being called so many different names—though he is obviously irritated by Heep's practice of calling him "Master Copperfield" and then assiduously correcting this to "Mister." By the last number of *Bleak House* one of the pet names for Esther becomes "Dame Trot" (60.714-15), which is but the short form of "Trotwood" in the previous novel. Indeed, David Copperfield's aunt sometimes calls him "Trot," and she has rechristened him Trotwood in the first place because she wanted him to be a girl-child named Betsey Trotwood Copperfield after herself. So also, for different reasons, is Steerforth's calling him "Daisy" effeminizing. Thus from "Trot" to "Dame Trot" for these narrator-protagonists was a passage already toyed with in *David Copperfield*.

It is hard to gauge what Dickens intended, if anything, by this small continuity between two very large novels. Quite possibly he repeated himself without noticing it, as Forster claims he had reversed the initials of his own name in choosing "David Copperfield" but failed to notice the conjunction until his friend pointed it out to him.[4] The more important thing to note is the skill with which he has his two protagonists answer to more than one name as different relationships come into play. For those, including myself, who believe that the literary inspiration for *David Copperfield* was probably Charlotte Brontë's *Jane Eyre*, similarly narrated in "autobiographical form," the switch from Copperfield's to Summerson's hand may seem less surprising or unprecedented.[5] Other scholars have looked at the possible bearing on *Bleak House* of Brontë's contemporaneous *Villette* and the narrator Lucy Snowe.[6] Brontë's narrators, of course, were often publicly identified with herself; Dickens, as a male, was ceded more distance from his fictional counterparts. Yet if Copperfield bore some carefully calculated resemblances to the author, so has Summerson a few intimate associations with her maker that may only be less deliberate.[7] A degree of self-pity for his early upbringing Dickens found no difficulty in venting both in the autobiographical fragment he supplied to Forster and in the early chapters of *Copperfield*. Sometimes his fantasy runs to pitifully dying in childhood, as if to serve parents and other grown-ups right: such are the substitute deaths of Little Dick in *Oliver Twist* and of David Copperfield's little brother, who lying in his mother's arms in their common grave somehow "was myself."[8] Little Esther experienced even less love, was harshly raised and explicitly left for dead by her mother, so that when the grown Esther mistakes her own dead mother for "the mother of the dead child" (59.713)—a child who actually dies in the novel like little Dick or David's baby brother—resonances build to a point where one begins to assume a connection with Dickens personally, in what seem to be fantasies that go beyond any one novel.

Because Miss Summerson frequently gives the keys of Bleak House a reassuring shake in the basket at her waist, it has seemed reasonable to suppose that she dedicates herself to housekeeping not for its own sake but for consolation, as if the jingle of the keys provided some cheer otherwise missing from her life. Possibly if Brontë had written the novel, readers would have been willing to put up with the symbolism to this day; but since Dickens was not a woman, and is not particularly admired for representing women, the jingling of the keys is more like a travesty of young spinsterhood, a change rung on the peculiarly Victorian rhyming of beauty against duty. That the author had some intimate acquaintance with housekeeping and erotic roles as separate and complementary in women is true, and at least since the early years of the twentieth century, when more became known about Dickens's family life, many have been persuaded that his sister-in-law Georgina Hogarth served as a model for Esther Summerson.[9] Genuine solicitude and gratitude need not preclude novelistic caricature; often the sincerities of an earlier age, let alone the humor, read like travesties at a later time. Michael Slater has summarized the case and shown how likely it is that Dickens sketched Miss Hogarth, who took care of his house and children both, as Miss Summerson, and plotted the novel so as to provide her with a bleak house and children of her own.[10]

If this were the end of the matter, the result would have been a heroine imagined by the novelist from the outside. With whatever motives, kindhearted or hopelessly officious, Dickens would have reinvented his busy sister-in-law objectively, according to his lights. Even if Miss Summerson's character and situation did depend upon Miss Hogarth's, the novelist has portrayed his heroine subjectively, as deeply representative of himself. Thus he relishes the pathos of the infant who might have died, reconciles himself to life again in spite of such neglect, and summons up forgiveness for parents who literally knew nothing about any of this. Take for example, Summerson's self-pity and justification the night following her first and only interview with her mother:

> I saw very well that I could not have been intended to die, or I should never have lived; not to say should never have been reserved for such a happy life. I saw very well how many things had worked together, for my welfare; and that if the sins of the fathers were sometimes visited upon the children, the phrase had not meant what I in the morning feared it meant. I knew I was as innocent of my birth as a queen of hers; and that before my Heavenly Father I should not be punished for birth, nor a queen rewarded for it. I had had experience, in the shock of that very day, that I could, even thus soon, find comforting reconcilements to the change that had fallen on me. (36.454–55)

Like the fantasy of being left for dead that Dickens easily takes to heart, the fact of illegitimacy is another way of divorcing the child from the sins of its parents. The business about a queen, too, is simply the feminized translation of numerous early modern sentiments to the effect that a king is no better than a gentleman. The telltale expression here is the brief concession, "I saw very well how many things had worked together, for my welfare," a softened echo of the half-reconciliation to Dickens's childhood days in the blacking warehouse that is then bitterly withdrawn again in the autobiographical fragment he left with Forster: "I know how all these things have worked together to make me what I am: but I never afterwards forgot, I never shall forget, I never can forget, that my mother was warm for my being sent back."[11] Though the narrator-heroine of *Bleak House* writes without resentment, the novel's ending may be thought to dispose of her mother no less fiercely.

As Q. D. Leavis observes, "We know more about Esther than we do about any other woman in Dickens."[12] The reason, I suggest, is that Dickens was able to throw himself into the part almost as readily as he had with Copperfield—assisted by Agnes Wickfield. In *David Copperfield*, note, his admission that his childhood suffering has helped to make him what he is was omitted from the chapter on Murdstone and Grinby's warehouse, though other paragraphs from the autobiographical fragment were incorporated word for word. Instead, much later in the novel another woman, Agnes, is empowered to inform the hero how "the endurance of my childish days had done its part to make me what I was."[13] Despite youth and inexperience Summerson is notably acute in her judgments of other characters; her closest competition in this regard comes from the much older Jarndyce, yet in the first test case—that of Harold Skimpole—Esther is almost immediately able to judge better than her guardian. She also knows about her own parentage before he does. In no instance in the long novel does her judgment appear to differ from Dickens's own. She is committed not only to "the duties and accountabilities of life" (6.66) but to the responsibilities of just narrative, with regard to both her access to the facts and suspense. Summerson indites her part of *Bleak House* according to what she knew or was told at the time, never hinting—except for some carefully suppressed hopes that Allan Woodcourt may notice her—at the outcomes of actions that she must be aware of even as she writes. (The evident arbitrariness of withholding the outcome is a liability of first-person narratives, even those, like Tristram Shandy's, that flaunt it. The small exceptions allowed for the protagonist's love interest are found in Copperfield's story as well.) No doubt Summerson shares with Copperfield and others certain polite hypocrisies, speaking and writing of less than she felt at the time; but the awkwardness, as Forster would have it, is not all on her side.

One wonders, if Esther had judged Steerforth's behavior, for example, whether the seducer of Little Em'ly would have been as assiduously forgiven as he is by David.[14]

Since this heroine bears such authorial responsibilities, her role should reflect the sense of mourning with which *Bleak House* introduces a new, more somber series of novels by Dickens. The affect from loss of his father and Dora Annie would not express itself merely in the Growlery, in John Jarndyce's despairing retirement and forced goodness, but in this female projection of the novelist. As Robert Newsom has speculated, the very irritating quality of Summerson's "busybody cheerfulness" and jingling of her household keys to reassure herself may be "a reaction against mourning and grief" and an "effort to overcome them." Newsom believes that the twentieth-century tendency to deny grief and distance ourselves from death has left readers uncertain what to feel. "More willing than we are to give way to the intense experience of despair, Dickens felt more urgency about bringing it to an end."[15] The potential for misunderstanding cannot be limited to present-day readers, however, since Forster and other contemporaries could also lose patience with Esther. Forced cheerfulness was also in evidence earlier in Dickens's novels: most extravagantly in the comic, and demonic, Mark Tapley of *Martin Chuzzlewit.*[16] Since Tapley, a strangely mechanical being, is a demon of unselfishness in the service of young Martin, it could be that Esther Summerson's insistent cheerfulness, equally mechanical at times, is medicine not just for grief but for self-pity again.

It has to be said that Esther's father, Nemo, who lives and dies without her knowledge as the novel gets under way, does not bear much resemblance to John Dickens. Nemo, later identified as one Captain Hawdon, the lover of Lady Dedlock, is still less like the great Wilkins Micawber; yet he is a haunting presence in *Bleak House* for all that. Literally no one, he has eked out his life unknown to any of the principals by copying law papers, before entering into the action as a corpse. J. Hillis Miller and Garrett Stewart have suggested that Micawber, with his oratory and endless letter writing, is a kind of rival wordsmith to David Copperfield, hence to Dickens.[17] Nemo's copying, on the contrary, counts as one of the lowly uses of literacy remarked in *Bleak House*. Irony suffuses Nemo's role in whatever direction we choose to take it. He is a ghostly, distant stand-in for John Dickens, perhaps, but even more oddly for the writers Dickens and Summerson, in that he is three times compared to an abandoned child. Thus in the impersonal, present-tense narrative, before the inquest, the policeman on his beat stops "now and then, at a street-corner, to look casually about for anything between a lost child and a murder," for example; "and, all that night, the coffin stands ready by the old portmanteau; and the lonely figure on the bed, whose path in life has lain through five-and-forty years, lies there, with no more track behind him, that any one can trace, than a deserted infant" (11.131). After the inquest, the father in the coffin is the same who was once a child; the child's mother is called to look upon the corpse she has given birth to; and this mother abruptly metamorphoses to the man's lover, Esther's mother, whose very absence from the bedside is an accusation:

> Then there is rest around the lonely figure, now laid in its last earthly habitation; and it is watched by the gaunt eyes in the shutters through some quiet hours of night. If this forlorn man could have been prophetically seen lying here, by the mother at whose breast he nestled, a little child, with eyes upraised to her loving face, and soft hand scarcely knowing how to close upon the neck to which it crept, what an impossibility the vision would

have seemed! O, if, in brighter days, the now-extinguished fire within him ever burned for one woman who held him in her heart, where is she, while these ashes are above the ground! (11.136)

Nemo's departure from the text is completed by the description of the "hemmed-in-churchyard, pestiferous and obscene" in which he is buried and by Dickens's scathing satire of the practice of burying anyone, no one, in the inner city's slums. These famous paragraphs, to be pronounced as from a stage, are not without their own echoes of *Macbeth:* "Come night, come darkness, for you cannot come too soon, or stay too long, by such a place as this! Come, straggling lights into the windows of the ugly houses; and you who do iniquity therein, do it at least with this dread scene shut out! Come, flame of gas, burning so sullenly above the iron gate, on which the poisoned air deposits its witch-ointment slimy to the touch!" Similarly, Lady Macbeth repeats "Come" three times in her apostrophes to "thick night" to hide the murder and to "spirits" to unsex her. The apostrophes are also the cue for Dickens's own version of the porter scene (left out of Macready's production of Shakespeare's play), in which the porter repeats "Come in" three times. The porter to hell's gate is none other than Jo the crossing sweeper, who has been acquainted with Nemo and present at the inquest. Just as Esther is the fatherless heroine who writes her story in *Bleak House,* Jo is the parentless, homeless, illiterate representative of the underclass, the innocent focus of the darker satire in the novel, whose orphaned existence crosses with hers and causes her illness. Until then he works as busily as she might, at this chapter ending, by tending Esther's father's grave:

> With the night, comes a slouching figure
> through the tunnel-court, to the outside of the

iron gate. It holds the gate with its hands, and
looks in between the bars; stands looking in for a
little while.

It then, with an old broom it carries, softly
sweeps the step, and makes the archway clean. It
does so very busily and trimly; looks in again, a
little while; and so departs.

Jo, is it thou? Well, well! Though a rejected witness, who "can't exactly say" what will be done to
him in greater hands than men's, thou art not quite
in outer darkness. There is something like a distant
ray of light thy muttered reason for this:

"He wos wery good to me, he wos!" (11.137–38)

The ironies of the least significant—ironies of the Sermon
on the Mount, if you will—were becoming more important to
Dickens. Blessed are the meek, blessed are the poor in spirit
and those who are blessed *by* the poor. Nemo is now someone
after all; in the novel that would follow *Bleak House* and *Hard
Times,* the protagonist becomes Nobody in some chapters, and
until Dickens thought of naming *Little Dorrit* for its meek,
impressive heroine, his working title was "Nobody's Fault"—
a painful and finally impossible attempt to fuse his code word
for the hero with what he saw as the refusal of responsibility
in the world at large.[18] Should Nemo, the scarcely significant,
unknown father of Esther Summerson, be a fictional emblem
of the novelist's own father, the chilling account of his disposal as the corpse in *Bleak House* is a moving, if depressing
tribute. "He wos wery good to me" indeed. In a novel that
frequently dwells on the outward failures of Christianity, the
title of this chapter, "Our Dear Brother," expresses a religiosity
both felt and contemptuously ironic. The barely buried body—
"They was obliged to stamp upon it to git it in," Jo later reports

(16.202)—rather than the spirit remains a presence through many more chapters, until Lady Dedlock dies at the iron gate to the same place of corruption. The disposal of the corpse is neither witnessed nor narrated by Dickens's heroine; only at the end of number 18—"And it was my mother, cold and dead" (59.714)—do the two narratives converge at this gate, and then without Summerson's full knowledge. One of the advantages of two narratives is the capacity thus to dramatize apprehension or ignorance. Summerson's story as narrator is that of initiation into the full story of the world in which the novel is set. As housekeeper at Bleak House she will never personally put hand to broom, I am sure; yet as a woman who might wish to know of her father's death, she is usefully supported by the still meeker orphan Jo, performing under the neuter pronoun. "It then, with an old broom it carries, softly sweeps the step, and makes the archway clean. It does so very busily and trimly . . ."

For the accomplishment of *Bleak House,* it is not only the resemblances of Miss Summerson to the author that count but the differences, starting with the differences of gender. Though no record has survived of how, when, or why Dickens determined to use a female narrator for half of his chapters, it is evident from the first number that he deliberately construed her voice, her style of writing, as feminine—different from his own style, or from Copperfield's, because it would be recognizably feminine. Copperfield had begun quizzically by putting it up to his readers to decide whether or not he was the hero of his own life: a modest opening that most likely invites us, by the novel's end, to join him in crediting his good angel Agnes for success and happiness. A modest female narrator can have no muse and must misdoubt her abilities, and thus Summerson introduces herself with the words, "I have a great deal of difficulty in beginning to write my portion of these pages, for I know I am not clever." Her second sentence insistently adds,

"I always knew that," and her third reveals her gender by refer-
ring to the doll she had "when I was a very little girl indeed."
This gendered voice Dickens studiously reinforces with a piece
of received wisdom about a woman's intelligence, that it may
be that she *is* clever when she loves. "I have not by any means
a quick understanding. When I love a person very tenderly indeed"—though there is no indication at this point that she has
ever been allowed to—"it seems to brighten." And again, "my
comprehension is quickened when my affection is" (3.17–18).
These qualifications are accompanied by half-confessions about
vanity, to which she knows she must be subject as a woman,
and her longing to be loved, in a manner that will preserve
her becoming passivity. Amid all this careful gender-casting,
she conveys enough information about her origins for the adult
reader to realize that she is illegitimate, without her ever saying
as much or hinting that she knows.

> Dear, dear, to think . . . how often I repeated to the
> doll the story of my birthday, and confided to her
> that I would try, as hard as ever I could, to repair
> the fault I had been born with (of which I confus-
> edly felt guilty and yet innocent), and would strive
> as I grew up to be industrious, contented, and kind-
> hearted, and to do some good to some one, and win
> some love to myself if I could. (3.20)

At this point Dickens has his fresh narrator drop a few tears
on the page, as if to summarize these several markings of her
sex. Yet to a good many readers the psychology seems right:
Esther propitiates those she meets because she lived in terror
as a child; she longs to be loved because she was abandoned as
a baby.[19]

Evidently Dickens felt that *he* was clever enough at playing
these games. Whether readers smile or snort, he was studi-

ously placing his female narrator at a distance, across the gender divide, at the same time that he was identifying with her. Noticeably, the affective center of Esther's life never shifts entirely away from her birth and her relation to those who might serve as parents. Dickens expends much cleverness in adumbrating her modest longing to be loved and her just-hinted interest in the doctor wistfully named Woodcourt. He does not succeed very well in imagining Allan Woodcourt as the love object, possibly because he is a man himself but more certainly because, in English novels, the object of a woman's interest in a man is partially censored. Apart from a nosegay that this putative lover leaves behind, without direction, on his departure for the Far East, the whole of Woodcourt's own concern with marriage is displaced upon *his* mother: a satiric portrait of snobbery that functions strictly with respect to the question of Esther's social standing. Undoubtedly the doctor is a figure of charity throughout *Bleak House,* so much so that Esther could hardly fail to win some share of his love by the end. But Dickens does not altogether imagine him as a real person. In a novel of so many habitations, for example, he never bothers to work out where the man lives: Woodcourt simply materializes, in the street or at the bedside, when needed, as if he were a figment of imagination in either narrative. In truth, the role is demonic, if one allows that there are good as well as bad demons in works of the imagination.

If Allan Woodcourt has demonic powers, he is a familiar of death more than he is of love. He presides over the deaths of Jo and Richard Carstone—two of the most portentous events in *Bleak House*—and his forebodings of the second exceed mere medical knowledge. More pertinent and mysterious, he gratuitously presides over the deaths of the heroine's father and mother. Thus he is intimately involved in the question of who Esther Summerson is; and he is entitled to accompany her, to wed her, and to enable her to have children because he can certify those deaths, because he has helped put to rest the sins of the parents. Indeed Jarndyce makes a special point of his importance to Esther's independent existence at the awkward moment of handing her over to Woodcourt and the new Bleak House: "My dearest, Allan Woodcourt stood beside your father when he lay dead—stood beside your mother. This is Bleak House. This day I give this house its little mistress" (64.753). Woodcourt did not exactly kill those prospective parents-in-law as a favor to his bride, yet their deaths are inseparable from her future contentment, and it is as if—Jarndyce is saying—the doctor has helped arrange all this for you. (The new Bleak House is pointedly not the old one, whose mistress would have been married to a man she once idly supposed might *be* her father.) Readers who thumb back through the pages of the novel to ascertain what Jarndyce means by "stood beside your father . . . stood beside your mother" will only be further impressed with the doctor's demonic presence. In number 4 Woodcourt literally materializes in the novel as a voice from behind Nemo's bed. Not he but a Scottish doctor is the one Miss Flite has summoned to the scene, and when the Scottish doctor hazards that Nemo has been dead about three hours, we learn of Woodcourt's presence for the first time:

> "About that time, I should say," observes a dark young man, on the other side of the bed.
> "Air you in the maydickle prayfession yourself, sir?" inquires the first.
> The dark young man says yes.
> "Then I'll just tak' my depairture," replies the other; "for I'm nae gude here!" With which remark he finishes his brief attendance, and returns to finish his dinner.

> The dark young surgeon passes the candle across
> and across the face, and carefully examines the law-
> writer, who has established his pretensions to his
> name by becoming indeed No one. (11.126)

In number 5, to be sure, Dickens has forgotten the Scottish doctor and rationalized Woodcourt's presence. It is then Summerson's narrative: Miss Flite introduces Woodcourt as her physician, and he comments politely that she brought *him* to the scene, "though too late for me to be of any use to the unfortunate man" (14.178). In this version, the first meeting of Allan Woodcourt and Esther Summerson recalls—in their first conversation—the death of Nemo, though neither knows anything of Nemo's relationship to Esther.

Woodcourt's appearance much later to Miss Summerson and Inspector Bucket in Chancery Lane, just before they come upon the body of Lady Dedlock, is less ominous but no more readily explicable: "We passed on in silence, and as quickly as we could with such a foothold, when some one coming towards us on the narrow pavement, wrapped in a cloak, stopped and stood aside to give me room. In the same moment I heard an exclamation of wonder, and my own name, from Mr. Woodcourt." He then accompanies them as far as the archway and iron gate of the burial ground, where the heroine, imagining that it is Jenny, "the mother of the dead child," who is lying there, "saw, but did not comprehend, the solemn and compassionate look in Mr. Woodcourt's face" (59.705,713). In Jarndyce's locution, it might seem that Woodcourt "stood beside" Captain Hawdon and Lady Dedlock at the wedding that never took place; but the text of *Bleak House* discovers him standing by their respective corpses, now linked but separated by the iron gate: an office that qualifies him to serve in the new Bleak House at the end.

Good demons in Victorian novels are more likely to be women—angels, as they are called—such as Agnes Wickfield. But Dickens so thoroughly identifies with his female narrator and her secret need to triumph that powers over death have in this case devolved on her male consort. Accordingly, instead of having male rivals such as Copperfield's Heep and Steerforth, Summerson will have female friends who at once embody what she would wish to be and will suffer for it, as Ada Clare does. Instead of a weak mother and strong stepfather, she will have a weak father and strong mother to overcome. Timothy Peltason has explored some of the far-reaching effects of Esther's "will" in a recent essay.[20] It is not a matter of mechanically shifting gender roles, as rough equivalences to *David Copperfield* may suggest, for only in the case of his heroine's relation to Ada Clare does Dickens deliberately focus on a stereotypical female concern, the desire to be beautiful. Nor is it a matter of projecting his own wishes in fiction—though there is some of that—for Dickens keeps a considerable distance from Copperfield and more distance from Summerson. Rather, he imagines his protagonist's part so intensely—whatever the biases of his own time and person—that *she* projects her feelings upon other actors in the drama, that *she* expresses her wishes without knowing it; and once these wishes are fulfilled with Dickens's help, Summerson proves just as dangerous a young person to be acquainted with as was Copperfield himself.

Often the self-aggrandizement is harmless enough. For example, Esther rather primly decides that she is "as innocent of my birth as a queen of hers" (36.454), and she is not the only one to give herself this little push. "When a young lady is as mild as she's game, and as game as she's mild, that's all I ask, and more than I expect," says the flattering Inspector Bucket. "She then becomes a Queen, and that's about what you are yourself" (59.704). Such royal intimations are very bourgeois sentiments, to be sure; yet after all, once upon a time Esther was a famous queen and a dazzling one at that. There cannot be much doubt that the conjunction of names and rivalry of persons between David Copperfield and Uriah Heep echo the ancient tale of King David and Bathsheba, the wife of Uriah the Hittite; Dickens may have tortured their history somewhat to preserve his hero's innocence, since in the Bible it is David rather than Uriah who lusts after another man's woman, but from where else but that history could these names have derived? So also it is hard to believe that Dickens's Esther does not reflect in some way or other, if only in her longing to be as lovely as Ada or as handsome as Lady Dedlock, her namesake Queen Esther in the Bible. In both novels the biblical allusions are very grand but inverted: the modern David never lusts and the modern Esther does not overwhelm with her beauty. Thus the biblical prototype flatters the low mimetic text—just to position the novels for a moment with respect to Northrop Frye's historical criticism [21]—but verges upon ironic commentary. The gender roles have remained constant, however, with the male learning to desire and the female hoping to become the object of desire.

And notwithstanding the coy treatment of physical beauty in *Bleak House,* the novel glorifies its heroine in ways that not even its modest female narrator can conceal. Because the glorification is of modesty and resignation, in fact, she is licensed to tell of it:

> "O, Mr. Woodcourt, forbear, forbear!" I entreated him. "I do not deserve your high praise. I had many selfish thoughts at that time, many!"
>
> "Heaven knows, beloved of my life," said he, "that my praise is not a lover's praise, but the truth. You do not know what all around you see in

Esther Summerson, how many hearts she touches
and awakens, what sacred admiration and what
love she wins." (61.731)

Miss Summerson may not be as sexy as Queen Esther or
hold the lives of quite so many in her power, but she'll do for
the nineteenth century. Her story resembles that of her biblical
namesake most simply in its unrestrained triumphalism. She
triumphs over not one Queen Vashti but over two women of
striking appearance, her friend and her mother; and it sometimes seems that the ambiguous figure of John Jarndyce, like
Mordecai, is powerless without her.

Allan Woodcourt and Honoria Dedlock appear in both narratives of *Bleak House.* Ada Clare and the heroine herself appear
only in Summerson's narrative. It is a nice critical question,
always, how to read the latter. Most readers seem to feel that
they know more than the heroine but also that the heroine
knows more than she lets on. As Audrey Jaffe puts it, "Her
narrative always knows more than she does," and hence we get
to know more than she does. "Readers pursue a system of signs
that define Esther as a character who does not know herself,
even at the very end of her narrative, when all she knows has
presumably been revealed."[22] But more than a system of signs is
involved—unless that expression refers so broadly to language
that nothing accomplished by the novel is excluded. The action
of a novel defines its protagonist, as do the interrelationships
of the characters. In *Bleak House,* as in other egocentric fic-
tions, displacement is an issue. The affective center of the action
may be conveniently signaled as Esther Summerson's story, but
that story, I shall argue, aggressively subsumes the stories of
Ada Clare and Honoria Dedlock and tries to subsume Caddy
Jellyby's story as well.

3

Ada Clare, Pride and Beauty

Dickens seems to have judged that a female narrator could not or would not describe herself. Summerson ventures no such carefully qualified opinion about her appearance as she does about her cleverness. Her resolve to be "industrious, contented, and kind-hearted" may indeed seem to discount her beauty. Though modest women are conventionally and purposively silent on this score, most readers probably feel that this heroine is but moderately good-looking, since she frames her narrative so as to leave this impression. At the very end she admits to her husband (who answers that she is prettier than ever), "I have been thinking about my old looks—such as they were" (67.770). Near the beginning, her attention to Ada Clare's looks—"such a beautiful girl!"—argues that she considers herself less special. Her first impression of this orphan, one of the wards in Chancery, is perhaps colored in the writing by Summerson's knowledge of the outcome: "With such rich golden hair, such soft blue eyes, and such a bright, innocent, trusting face!" (3.30). Thus she writes in full consciousness of the importance the culture gives to female beauty and leads her readers to believe that she is not as beautiful—or as vulnerable—as her friend. Yet in the very center of the novel, the spoiling of her own face by disease is the determined turning point of the heroine's story.

The turn occurs between the tenth and eleventh numbers while the narrating heroine is unconscious and near death. Her fever has been contracted from Charley, her maid, who received it from Jo the crossing sweeper, who is eventually to die from it and other deprivations besides. In both the style and evident virtue of his heroine in this episode, Dickens may have mimicked novels written expressly for girls: *Bleak House,* after all, was nearly contemporaneous with the American novel, Maria Cummins's *The Lamplighter,* that Joyce singled out for parody in the Gerty MacDowell episode of *Ulysses.*[1] Yet the disfigurement of Esther's face has a number of important consequences for the plot. First, the resemblance of this face to that of Lady Dedlock, and Lady Dedlock's portrait, must soon reveal their relationship to others besides young Guppy; Esther's meeting with her mother becomes possible only after the resemblance is erased, supposedly a boon to both women. Second, the spoiling of the heroine's face is John Jarndyce's opportunity, since he can propose to make her "mistress of Bleak House"—neither of them uses the word "wife" until the engagement is at an end—without taking advantage of her: no young Guppy will want her now. Third, Allan Woodcourt can prove his attachment by marrying Esther in spite of her face—a sentimental more than a practical issue perhaps. Thus each of these principal actors and Esther herself, who must sooner or later have a look in the mirror, make their terms with the new face; and as heroine and narrator both she is acutely aware of this crisis when she next appears in number 11 and when Woodcourt returns in number 14. Moreover, all three—mother, guardian, and future husband—have more power to affect Esther's happiness than a fourth principal she must also look in the face, her friend Ada. Yet Ada proves still harder to confront than any of the others.[2]

Doubtless Dickens continues to rely on conventional ideas of how one young woman might behave to another. Ada is still "my darling," "my angel girl," "my sweet beautiful girl" (36.456). But in comparison to Esther's much calmer behavior with those closer to her interests, this relationship is overdetermined, compounded of identification and hostility. For as should become clear, Ada is both double and rival to the heroine: a sure index of the degree to which the novelist subjectively construes the plot, for which Ada Clare is otherwise not very interesting. Ada exists only for Esther Summerson, for her projection and her narrative. As Timothy Peltason puts it, "Esther has made Ada's romantic and sexual nature a symbol of her own." Ada is the heroine's "licensed emissary in the world of youthful, romantic desire."[3]

No reader of *Bleak House* is asked to feel deeply sorry for this woman, whose unswerving love for Richard Carstone is so absolute that it would be awkward to think of warning her and thereby imagining a self-interest that she simply does not possess. She is not a character in her own right: unlike George Eliot or Thackeray, Dickens will not develop and make understandable the psychology of several characters as they interact but rather reveal the psychology of his protagonist as it is projected upon, or aimed against, some other invented figure. Therefore the more interesting Esther Summerson becomes for a thoughtful reader, the less interesting will be Ada Clare. But Dickens doesn't care about this sacrifice of the double and rival; on the contrary, he moves in behind his heroine and makes her win, he backs Summerson as willingly as he backed Copperfield, with similarly fatal results to those who come in her path. The value of this procedure is its depth psychology, a study of what someone does not know about her- or himself, rather than the sum of experience among several actors.[4]

Even before anything has happened to Esther's face, the fascination with Ada intensifies and stiffens with antiseptic precaution. In one moment Esther senses that she is ill, and in the next she bars the door: "I heard Ada's voice outside, and I hurried to the door . . . and locked it" (31.388). Charley is then instructed to keep out the other woman at all costs, always with the unspoken implication that her beauty, so much finer than Esther's, must not be infected.

> On the second morning I heard her dear voice—O how dear now!—outside; and I asked Charley, with some difficulty (speech being painful to me), to go and say I was asleep. I heard her answer softly, "Don't disturb her, Charley, for the world!"
>
> "How does my own Pride look, Charley?" I inquired.
>
> "Disappointed, miss," said Charley, peeping through the curtain.
>
> "But I know she is very beautiful this morning."
>
> "She is indeed, miss," answered Charley, peeping. "Still looking up at the window."
>
> With her blue clear eyes, God bless them, always loveliest when raised like that!
>
> I called Charley to me, and gave her her last charge.
>
> "Now, Charley, when she knows that I am ill, she will try to make her way into the room. Keep her out, Charley, if you love me truly, to the last! Charley, if you let her in but once, only to look upon me for one moment as I lie here, I shall die."

Then—apparently the last thing she realizes before the fever overtakes her—she tells Charley, "I cannot see you . . . I am blind" (31.391). As to this eventuality, Dickens left his original readers in suspense for a month; but readers duly discover in the next number that though her face is disfigured, the heroine does not remain blind. The blindness, reinforced by the chapter ending, is like a psychosomatic response to the frenzy about seeing and not being seen that commences here: not peeping and peeping by proxy through the window curtain, the fear of having to look upon "my own Pride" while possessed of the power to infect that beauty, or of being punished for not possessing such blue eyes—"always loveliest when raised like that!"

After this number, Phiz—the illustrator Hablot Browne—no longer portrays the heroine's face.[5] But though Summerson's readers are thus deprived of looking, her fictional acquaintances must eventually look upon her, and likewise she must face them. The easiest and first person to be confronted after the illness, in the second half of the novel, is "my guardian." Esther and Jarndyce are quickly at ease with one another again, and he sensitively raises the question of when Ada shall see her:

> I had been thinking of that too. A little in connexion with the absent mirrors [removed so as not to distress Esther], but not much; for I knew my loving girl would be changed by no change in my looks.
>
> "Dear guardian," said I, "as I have shut her out so long—though indeed, indeed, she is like the light to me———"

Esther admits to herself that her appearance will make no difference to Ada, yet cannot finish her sentence. Summerson the narrator understands that the reluctance to confront Ada lay on her side, though she cannot explain it and could not at the time: otherwise she would not describe so carefully this delicate conversation with her guardian, who gently advises her to rest before speaking further.

> "As I have kept Ada out so long," I began afresh after a short while, "I think I should like to have my own way a little longer, guardian. It would be best to be away from here before I see her. If Charley

and I were to go to some country lodging as soon as I can move, and if I had a week there, in which to grow stronger and be revived by the sweet air, and to look forward to the happiness of having Ada with me again, I think it would be better for us."

I hope it was not a poor thing in me to wish to be a little more used to my altered self, before I met the eyes of the dear girl whom I longed so ardently to see; but it is the truth. I did. (35.436)

Readers need to appreciate what a strong antipathy to seeing and being seen is represented here: never in the first half of the novel has the character narrating so asserted herself as to propose, as if she truly were the mistress of Bleak House, any favor for herself. Jarndyce registers the change when he begins his response by jokingly calling her "our spoilt little woman," and in the dialogue he is more mindful of Ada's possible feelings than Esther is. The latter's account of these days is helplessly contradictory. She "longed so ardently to see" her friend but prohibits seeing. By "a week or so more" she has treated herself to "long talks with Ada, from behind the window-curtain." Presumably Ada remained on the outside looking in, her blue eyes lifted in vain. "Yet I never saw her; for I had not as yet the courage to look at the dear face, though I could have done so easily without her seeing me" (35.436–37). And why not peek at Ada? Because now that her own face is disfigured it must be as painful to see her friend's beauty as to be seen by her.

To be fair to Esther, she has not yet looked upon her own face in a mirror: it is as if Ada truly were her double, as far as wishful looks and looking are concerned. After she receives a visit from Miss Flite (by the end of which Miss Summerson seems quite in her old form) and after she and Charley have gone off to stay at Boythorn's home in Lincolnshire near Chesney Wold, she does persuade herself to look: "I put my hair aside, and looked at the reflection in the mirror; encouraged by seeing how placidly it looked at me" (36.444). More time passes (among other pastimes, she writes to Ada every day) before the momentous meeting in the open with her mother. But Esther's altered face does not figure in that encounter except as a palliative: Lady Dedlock throws herself at her daughter's feet to beg forgiveness, and "I felt, through all my tumult of emotion, a burst of gratitude to the providence of God that I was so changed as that I never could disgrace her by any trace of likeness"; and more neutrally, as if there were a second advantage to be gained for herself, "that nobody could ever now look at me, and look at her, and remotely think of any near tie between us" (36.449). A contrite Lady Dedlock says not a word about her daughter's appearance, nor does the narrator of the scene recur to it among her many other reflections. From a letter prepared in advance, Esther learns that she "had not been abandoned by my mother," but rather "laid aside as dead," before recovering her infant life and being cared for "in rigid secrecy" by her aunt (36.452).

In the midst of still more reflections on the heroine's birth, the reader finds that Ada is coming at last: "But from my darling who was coming on the morrow, I found a joyful letter, full of such loving anticipation that I must have been made of marble if it had not moved me" (36.454). The next day, Summerson recalls, with only two hours remaining, she could not decide whether to advance along the road by which her friend would come or to wait in the house, and consequently put herself in a sweat by trying to do both. Now the anxiety "about my altered looks" and about Ada's looks rises to a pitch, for "I knew the various expressions of my sweet girl's face so well and it was such an honest face in its loveliness, that I was sure, beforehand, she could not hide that first look from me" (36.455).

While our heroine is "trembling in the garden," Charley cries out, "Here she comes, miss! Here she is!":

> I did not mean to do it, but I ran up-stairs into my room, and hid myself behind the door. There I stood trembling, even when I heard my darling calling as she came up-stairs, "Esther, my dear, my love, where are you? Little woman, dear Dame Durden!"
>
> She ran in, and was running out again when she saw me. Ah, my angel girl! the old dear look, all love, all fondness, all affection. Nothing else in it — no, nothing, nothing!
>
> O how happy I was, down upon the floor, with my sweet beautiful girl down upon the floor too, holding my scarred face to her lovely cheek, bathing it with tears and kisses, rocking me to and fro like a child, calling me by every tender name that she could think of, and pressing me to her faithful heart. (36.456)

And so the chapter ends: the two friends cheek to cheek but still not eye to eye perhaps. The tremendous buildup has collapsed in writhing on the floor, in a scene that anticipates the ambivalence of Pip's struggle on the floor with Miss Havisham, as he vainly attempts to save the wretched woman from the flames: the intentions are all positive but the results mixed — even negative.[6] In the instant before the two friends entwine, Esther has checked for "the old dear look" and found nothing but what she wanted, and has always wanted, love. But of this love she has intellectually, consciously been assured all along, so her manifest relief — if it is relief — is from whatever it is that lies behind her negative, something that has not turned up in her swift glance. "Nothing else in it — no, nothing, nothing!"

But what else, precisely? Throughout weeks of anxiety and more than two chapters of narration, either Esther has never known or Summerson will not write directly of the cause of near panic, and in this outcome and resolution of the suspense at the end of chapter 36 the cause is still not explicit. Very possibly Esther fears she will see pity in Ada's look, pity that might weigh heavily, along with her invalid's self-pity, upon her fragile pride. But as with the shock and disappointment she wishes to spare her friend and the love she hopes to preserve, a fear of being pitied applies to her other friends as well. After a little time, in fact, she is pleased that Allan Woodcourt feels sorry for her when he sees her face; and if pity may sometimes seem an offense to pride, it is also expressive of the character and affection of one's friends—Woodcourt's case exactly (45.549).

The question is what is special to the relation to Ada that induces panic in their meeting face to face that she does not experience with the others. Ada is another young woman, obviously: cheek to cheek or eye to eye, a comparison may be at issue. In the case of Esther's mother, a famously handsome but older woman, the new difference of appearance in the daughter works in the direction of a desired separation; but in the case of the friend the difference in appearance has been evident, at least to Esther, all along and now is greater than ever. Ada Clare serves as an icon of female attractiveness in the novel, entirely within Summerson's narrative. Since this icon exists, how should a heroine not wish to be like her? (A few feminists might protest that women do not make such icons, but this one was in any event made by Dickens.) The confronting of Ada's face, in the crisis of Esther's illness, comes closest to the problem of confronting the self in the mirror, and Ada has been a mirror all along: the mirror of all female beauty, as she might have been called in the Renaissance, when mirroring in this sense was often comported with by queens and courtiers, not to say kings. The giveaway in the text is the extended opportunity for looking *at* Ada that Esther refuses after her disfigurement: the comparison has now become too painful to cover with fondness. No wonder, when the time arrives, that Esther instantaneously perceives "the old dear look, all love, all fondness, all affection." Quite possibly she persuades herself of this old look and its trail of associations without actually looking Ada in the face.

But it is also uncertain how friendly the heroine is to the one who has been kept waiting, first outside the room and latterly at a distance of two days' journey. Hostility—which in truth, Dickens cultivates here and there for harvest in the denouement of *Bleak House*—may underlie the heightened anxiety that the narrator associates with Ada's face. Perhaps the something else that she madly fears ("Nothing else in it—no, nothing, nothing!") is a look of triumph in her friend's eyes, in which case she would be justified in hiding, delaying, and striking back. Esther's goings-on about Ada do seem a little mad, in both senses of the word: irrational, in view of Ada's obvious goodwill, and angry at her beauty. Men and women certainly are capable of resenting very beautiful persons of either sex—persons, that is, in the Victorian, physical sense—and resenting them precisely because of the fierce attraction they hold. A double or duplicit response to an especially attractive woman may be more common in males, and if so Dickens may have compromised his protagonist's calculated femaleness in this respect. Even so, over the course of the novel Esther Summerson will prove superior to misfortune and triumph over all her friends; her timorousness may be genuine and still disguise a preemptive superiority or secret condescension. The panic in chapter 36, from this point of view, could be a charade for her own and her reader's benefit, as if to say that my Pride, the blue-eyed one, is only capable of trading looks, comparing faces, regarding beauty, and thus has to be treated with these exaggerated precautions, whereas my other friends are deeper and prepared to understand me. Dickens designed some such ambivalence to reveal the character, and the reticence of his narrator allows for it. At the same time, Esther Summerson may have become secretly more aggressive than he expected her to be.

The narrator's silences are largely dictated by her feminine role throughout. Conventionally, we should not expect her to write of loving any man, and her general longing is that of a receptacle—the passive aim to "win some love to myself if I could" (3.20). Her adult relation to men nevertheless begins in the same chapter that tells of her childhood, when she, Ada Clare, and Richard Carstone meet in London for the first time. Proleptically she writes of "my darling" here and apologizes to the reader in tones faintly reminiscent of Uriah Heep: the expression "is so natural to me now, that I can't help writing it" (3.31). But a certain recollection from that day brings her into relation with Carstone, too, when the two wards are presented to the Lord Chancellor and this exchange takes place:

> "Mr. Jarndyce of Bleak House, my lord," Mr. Kenge observed, in a low voice, "if I may venture to remind your lordship, provides a suitable companion for——"
> "For Mr. Richard Carstone?" I thought (but I am not quite sure) I heard his lordship say, in an equally low voice, and with a smile.
> "For Miss Ada Clare. This is the young lady. Miss Summerson." (3.31–32)

With rare touches like this, Dickens just hints at his narrator's own desires. Esther's main initiation into love between the sexes is that of a bystander as she watches the two very handsome wards in Chancery select each other almost without words. Never is there any overt desire for Richard on her part—on the contrary, he will remorselessly be exposed as a disaster in store for any woman—but the narrative becomes quietly infused with envy of the chance of being loved.

Miss Summerson's chance waits upon Allan Woodcourt, a young doctor as circumspect as she herself and, needless to say, far more dependable over the long haul than Carstone. The chance materializes in the novel only when Woodcourt calls to announce that he is embarking for the Far East as a ship's surgeon: "And so he put his lips to Ada's hand—and to mine; and so he went away upon his long, long voyage!" Apparently Woodcourt would court if he could court, but the only sign he leaves behind is a nosegay—at another location.[7] Summerson's narrative fails to discern whether the flowers were left for herself or Miss Flite, but Caddy Jellyby, who has brought them along, and Ada determine that they are meant for Esther (17.215–16). Subsequently, the dead flowers provide an emblem for the heroine's lost chance and—like a corpse that keeps turning up in a mystery story—always in relation to Ada. After Esther has traveled to Lincolnshire and looked herself in the glass, she informs the reader that "one thing troubled me." She has apparently kept and dried the withered flowers, has "put them in a book that I was fond of. Nobody knew this, not even Ada." Now her question is whether she has "a right" to keep them, or whether keeping them is "generous" to a man who knew her before her illness. But she confesses that she "could have loved" Woodcourt and decides to keep the flowers "only as a remembrance of what was irrevocably past and gone" (36.445). With this little matter of the flowers out of the way, she is finally prepared for the terrific meeting with Ada.

The unexpected meeting with her mother and the secret of her birth Esther keeps to herself—it makes surprisingly little

difference to the panic over Ada. An unrelated call by Sir
Leicester Dedlock at Bleak House later prompts her to confide in Jarndyce, lest the latter unwittingly bring her into closer
contact with either of the Dedlocks. Encouraged by his new
knowledge of her illegitimacy and loss of good looks, Jarndyce
invites her to become "the mistress of Bleak House" in the letter that "was not a love letter," which she recounts entirely in
indirect discourse (much as Copperfield treated Agnes Wickfield's letters in his narrative). Two things that Jarndyce does
not write, Esther nevertheless understands perfectly: "That the
discovery of my birth gave him no shock. That his generosity
rose above my disfigurement, and my inheritance of shame"
(44.537–38). Notoriously, Jarndyce never does speak, and waits
patiently two weeks before Esther intimates her answer with
a kiss—the one erotic moment in their relationship. Yet she
speaks to her own face in the mirror the night she receives the
letter, when her decision to accept this proposal requires that
the dead flowers be cremated:

> Perhaps the name [Woodcourt] brought them to
> my remembrance. The dried remains of the flowers.
> It would be better not to keep them now. They
> had only been preserved in memory of something
> wholly past and gone, but it would be better not to
> keep them now.
>
> They were in a book, and it happened to be in
> the next room—our sitting room, dividing Ada's
> chamber from mine. I took a candle, and went
> softly to fetch it from its shelf. After I had it in my
> hand, I saw my beautiful darling, through the open
> door, lying asleep, and I stole in to kiss her.
>
> It was weak in me, I know, and I could have no
> reason for crying; but I dropped a tear upon her

dear face, and another, and another. Weaker than
that, I took the withered flowers out, and put them
for a moment to her lips. I thought about her love
for Richard; though, indeed, the flowers had nothing to do with that. Then I took them into my own
room, and burned them at the candle, and they
were dust in an instant. (44.539)

In such a passage, the Summerson narrative outdoes itself. It
reveals even as it comes apart. Involuntary thoughts and actions
are recalled together with analysis, but analysis too is incomplete. "The dried remains of the flowers," without a predicate,
is the image that imposed itself on her mind—for the first sentence is retrospective analysis of the association. The handling
of tense and the indirect style of the rest of that paragraph
carry the Esther who is writing, and her reader reading, back
to that time and to the still earlier time of deciding to keep
the flowers; the reasoning, though exemplary, gives the lie to
her earlier reasoning: the flowers were not preserved in remembrance but in hope. "They were in a book, and it happened to
be in the next room . . ." Though a conscious decision draws
her to the flowers, to the place where she put them, they have
a fixity in the dark that is not ordinarily disturbed. She moved
"softly" then from an awareness of Ada's presence before the
reader can be aware of it, and before she so inadvertently "saw
my beautiful darling" and "stole in to kiss her." Retrospectively,
she is full of the consciousness of significance, and therefore
of the need to narrate what just "happened to be"; typically,
she deflects the significance by moralizing instead of being explicit. "It was weak in me I know" precedes what she involun-
tarily did, which was to cry over that face. Again she puts aside
analysis, with intensified self-criticism—"weaker than that"—
before narrating the most extraordinary action of that night,

contriving to make Ada kiss the dried remains of those flowers. Then, for her own and the reader's enlightenment, she recalls one bit of association at the time that might be useful for interpreting this gesture—"I thought about her love for Richard"; and this association is checked, not by moralizing this time, but by naive denial of its significance—"though, indeed, the flowers had nothing to do with that."

The denial, coming near the end of what is in effect Summerson's defense of this spontaneous ceremony, asks to be denied in turn. She has, after all, pointedly recalled and called to our attention a process of association and analysis that she herself cannot or will not complete. Furthermore, since the ceremony begins by betraying her previous contention that the flowers were merely a remembrance, we have to wonder if this analysis is any more valid than the last. Positioned as it is between Jarndyce's proposal, which promises to alter their relationship not at all, and Esther's acceptance two weeks later with a kiss and a yes, which "made no difference presently" (44.540), it is fair to say that her involuntary recollection of the flowers, the inadvertent ceremony, and the deliberate move to burn them signify the giving up of Woodcourt in particular and of sexual relations in general. Her friend Ada comes into it because Ada, along with Caddy, first perceived that Woodcourt might be interested in her, and her friend Ada's love for Richard comes into it because their engagement represents for Esther a sexual relation between a man and woman of more nearly the same age.

But the extraordinary action is to make Ada kiss "the withered flowers" without knowing it, even though the flowers have admittedly nothing to do with her love. The passage calls out for interpretation, for help from the reader in completing the faltering analysis, so that the last sentence too—after which

Dickens instructed the printer to leave a blank line[8]—is best read in the context of Esther's ambivalent feelings and the outcome of Ada's love for Richard. "Then I took them into my room, and burned them at the candle, and they were dust in an instant": symbolically Esther puts an end to the idea, never expressed in so many words, that Woodcourt is her proper suitor; but on a second or third reading of *Bleak House,* in the biblical finality of this return to dust, after the dead flowers have been touched to Ada's lips rather than her own, there seems to be a fateful anticipation of the end of Richard's availability as well.

Dickens and Summerson at the time of writing already know that Richard will die, and the intelligent reader will be advised of his fate by the next chapter. There Esther confers with Richard at Deal about his latest failure of will and coincidentally runs into Woodcourt, returning that very day from his long absence (burning the flowers now takes on a new irony). In fact, Woodcourt's concern for what has happened to Esther is on this occasion overshadowed by the inward change he perceives in Richard's face:

> "I saw you observe him rather closely," said I. "Do you think him so changed?"
>
> "He is changed," he returned, shaking his head.
>
> I felt the blood rush to my face for the first time, but it was only an instantaneous emotion. I turned my head aside, and it was gone.
>
> "It is not," said Mr. Woodcourt, "his being so much younger or older, thinner or fatter, paler or ruddier, as there being upon his face such a singular expression. I never saw so remarkable a look in a young person. One cannot say that it is all anxiety, or all weariness; yet it is both, and like ungrown despair." (45.550)

Our heroine's face beautifully betrays her personal application of "changed" in this blush; yet given the nature of the change in store for Carstone and foreshadowed here by Woodcourt's words, she might well blush from a secret enmity, as if "such a singular expression" in their friend's face resulted from her playing with those flowers and the candle. Dickens, I suggest, does not purpose to endow his heroine with witchlike powers; but such are his own powers of projection that between his design and Summerson's reticences not a few passages of her reporting are overdetermined.

With the burning of the dead flowers and the return of Woodcourt alive, a longer-term opportunity for Esther begins to open before the reader. At the same time, a gap widens between the two women friends. As for her engagement to become mistress of Bleak House, "I said nothing to my precious pet"—to Ada, that is—"about it" (50.540). But once Esther has returned from Deal and taken to visiting Caddy Turveydrop, who now is mother to an odd little baby named after Esther, she recalls that Caddy was the one who "had brought me the little parting token"—the last reference of all to the nosegay (50.601). This memory and Ada's close association with the same occasion prompt Esther to tell them both of her engagement at last; and with characteristically mixed motives she does so. More time passes in London, where the heroine is mainly occupied with Caddy, before she begins to notice a "change" in Ada that, like the change in Richard, portends more serious matters than the change of her own face wrought by disease. At first she imagines—one of the many touches that reveal her as not entirely happy "about Bleak House"—that Ada must be unhappy for *her* (50.604). She fails to realize, it seems, that if she has had secrets from her darling girl, the reverse may also be the case; and a surprise awaits her in the next chapter when she accompanies Ada to Richard's new lodgings in

Symond's Inn near Chancery Lane. Death is palpably present in the streets that day: "I thought there were more funerals passing along the dismal pavements, than I had seen before"; and when they arrive at the door, she sees "Richard's name in great white letters on a hearse-like panel" (51.611). With this ominous prelude for the scene to follow, the two women enter Richard's rooms, and Ada reveals the first of her secrets by means of the same gesture poor Esther had used to signal her acceptance to Jarndyce, in the same words: "her two arms round his neck" (51.613; cf. 44.540). So the first change in question is that Ada has secretly married Richard Carstone as soon as she was twenty-one; and the second change, since this placing of her arms around the man's neck has been more metonymic than in Esther's case, is that Ada is pregnant.

Such ironies would seem to tell against the heroine. But consider that it is Summerson who relates them, and how she turns up the power—ultimately the power of the plot that Dickens has placed in her service—when these discoveries are made. While Ada continues to embrace her husband and announces that she will not return home with Esther any more, the narrator, who has already seen death in the streets and on the panel of the door, to say nothing of Richard's changed face, reports calmly that "if ever in my life I saw a love that nothing but death could change, I saw it then before me." And again, "I pitied her so much. I was very fond of Richard, but the impulse that I had upon me was to pity her so much" (51.613). These sober reflections, to be sure, do not quite match with her behavior in the scene, which she characterizes as inadequate, fond, and foolish—so much so that she resolved "to hide my plain old face as much as I could, lest I should put them out of heart." In parting, it is Ada's "precious face, which it seemed to rive my heart to turn from." And with a joke about whether the married pair will welcome her any more, "I folded her lovely face between my hands, and gave it one last kiss, and laughed, and ran away" (51.614–15). But Esther neither stays away nor waits until she is invited to return. In another overdetermined demonstration of ambivalence, she returns that night after dark with Charley, walks by looking up at their light, and sees Vholes go past (the whole chapter is distinctly operatic). As if not wishing Ada to have the last secret, she leaves Charley and steals up the stairs.

> I listened for a few moments; and in the musty rot-
> ting silence of the house, believed that I could hear
> the murmur of their young voices. I put my lips to
> the hearse-like panel of the door, as a kiss for my
> dear, and came quietly down again, thinking that
> one of these days I would confess to the visit.

The kiss to the hearselike panel recalls the holding of the dead flowers to Ada's lips: these actions, fraught with death for Richard, do make Dame Trot or Dame Durden seem rather witchlike.[9] "And it really did me good," Summerson recalls. She returns home to commiserate with her guardian about the two married ones. Jarndyce looks at her with "his old bright fatherly look," and after this exciting day she is even "rather disappointed" that her engagement has changed nothing (51.615–16).

In the last number of *Bleak House,* when the infamous case of Jarndyce and Jarndyce—"a Monument of Chancery practice," in the words of Conversation Kenge—goes up in costs and laughter, Summerson gets another glimpse of Vholes: "He gave one gasp as if he had swallowed the last morsel of this client, and his black buttoned-up unwholesome figure glided away to the low door at the end of the Hall" (65.759,760). Right enough, the end of the lawsuit is the end of Richard Carstone, whose own mouth, instead of Vholes's, fills with blood. Incongruously, Summerson observes that "he looked handsomer than I had seen him look for many a day." Indeed, he dies "with a light in his eyes," having mended his wrong opinion of John Jarndyce and desired to see the new Bleak House, "their house—Dame Durden's and Woodcourt's house" (65.761–63). Though Richard never travels as far as the new Bleak House in this life, his child by Ada will, as Summerson reports in the last chapter of all. "It was a boy; and I, my husband, and my guardian gave him his father's name" (67.767). The boy is seven at the time of writing: "I call him my Richard! But he says he has two mamas, and I am one" (67.769). Who might the other be? The biological mother has meanwhile taken Esther's place at the old Bleak House, which "claims priority" according to Jarndyce. In order to get used to this exchange of places, Ada is no longer to call him cousin John but guardian. "So she called him guardian, and has called him guardian ever since" (67.767). Such a triumph for the heroine could scarcely be told without irony: Esther now has her Woodcourt and her beautiful darling has a guardian, the same guardian. As Lawrence Frank puts it, "Ada becomes the captive of Jarndyce's coercive benevolence." [10] Yet Summerson the narrator betrays no consciousness of irony or recognition that her happiness is starkly set off by Carstone's death and her friend's permanent state of mourning. "Sometimes, when I raise my eyes and see her, in the black dress that she still wears, teaching my Richard, I feel— it is difficult to express—as if it were so good to know that she remembers her dear Esther in her prayers" (67.769). But the prayers devoted by Ada, in her role of pure love, to *her* Richard were in vain. Summerson shows no particular awareness of her own mortal danger, as she had during her illness, and forgets that her rival's prayers most likely are directed elsewhere.

The question of Dickens's consciousness of all this is a more difficult matter. Surely he deserves more credit than is generally accorded him for exploring at least this one character in

Bleak House in depth. And surely he distances himself from his narrator-heroine. Just as she always envied Ada and once vicariously imagined sexual union by the same mediation, she now imagines herself the mother of her friend's male child. Pointedly, she has no male child by Woodcourt: "I have two little daughters" (67.767). Dickens expects his readers to understand all this, along with the petty vanity of his heroine, and he has been able to suggest some underlying hostility reflected in the action. But as with many novels with happy endings, the egocentric construction rather than the egotism of the character seems to clash with the received morality of the culture. If we smile at "my Richard" or the heroine's last little conceit about her face, "even supposing———" as her narrative breaks off (67.770), presumably we are not to worry too much about the remorseless way in which the plot has worked to elevate her fortune at the expense of others'. The self-aggrandizement wound up in the last chapter poses a problem not unlike that of the ending of *Jane Eyre.* I have to believe that Brontë quite intended to blind and maim Rochester and that Dickens was just as determined to kill Richard and enslave Ada, however jollily the novelists distance themselves from their protagonists in lesser ways. And for Dickens to have engaged in wish fulfillment on Summerson's behalf just as eagerly as he had with Copperfield argues that this vector of narratives in the first person is no respecter of gender.

4

Honoria, Lady Dedlock

The novel's other great beauty has a different style altogether: so different that, even though Esther and her mother look alike, relatively little fuss is made about the heroine's disfigured face—a relief to Esther now—when they meet in Lincolnshire. Summerson's readers have seen more of the mother than she has, since we are made acquainted with Lady Dedlock before the Summerson narrative is born: "She had beauty, pride, ambition, insolent resolve, and sense enough to portion out a legion of fine ladies," yet is "bored to death" (2.12,11). The list of her qualities begins, interestingly, with two that Summerson faithfully confers on her coeval, Ada. The character functions, in fact, as a principal cross-over between the two narratives of *Bleak House*. Lady Dedlock's boredom seeps into the satire of privilege much as the fog infects the Court of Chancery, yet she proves to be the mother of the self-effacing narrator of all those other chapters. A few characters associated with her also move between the two narratives: most notably Inspector Bucket, but also Hortense, George, Guppy, and—satisfyingly somehow—Mrs. Chadband, who as the housekeeper Mrs. Rachael helped raise Esther. Only Jo the crossing sweeper, and Allan Woodcourt, of all the characters in *Bleak House,* have roles comparable to Lady Dedlock's in traversing both narratives. To reflect on her story, therefore, is to start somewhere beyond Summerson's ostensible control and then to circle back within it.

A person Esther never encounters is Mr. Tulkinghorn, though the rusty old lawyer is critical to the main action involving Lady Dedlock. There indeed would be no compelling reason to introduce a Tulkinghorn in *Bleak House* if it were not the novelist's determination to approach Esther's mother from the outside in. The lawyer turns up very early to observe my Lady's startled response to a particular piece of handwriting. "She supposes herself to be an inscrutable Being . . . seeing herself in her glass"; yet, "while Mr. Tulkinghorn may not know what is passing in the Dedlock mind at present, it is very possible that he may" (2.14–15). Esther later hears about Tulkinghorn in the course of her only interview with her mother, and what she hears concerns her birth—concerns, that is, mother and daughter both. In fact, it is she who prompts discussion of the man, whose name is never mentioned between them. " 'But is the secret safe so far?' I asked." To this Lady Dedlock replies that she dreads especially "Sir Leicester Dedlock's lawyer; mechanically faithful without attachment, and very jealous of the profit, privilege, and reputation of being master of the mysteries of great houses." "Has he any suspicions?" Esther asks, without needing to specify suspicions of what. "Yes! He is always vigilant, and always near me." Nor can he be won over, for "his calling is the acquisition of secrets, and the holding possession of such power as they give him, with no sharer or opponent in it" (36.450–51). The subsequent murder of this man is pivotal to the action as far as the older woman is concerned. She has given birth to Esther years before the novel properly commences; yet when the murder occurs, she will run away, vainly pursued by her daughter and Inspector Bucket. I stress the conversation of chapter 36 because there, Dickens informs us, his heroine finds out about Tulkinghorn: Esther never encounters him, but her questions call up his troublesome role.

Thus the meeting of mother and daughter in chapter 36 completes one line of suspense in *Bleak House* (Esther Summerson's identity) and places renewed emphasis on a second line that also winds its way all the way back to the first number: a threat to Lady Dedlock and, it would now seem, to Esther, the root of which threat is Tulkinghorn's "acquisition of secrets, and the holding possession of such power as they give him." The murder, which I have anticipated, will occur on a certain "very quiet night" twelve chapters on, in number 15:

> When the moon shines very brilliantly, a solitude and stillness seem to proceed from her, that influence even crowded places full of life. . . . In these fields of Mr. Tulkinghorn's inhabiting, where the shepherds play on Chancery pipes that have no stop, and keep their sheep in the fold by hook and by crook until they have shorn them exceeding close, every noise is merged, this moonlit night, into a distant ringing hum, as if the city were a vast glass, vibrating. (48.584)

In the mock pastoral stillness a sound is heard that may have been a pistol shot, but the body is not found—beneath Allegory's pointing finger—until the next morning. At such a turning of the action, in such a setting and determined allegory, it is obviously a mistake to read Tulkinghorn as Dickens's example of wicked professional behavior *or* as his true portrait of a family lawyer, though two American lawyers have recently disputed the novelist's intentions along these very lines.[1] Tulkinghorn's role is to be murdered, so that the question can arise of who killed him—which of three possible women or, if anyone could believe it, the trooper George. And at some generalized level the murder is an allegory: this lawyer's power when living is rooted in the possession of threatening secrets, a power akin to blackmail. A social if not political issue is being addressed here, since Dickens as well as Phiz's illustration for this number insist on the Roman figure painted on the ceiling. The mock pastoral setting and pointing Roman draw upon a long tradition of covert commentary on public as well as private affairs.[2]

Tulkinghorn's life plays out just when he is preoccupied with "the" secret of Esther's conception and birth. Though he has latterly been able to put his hands on some incriminating letters, he first came upon the secret by a combination of symbiosis and osmosis: "She passes close to him. . . . They meet again at dinner—again, next day—again, for many days in succession. . . . But whether each evermore watches and suspects the other . . . whether each is evermore prepared at all points for the other . . . what each would give to know how much the other knows—all this is hidden, for the time, in their own hearts" (12.150). Because Tulkinghorn's calling is the acquisition of secrets, it seems he cannot do better than keep a watch on women: "There are women enough in the world, Mr. Tulkinghorn thinks—too many; they are at the bottom of all that goes wrong in it, though, for the matter of that, they create business for lawyers. . . . They are all secret. Mr. Tulkinghorn knows that very well" (16.200). Consistent with his principles, even though against his interest as a family lawyer, the enemy of womankind disapproves of marriage. As he pointedly threatens the wife of Sir Leicester, having learned her secret, "Most of the people I know would do far better to leave marriage alone" (41.512). Tulkinghorn is not so vulgar an operator as to shake down a fine lady: that would be a risky business, against his client's interest as well as his own. But it should be remembered that every blackmailer, even the weakest, intends first and foremost to hold on to the secret in question, since its disclosure spells the end of income or power, either one. Just because Tulkinghorn holds his secrets close doesn't mean that he is not what would soon come to be called a master blackmailer.[3]

As Tulkinghorn's misogyny fairly predicts, it is no accident that his victim is a woman and a woman of distinctly lower class origins than her husband. If Lady Dedlock had been Lady Honoria—that is, held the title in her own right—her name would convey a different set of ironies, and it is less likely that a premarital affair with Captain Hawdon (if he were handsome enough and belonged to the right regiment) would have caused her beauty to be treated as spoiled goods. The whole scandal of the heroine's mother in *Bleak House* has to be seen against the background of changing conditions of class mobility and publicity in the period, conditions that novelists were studying even before "blackmail" attained its modern meaning of threatening to reveal secrets or was criminalized in the common law.[4] Dickens, in fact, represents some of this background in his novel, and in number 17 vulgar blackmail pronounces its demands with impertinent exuberance. Smaller fish than Tulkinghorn have been nibbling at Lady Dedlock's secret, and sure enough, the comic extortioners turn up at the critical moment: Bucket has to handle their interruption in an interval between his telling Sir Leicester of the premarital affair and his arrest of Hortense, the French maid, for the murder. Smallweed, the Chadbands, and Mrs. Snagsby abruptly arrive at the door, all clamoring to be paid off by the baronet. Smallweed, who demands five hundred pounds, makes the novel's only direct sneer at the name "Honoria." Mrs. Snagsby has stumbled on information during her ceaseless and suspicious watching of her husband. And Chadband delivers the most curious blackmail threat ever uttered:

> My friends, we are now—Rachael my wife, and I—
> in the mansions of the rich and great. Why are
> we now in the mansions of the rich and great, my
> friends? Is it because we are invited? Because we are
> bidden to feast with them, because we are bidden

to rejoice with them, because we are bidden to play
the lute with them, because we are bidden to dance
with them? No. Then why are we here, my friends?
Air we in possession of a sinful secret, and doe we
require corn, and wine, and oil—or, what is much
the same thing, money—for the keeping thereof?
Probably so, my friends. (54.643–44)

The Chadbands thus marvelously threaten, even as they represent in their own persons, the danger from low connections of the woman who married Sir Leicester. And still another comic seeker of secrets in *Bleak House*, not present in this tumultuous scene, is Guppy. While Guppy's motives are more ambiguous, like Tulkinghorn's but of the amorous rather than the legal way of profiting, his persistence also threatens privacy with publicity.

In rendering blackmail comic, Dickens represents the extortion, reproves it, but by no means eliminates it. The worldly Inspector Bucket simply recommends that this crowd be paid off, and the implication seems clear that should the blackmailers stumble upon some new scandal, they will be at it again. With his mock pastoral, his pointing Roman, and the decisive murder of the master blackmailer Tulkinghorn, Dickens is up to something different—and allegorical. As Michael Steig has shown, when the Roman figure first appears in number 3, it "sprawls among balustrades and pillars, flowers, clouds and big-legged boys, and makes the head ache—as would seem to be Allegory's object always, more or less" (10.119); and Phiz initially followed this description in the working drawing for number 15.[5] He had apparently missed the change to a pointing figure that Dickens imposed in number 5. Originally the fresco on Tulkinghorn's ceiling served to characterize the occupant and permitted the novelist to take a crack, as he sometimes would, at art styles he didn't like. But in number 5, Lady Dedlock and the crossing sweeper Jo, Tulkinghorn's chambers and Tom-all-Alone's come together in a single chapter, while Dickens hints broadly at their relatedness. "What connexion can there be . . . What connexion can there have been between many people in the innumerable histories of this world, who, from opposite sides of great gulfs, have nevertheless, been very curiously brought together!" There, after Lady Dedlock leaves Tulkinghorn, "foreshortened Allegory, in the person of one impossible Roman upside down, points with the arm of Samson (out of joint, and an odd one) obtrusively toward the window" (16.197,199–200). Dickens is again badgering bad art, but the pointing arm seems directed toward Lady Dedlock in the street outside. The further connection to be made is with Jo pointing to Nemo's grave at the end of the chapter, as drawn by Phiz in the illustration "Consecrated Ground."

Whether it is possible for a reader to realize the intention here is doubtful, but that Dickens connected the two pointing arms we know from his summary notes on the chapter, one line from which reads "Pointing hand of Allegory—Consecrated ground."[6] When the Roman on the ceiling reappears in number 15, Phiz has duly foreshortened him and nearly stood him on his head, and he points at the deserted murder scene. Furthermore, he shall keep on pointing "so long as dust and damp and spiders spare him, with far greater significance" than before— whether at Tulkinghorn's body or Lady Dedlock's look-alike or both (48.585). Allegory is also pointing the moral. Though petty blackmailers still go about the world seeking whatever secrets they can use, this secret is out. The death of the master blackmailer releases Esther Summerson's mother; so does the general knowledge of her secret release her; and so will death release her, the death she is headed for in full flight to the same burial ground. This action is scarcely comic, but killing the possessor of a threatening secret nevertheless feels good. An arm points at Honoria, an arm points at Nemo, but the lawyer who fancied this bad art is finished.

When Inspector Bucket has gone so far as to tell Sir Leicester of the murder, "It was a woman," but not yet told him which woman or what Lady Dedlock was guilty of long ago, he prepares his aristocratic client for a blow by appealing to his sense of "family": "You ask yourself, how would all them ancestors of yours, away to Julius Caesar—not to go beyond him at present—have borne that blow" (54.637). (Perhaps the pointing Roman *is* Julius Caesar or some such ancestor: he wore a helmet in number 5.) Ostensibly Bucket tries to mitigate the blow by first raising the worse case, that Lady Dedlock, besides having had a lover, has herself murdered her tormentor; then when he dramatically ushers in Hortense, of course, he brings on a stroke. Sir Leicester's stroke is anticipated by Allegory's reaction to the murder "as if he were a paralyzed dumb witness" (48.585). The death of Tulkinghorn, whatever the significance Dickens imputes to it, is nothing if not emphatic:

> So, it shall happen surely, through many years to come, that ghostly stories shall be told of the stain upon the floor, so easy to be covered, so hard to be got out; and that the Roman, pointing from the ceiling, shall point, so long as dust and damp and spiders spare him, with far greater significance than he ever had in Mr. Tulkinghorn's time, and with a deadly meaning. For, Mr. Tulkinghorn's time is over for evermore; and the Roman pointed at the murderous hand uplifted against his life, and pointed helplessly at him, from night to morning lying face downward on the floor, shot through the heart. (48.585–87)

This narrative end, like the passages that have preceded it and the pastoral setting, mocks allegory and at the same time is allegory. The deadly art form has begun to signify at last, while the narrator allegorizes right and left, with retarding speculations and concealments that delay the indicative moment until the last four words of the chapter, "shot through the heart." Murder by itself is not the issue here: a "stain upon the floor, so easy to be covered, so hard to get out," may be from the lawyer's blood but is also the stain of Lady Dedlock's sin. Most notably in the last sentence, Dickens's allegory accuses both murderer and victim: the relentless collector of secrets has invited his fate. Thus the Roman motif "helplessly" points a moral. As John Kucich puts it, "Social power in *Bleak House* consists entirely in the ability to invade the privacy of others, and to protect one's own privacy."[7]

Even if Dickens had not led up to the murder so beautifully with his "Don't go home!" and pistol shot muffled by the "distant ringing hum, as if the city were a vast glass, vibrating," most readers would find Tulkinghorn's death resistlessly satisfying. The rusty old lawyer is the prototype of the master blackmailers who captured the imagination of the Edwardian era, when reputational blackmail was popularly known as "moral murder." It became, in George Orwell's words, "a fairly well-established convention in crime stories that murdering a blackmailer 'doesn't count.'"[8] Like the detectives in *Martin Chuzzlewit* and *Bleak House,* the blackmailers in these novels introduced a new convention of crime stories. The interest for the reader of the murder plot depends on the suspicion cast on good citizens like George Rouncewell, the ex-soldier who runs the shooting gallery, or appropriately motivated persons like Lady Dedlock who are nevertheless innocent of this particular crime. Dickens can even be said to initiate the convention of using a particularly unsympathetic nonentity like Hortense to pull the trigger. Hortense is just barely motivated at all, but she is of a murderous temperament and a foreigner to boot: Tulkinghorn's murder is treated as a telling accident of his fate, not of hers. And a very jolly murderess she is, for Mr. Bucket to take in: she chortles that her victim cannot be restored to life, nor Lady Dedlock made honorable, nor Sir Leicester proud again, by her arrest and execution (54.652–53). Nothing can touch Hortense, so no one cares what happens to her, while her words serve to underline the finality of her intervention in the plot.[9]

The displacement of what should be Lady Dedlock's crime upon her sometime maid Hortense enables the novelist and his readers to contemplate the justice of the act without practical guilt or danger. More as if in a theater than in a dream, the displacement is facilitated by exchanges of costume between the two women. The murder would make better sense if it were committed by Lady Dedlock, as her daughter registers — "immediately my mother's dread of him rushed into my remembrance" (52.616) — though she never quite says why. (For this reason, the reader may infer, Esther is all the more concerned by the arrest of the innocent George.) Though Dickens takes some pains with Hortense's dislike of the lawyer, he takes greater pains with Lady Dedlock's motivation to murder. But in order to keep his heroine's mother technically in the clear, he saves his full account of this motivation until after Hortense's arrest. Lady Dedlock learns from Guppy that the secret of her affair with Captain Hawdon is circulating among would-be blackmailers and from Mrs. Rouncewell that she is being anonymously accused (by Hortense) of killing Tulkinghorn. Only then do we read of Lady Dedlock:

> Her enemy he was, and she has often, often,
> often, wished him dead. Her enemy he is, even in

his grave. This dreadful accusation comes upon her, like a new torment at his lifeless hand. . . .

She has thrown herself upon the floor, and lies with her hair all wildly scattered, and her face buried in the cushions of a couch. She rises up, hurries to and fro, flings herself down again, and rocks and moans. The horror that is upon her, is unutterable. If she really were the murderess, it could hardly be, for the moment, more intense.

Dickens contributes another two paragraphs—partly in the conditional mood, to be sure—delineating what he takes to be the psychology of a murderer, as he had previously done for Bill Sikes and Jonas Chuzzlewit. It is as if someone else—Bucket, perhaps—made up the idea of Hortense committing the crime. The lady has killed (as it were) and failed to find relief in killing:

So now she sees that when he used to be on the watch before her, and she used to think, "if some mortal stroke would but fall on this old man and take him from my way!" it was but wishing that all he held against her in his hand might be flung to the winds, and chance-sown in many places. So, too, with the relief she has felt in his death. What was his death but the key-stone of a gloomy arch removed, and now the arch begins to fall in a thousand fragments, each crushing and mangling piecemeal! (55.666)

Is that why Allegory's arm "pointed with the arm of Samson" as well as a good Roman arm? Are we dealing here with a Delilah Dedlock? The passage confirms that it is finally Guppy's news that drives the lady to flight; Tulkinghorn the chief possessor of secrets was but the keystone, and removing him has only made room for the petty blackmailers. At the same time "the key-stone of a gloomy arch removed" prefigures the denouement of this action, which terminates beneath the arched gateway to the burial ground in Tom-all-Alone's. Lady Dedlock—"my mother, cold and dead" (59.714)—lies there because she would be crushed and mangled by infamy if she attempted to rise.

The French maid in Lady Dedlock's clothing killed Tulkinghorn: well and good. Displacement in the murder mystery does not stop here, however, for it reaches to a third look-alike, the person only less interested in the secret than her mother, Esther Summerson. She too must fear the old lawyer, of whose existence she was told precisely because of her solicitude ("Is the secret safe so far?"). One reason this action in *Bleak House* provides such a good detective story is that any number of people might have wished Tulkinghorn dead; another is that three, not two, of these people resemble one another enough that witnesses could mistake them.[10] It is given to Jo to remark the resemblance early on, since he has seen both Hortense and Lady Dedlock in Hortense's clothing by the grave of Nemo. When Jenny the brickmaker's wife—"the mother of the little child who had died"—introduces Esther to the ailing Jo—"This is *my* lady, Jo"—he responds "doubtfully": "She looks to me the t'other one." And the last words he speaks on this fateful encounter are "hoarsely whispered" to Charley: "If she ain't the t'other one, she ain't the forrenner. Is there *three* of 'em then?" (31.380–83). The bafflement he recalls with touching contrition on his death bed: "I went and giv a illness to the lady as wos and yit as warn't the t'other lady" (47.569). The question "Is there *three* of 'em then?" was of course overheard by Summerson, at a time when she had met both Lady Dedlock and Hortense with some emotion, though without distinctly knowing anything of their relation to herself. She has had plenty of time to think of these things before Woodcourt calls with the news that George has been apprehended for murder.

As we have seen, when Esther hears that the murdered man was Sir Leicester's lawyer, "my mother's dread of him rushed into my remembrance"; and something like guilt mixes with compunction for the innocent:

> I had that secret interest in what had happened, which was only known to my guardian. I felt as if it came close and near to me. It seemed to become personally important to myself that the truth should be discovered, and that no innocent people should be suspected; for suspicion, once run wild, might run wilder. (52.618)

The unspoken comparison of the last clause is undoubtedly to her mother's suspect position, yet Esther herself has an uncanny relation—a refused relation, to be sure—with the actual murderer. Much earlier, in number 8, after leaving Lady Dedlock's service in a pique, Hortense went out of the way to offer her services to the daughter. Summerson cannot explain this visit: it is simply an "incident that . . . I had better mention in this place," presumably because she writes with the after knowledge of Hortense's crime. The uncanniness, together with the initiative—as in the murder—resides in the devilish French maid. Esther "drew back, almost afraid of her." Hortense acts on some perception of the still undisclosed relationship of the other two and promises to serve the daughter well—"You don't know how well!" Very likely Hortense has in mind revenge, and inwardly Summerson thinks of "some woman from the streets of Paris in the reign of terror" (23.284–86). In the event— that is, by murdering Tulkinghorn—Hortense avenges not only herself but the mother and child. Yet in that earlier "incident" she came to Miss Summerson bristling with resentment against Lady Dedlock. One wonders how far Hortense's demonic energy can thus extend itself, or how she imagines she can serve the heroine better than the heroine knows. By framing Lady Dedlock, as she later attempts to do? The three of them, though they may share Tulkinghorn as the common enemy, do not have identical interests by any means.[11]

Though Esther Summerson openly sympathizes with her mother and both have an interest in keeping their secret, she too has her revenge, for she discovers at the climactic end of number 18 "my mother, cold and dead," and yet lives happily ever after: the long chase that affords *Bleak House* such a stirring climax has its own ambiguities. Lady Dedlock's flight begins from her knowledge that she always wanted to kill Tulkinghorn and from Guppy's information that her letters to Captain Hawdon were not destroyed but are being hawked about by the lesser blackmailers, with whom he is connected through his friend Smallweed. A letter that she leaves behind for Sir Leicester states that she followed Tulkinghorn home to beg him not to "protract the dreadful suspense" but "mercifully strike next morning." Since Tulkinghorn did not, or could not, answer her ring that night, it remains unclear what scenario she had in mind; but she did not kill him. And now she avoids her husband "only with a deeper shame than that with which she hurries from herself" (55.666–67). The last clause may hint at suicide, and indeed she leaves all her possessions behind. So when the stricken husband writes on his slate, "Full forgiveness. Find———" (56.669), and Bucket swiftly takes up the pursuit with Esther (he infers the usefulness of Esther from finding her handkerchief), the presumption is that the hunting down of Lady Dedlock purposes to save her from taking her own life. But it is not clear where the latter is headed, how she knows that she is being pursued, or why she dresses herself in

Jenny's clothes and reverses direction, if her object is suicide. The distance she travels through the wet snow and Bucket's failure to see through her ruse at first seem intended to make it plausible for her to die of exhaustion—of natural causes, so to speak—at the archway to the burial ground in the city. Dickens glosses over rather than resolves the ambiguity by (awkwardly) having her indite another, last-minute letter to no one in particular allowing that it is right "that I should die of terror and my conscience" (59.710).

The reader is obliged to step back from the narrow issue of Lady Dedlock's motives and physical condition to view the climactic chase as a whole. Are the detective and the daughter saving the wayward lady for Sir Leicester's full forgiveness or hounding her to her death?

> The gate was closed. Beyond it, was a burial ground —a dreadful spot in which the night was very slowly stirring; but where I could dimly see heaps of dishonoured graves and stones, hemmed in by filthy houses, with a few dull lights in their windows, and on whose walls a thick humidity broke out like a disease. On the step at the gate, drenched in the fearful wet of such a place, which oozed and splashed down everywhere, I saw, with a cry of pity and horror, a woman lying—Jenny, the mother of the dead child.

It takes a while, even with Bucket's explanations in her ear, before Esther moves closer, puts "the long dank hair aside," and identifies her mother as the one who has come to this wretched end (59.713-14). The misidentification momentarily saves Lady Dedlock from the associations of the dreadful place but also deprives her of Esther's expression of pity and even remotely sanctions her death, by recalling that she once abandoned a "dead child."[12] The mounting suspense and gathering affect remind one of the "Tempest" chapter in the corresponding number of the previous novel, in which David Copperfield struggled in his mind to save both Steerforth and Ham but was forced to be content with their deaths.

Some might say that convention governs the deaths of Steerforth and Ham: the seducer of Little Em'ly deserves to die, and the plighted lover of the same innocent, who will never love another woman, is happier dead. But in Dickens's *Copperfield,* with its egocentric design, these two also die because they got in the way of the hero's would-be love for Little Em'ly, whom he saw first. Dickens arranges the plot so as to satisfy even silent wishes of his narrator-hero. Similarly, for *Bleak House,* one can say that Lady Dedlock must never enjoy full forgiveness and live beyond the pages of the novel, the way her daughter does, because conventionally fallen women never do. Nonetheless, by subtle signs, she dies because she deserted her daughter and tainted the latter's life with illegitimacy. The remarkable thing is that the egocentric and overdetermined action rises above — or courses beneath — the difference of gender in the two novels. Hero or heroine, Dickens endows his protagonists with winning ways; so naturally there are also losers. (Though the way the bodies begin to pile up can still be a little startling.) In *Bleak House,* at least, some of the deaths that Ruskin complained of do not answer directly to the heroine's needs. In this novel Dickens returned to social themes, satiric and prophetic, that he had downplayed in *Copperfield.* Yet even the most portentous of these deaths — "Dead, your Majesty. Dead, my lords and gentlemen. . . . And dying thus around us every day" (47.572) — has its ties to Esther Summerson. In number 15, immediately preceding the mock-pastoral demise of Tulkinghorn, the death of Jo sends a message of dire connectedness to all inhabitants of the modern metropolis. But the message has already been inscribed in part on the heroine's face in number 10. Thus Jo too could be said to die because of what he has done to Esther.

Possibly because Dickens was working with a female consciousness, as he construed it, the wish fulfillment in *Bleak House* has become more coded than that in the previous autobiographical novel. Thus, in order to grasp the narrator-heroine's sexual interest and her relation to Ada Clare, the reader must follow the trail of the dead flowers wherever it leads. Thus, too, a handkerchief disappears and resurfaces as a clue to the filial connection and Lady Dedlock's maternal feelings, such as they are. Esther never lost her handkerchief: she placed it over the face of the baby who died before her eyes in the brickmaker's cottage, in the chapter called "Covering a Multitude of Sins" (8.100). It surfaces again with a story attached to it during the visit of Miss Flite to Bleak House, just after the heroine has revealed her stricken face to Jarndyce but before she has gone to Lincolnshire and faced her mother and Ada. Miss Flite and Charley have the story from Jenny: "a lady with a veil" has made off with the handkerchief. "Jenny says that when her baby died, you left a handkerchief there, and that she put it away and kept it with the baby's little things . . . partly because it was yours, miss, and partly because it had covered the baby." "And Jenny wants you to know," Charley continues, "that she wouldn't have made away with it herself for a heap of money, but that the lady took it, and left some money instead" (35.438–39). It would be a dull reader who could not guess that the agent here was Lady Dedlock, and true enough, that lady shows up in Lincolnshire, in the next chapter, with the handkerchief as a kind of token of her relation to the narrator, who duly records the effect of this mode of communication: "I cannot tell in any words what the state of my mind was, when I saw in her hand my handkerchief, with which I had covered the dead baby" (36.449). The usefulness of the handkerchief motif, obviously, resides in its covering of more than one sin: the social sin of poverty beneath the subsistence level in that brickmaker's hovel, exacerbated by the temper of the brickmaker and by Mrs. Pardiggle's false charity; the sexual sin of giving birth to Esther, exacerbated by mistakenly deserting her for dead and living well with the ignorance of the fact ever since; and indirectly the multitude of sins associated with Jarndyce and Jarndyce, with Skimpole, and with Mrs. Pardiggle's treatment of her own children. The handkerchief is the sign of the mother-daughter relationship (easily read by Inspector Bucket) but always with the emphasis on covering, which powerfully comes to a halt with the last perception of Lady Dedlock as mother of the dead child: Lady Dedlock herself dead, in the despicable resting place of Nemo and company. Dead baby, dead mother!

In this coded narrative of poetic justice, the mother is not the only person close to the heroine who pays. The face of Jenny's child may have been critical: the handkerchief covered that face, and strangely enough, the little face was its vulnerable spot. In Summerson's narrative generally, the heroine's own disfigurement has been linked to dead flowers and contrasted with Ada's striking looks. But for one moment in that narrative, Ada directly touched Jenny's dead child in the same part, as if inadvertently killing it. "Ada, whose gentle heart was moved by its appearance, bent down to touch its little face. As she did so, I saw what happened and drew her back. The child died" (8.100). Here is an example of the rather frightening logic of Esther Summerson's story. Not only will the heroine's glamorous mother be faulted for metaphorically killing her child, but even earlier the beautiful Ada has touched the other child's face and seemingly killed it. Of the three women most concerned in this elaborate metaphor, only the heroine herself—notwithstanding her disfigurement—emerges unscathed by the subsequent action. Not that Esther, who both as a child and as a woman longs "to be industrious, contented, and kind-hearted," does not deserve her happiness; but poetic justice is ever more vigilant with the other two.

There is one rivalry in Summerson's telling for which the outcome is less certain, even though superficially it follows the same egocentric pattern. Like Ada Clare, Caddy Jellyby manages to have a love life, however unpromising, entirely on her own and similarly gets married and pregnant. Dickens tends to frame Caddy in satiric and then comic scenes, but as with comic characters of Shakespeare or Scott, his are capable at times of subverting the main action. Caddy talks back alarmingly on her first appearance in the first number, even though she soon comes to worship the well-meaning Miss Summerson. The heroine, it has to be said, treats her with condescension: there are both the class difference and the appalling chaos of the Jellyby home to warrant this distance, and later on, the Turveydrop connection. The satire against condescension in the person of Mr. Turveydrop is strong medicine, yet Esther herself never treats Caddy as an equal. The heroine, in effect, denies this friend's marriage to the unfortunately named Prince Turveydrop by continuing to call her Caddy Jellyby—"her maiden name was so natural to me that I always called her by it"—but so does the heroine as narrator continue to write "Caddy Jellyby" (38.472). Dickens twice has her catch herself in this mistake; he possibly committed the error to paper himself, then found it appropriate to Summerson. If so, one can hope that he stands outside the gravely concessive clauses of her estimation of Caddy: "I encouraged her and praised her with all my heart. For I conscientiously believed, dancing-master's wife though she was, and dancing-mistress though in her limited ambition she aspired to be, she had struck out a natural, wholesome, loving course of industry and perseverance that was quite as good as a Mission" (38.474). Granted that the favorable comparison to having a mission is a hit against the Jellyby parent this time, the putdown of Caddy's marriage and "limited ambition" seems callous for someone who is about to fancy herself mistress of Bleak House.

Since young Mrs. Turveydrop's room for maneuver is severely constrained by one of literature's most neglectful mothers ("educating the natives of Borrioboola-Gha") on the one hand and a cruelly fatuous father-in-law ("Wooman, lovely Wooman") on the other, it is difficult to understand why her bravely seized happiness should turn so darkly against her as it has at the beginning of number 16:

> It happened that when I came home from Deal, I found a note from Caddy Jellyby (as we always continued to call her), informing me that her health, which had been for some time very delicate, was worse. . . . Caddy was now the mother, and I the godmother, of such a poor little baby—such a tiny old-faced mite, with a countenance that seemed to be scarcely anything but cap-border. . . . Whenever it was moved it cried; but at all other times it was so patient, that the sole desire of its life appeared to be, to lie quiet, and think. It had curious little dark veins in its face, and curious little dark marks under its eyes, like faint remembrances of Caddy's inky days; and altogether, to those who were not used to it, it was quite a piteous little sight.
>
> But it was enough for Caddy that *she* was used to it. The projects with which she beguiled her illness, for little Esther's education, and little Esther's marriage, and even for her own old age, as the grandmother of little Esther's little Esthers, was

so prettily expressive of devotion to this pride of her life, that I should be tempted to recall some of them, but for the timely remembrance that I am getting on irregularly as it is. (50.599)

These paragraphs are extraordinary, from their sudden announcement of this development in Caddy's life to the self-amendment of the narrator for proceeding thus "irregularly," as if these things didn't quite fit into her story anywhere. Yet here is a little Esther with a congenitally marked face, "like a faint remembrance of Caddy's inky days," and a succession of pathetic little Esthers still to come—"this pride" of Caddy's life that Summerson hasn't time for.

Nor does the narrator waste more time on the business, which takes her to London but quickly devolves upon questions of whether she should tell Caddy and Ada about Bleak House. The chapter begins with this unexpected intelligence about Caddy and moves toward the change in Ada that signals the latter's secret marriage. Not until the last chapter, "The Close of Esther's Narrative," do we hear any more irregular news of Caddy's family. There, just as unexpectedly, we find that this friend who has successfully worked her own way in life is working even harder, "her husband (an excellent one) being lame, and being able to do very little." There seems to be a bitter lesson here for women who work for a living; being lame seems a crueler fate for a dancing master than spontaneous death is for a Richard Carstone. Yet wait: "I had almost forgotten Caddy's poor little girl. She is not such a mite now; but she is deaf and dumb. I believe that there never was a better mother than Caddy, who learns, in her scanty intervals of leisure, innumerable deaf and dumb arts, to soften the affliction of her child" (67.768).

It is as if these brief messages about Caddy, two paragraphs at the beginning of number 16 and one paragraph at the end of the novel, were blurted out—if such expression can be used of Summerson's pen on inky days. Here the narrator seems helplessly at her most witchlike, as when with more art she recalls imprinting a kiss on the hearselike panel of the door to Richard and Ada's chamber. But Caddy's career in *Bleak House* began with the jolly satire of "Telescopic Philanthropy" and continued with "Deportment," and the mischief of those chapters may infect even these dark passages of Caddy's heroic fate. The hardships inflicted on Miss Jellyby, whose marriage remains unrecognized, go well beyond that which might be needed for still another pleasing contrast with the narrator's happiness. The inflictions, I believe, are meant to be darkly funny, but how? The key is this second seemingly illegitimate child named Esther, who telegraphs another relation between Caddy and our Esther—that of mother and child.

The explanation of this strange feature of Summerson's narrative lies in a redoubling of Dickens's already impressive powers of projection. Though as a coeval of the heroine, Caddy is a young woman who determines her own course by marriage, she is also a mother, like Lady Dedlock, of a sorrowful child named Esther: a barely surviving infant, so weak that it cries when it is moved, "but at all other times . . . so patient, that the sole desire of its life appeared to be, to lie quiet, and think." Within this daring comparison, Dickens and Summerson go to work to redress some injustices on their side. The condescension implicit in Lady Dedlock's position vis-à-vis that of her illegitimate daughter is paid back with condescension to Caddy; the illegitimacy itself is paid back by forgetting that Caddy is married and by eventually dropping her husband from the scene. At the same time, Lady Dedlock's neglect of our heroine compares very poorly to Caddy's "devotion to this pride of her life," the strange-looking and severely handicapped new little Esther. Even if I had been congenitally defective, this narrative contends, I ought to have been cared for. Even if she had no father—as we say of illegitimate little girls—Esther's mother should not have abandoned her.

The narrative is sensitive here to a gender difference. The lore and literature about bastard boys give leeway for more jokes. The male bastard may inherit the carefree wickedness of the father who engendered him, who had the fun and got away with it. If the female of the species goes to the bad, it is because she is stigmatized by her birth. Her succor lies in the mother's love that a woman circumstanced as Lady Dedlock fails to give. But Caddy gives that love and, according to Summerson, can fancy herself "the grandmother of little Esther's little Esthers"—a female line of succession without end, to which our Esther is godmother.

5

Jarndyce and Skimpole

Esther Summerson makes a great deal of her "guardian," as she is invited to call Mr. Jarndyce. She not only defers to his judgment but is apt to tremble in his "benevolent presence" (8.87). She owes her schooling to his benefaction and accepts the housekeeping keys to Bleak House from his trust. No man or woman in her life has treated her with so much kindness. Yet as a practical matter, he depends much of the time on her, and his presence in the novel depends on her narration. Jarndyce is not nearly as inclined to exercise power as Mordecai, the guardian of the biblical Esther before she becomes queen, but neither does he have any enemies. Like Mordecai, he does operate through his ward to some extent. He may know and be distressed by the world about him, but he leaves Esther to find her way among the Jellybys and Pardiggles, to foray in brickmakers' cottages or track down Richard Carstone at Deal. Excused from any bedwork, this Esther performs a lot of footwork. Jarndyce never really needs to tell her anything she cannot discover for herself. On two salient matters, the first of importance to her and the second to him, Esther is well ahead of her guardian: she learns the secret of her birth before he does; and she sees through Harold Skimpole, who has a marked attraction for Jarndyce.

Benevolence on the one side and gratitude on the other become focused, then eroticized in Esther and Jarndyce's relationship. While the text of *Bleak House* is open to interpretation on the point, it will not do to disparage the older man's proposal as a choice for Esther between spinsterhood and a sexless marriage or, with quite opposite implications, as an attempt by Jarndyce to gain sexual advantage over her. I think we have to concede that whatever case Dickens thought he was making, he makes it with care. One reason it remains authentically puzzling is that the proposal and the entire relationship are told by Summerson, who must interpret her guardian's feelings and intentions while guarding her own. Jarndyce is unusual for Dickens in that he is a character not easy to read: technically, this added interest is gained by representing him as deeply thoughtful but not describing those thoughts directly. In Dickens's other novels of this time, he also examined the possibility of love between an older man and younger woman. In *David Copperfield* he wrote a happy ending to the tale of January and May by portraying the passionate loyalty of Annie Strong to Dr. Strong and by making a scoundrel of Jack Maldon (in pointed contrast to the soft landing he provided for Steerforth). But the Strongs were minor characters, even if Mrs. Strong's reflections on her earlier, mistaken feelings for Maldon furnish the moral about the "undisciplined heart" that is gradually applied by Copperfield to his first marriage (an appropriation that incidentally reverses sexes and has Maldon parallel to the hero's Dora).[1] *Hard Times* would go to the opposite extreme and join Louisa Gradgind to Mr. Bounderby, in a loveless marriage that breaks up when pressured by a more sophisticated type of Maldon named Harthouse. For *Bleak House,* however, Dickens chose to develop an intricate courtship, in which the woman over a course of time expresses her willingness to marry a man she once imagined might be her father (6.76), but the man holds himself in check, deploying the proposal itself as a test not only of her will but of her feelings and happiness. Certainly by the completion of this action readers are supposed to understand that Jarndyce has observed Esther carefully enough to know—what she never improperly states outright—that she would like to be free to love Woodcourt. Thus Esther's guardian is left with a subdued version of Sydney Carton's sacrificial spell—practiced on the stage by Dickens himself in Wilkie Collins's play *The Frozen Deep*.[2] Jarndyce plays the part not entirely without fanfare, since the day he turns over his love to Woodcourt is "before God . . . the brightest day in all my life!" (64.753). Just so, Summerson reports after seven years of being what she persists in calling, coyly or considerately, "mistress of Bleak House": with that new house, young husband, "I was the happiest of the happy" (67.767). Only in *Little Dorrit*, under the aegis of a Shakespearean plot as he imagined it, would Dickens contrive the marriage of an older hero to his "child."

Given these wider interests of the author's, it would be surprising if John Jarndyce were not in some passages a second affective center of the novel. The emotions in question apparently do not conflict with Esther Summerson's triumph; the pleasures of self-sacrifice, at least, complement that triumph. Dickens may have experimented with a character whose point of view is not expressed directly in order to create a muted, more truly modest impression of suffering. If mourning for his father and for Dora Annie casts a shadow over the novel, it probably accounts for the sadness of the master of Bleak House as well as the mistress's sense of unfulfillment. The remarkable trait in Jarndyce is the hiddenness, not just of his love, but of all his inward life—again, the effect of Dickens's technique but also in accord with the character's wishes. Grief tends to hide itself, whether because it leaves one feeling vulnerable or because it is fraught with guilt. Quite apart from mourning, or in conjunction with it, there may be something in Jarndyce's mood akin to Summerson's longing to "win some love" if she can, and definitely akin to Copperfield's "vague unhappy loss or want of something," which later becomes confused with mourning for *his* Dora, for Steerforth and Ham.[3] About a year and a half after *Bleak House* was completed, the author queried his friend Forster, "Why is it, that as with poor David, a sense comes always crushing on me now, when I fall into low spirits, as of one happiness I have missed in life, and one friend and companion I have never made?"[4] Forster cited this letter to help explain Dickens's separation from his wife three years later still, but it is also suggestive of Jarndyce's subdued spirits. Jarndyce, like his author, apparently has everything he needs in life yet misses something.

The erotic component of this man's life is never far from its charitable impulse. Presumably he comes to love Esther first by making her a focus of his benevolence; conversely, a problem for her (and the reader) is whether she simply remains an object of charity, since he proposes only after she has been disfigured and has confessed her illegitimacy. Characteristically, both his love and his charity are hidden. Like the purest of Christians, he lets not the left hand know what the right hand doeth, and if any recipient of charity expresses gratitude in his presence he positively cringes. His withdrawal from the world, let alone from Chancery and the case of Jarndyce and Jarndyce, is Christian as well—most like an anchorite's but with a shading of the satirist's without the voice. The forms of telescopic and intrusive charity that his genuine benevolence has attracted are as dreadful to him as cruelty, and he falls silent before them also. In truth his charitable efforts are largely ineffective, or hopelessly entangled with frailer humankind. In one unexpected encounter, Lady Dedlock alludes to his reputation as a quixotic figure, thereby fixing him as one who both loves and performs good deeds. Though Esther is present, it is Lady Dedlock's first glimpse of Ada that prompts this cynical remark: "You will lose the disinterested part of your Don Quixote character . . . if you only redress wrongs of beauty like this" (18.229). This gibe approaches meanly close to home, as regards both

Jarndyce and the original Quixote. If Jarndyce is quixotic, however, he is more like Dostoevsky's reincarnation than Dickens's earlier character and first hero, Pickwick.[5] Prince Myshkin in *The Idiot* suffers, often silently, for the human casualties around him and seems to be brooding over the whole unhappy course of nineteenth-century civilization. So too does Mr. Jarndyce react with pained silence rather than sally forth against injustice in the world.

As champions of repression in *Bleak House,* without question Esther Summerson and her guardian win the field. Esther's victories over herself are eased by her gender, facilitated by displacement, and rewarded by the plot; but Jarndyce is subject to opposite conventions, less displacement, and the more doubtful satisfactions of sacrifice. His is a modest, never laughable, quixotic role that is enhanced by Summerson's narrative, since the reader can only infer the champion's thoughts. Male heroes, including quixotic ones, are at least permitted anger, and that Jarndyce is angry we know well enough from his adversions to the east wind, his silences and retreats to the Growlery—and no doubt his strictly self-enforced withdrawal from Jarndyce and Jarndyce. Besides the ruin presided over by the Court of Chancery he is most involved with, and disturbed by, the supposed philanthropies of Mrs. Jellyby and Mrs. Pardiggle. In those cases the anger Jarndyce presumably feels, or knows he ought to feel, is expressed by the Jellyby and Pardiggle children: Caddy, whose "I wish Africa was dead!" cannot be suppressed (4.43), and Egbert, Oswald, Francis, Felix, and Alfred, who take out their rage on Esther by pinching, demanding money, and otherwise terrifying her (8.97). Likewise, in the Chancery arena deep, abiding anger is partially displaced on Gridley, whose wrath is not content with Jarndyce's reproof to the "monstrous system" but wants to go for the jugular of those in charge of the system, and who teaches our repressed Quixote the helpless Lear-like lesson "that if I took my wrongs in any other way, I should be driven mad!" (15.192–93). Subsequently, on his death bed, Gridley honors Jarndyce as a man "superior to injustice" (24.313)—no mean compliment from one who understands what that superiority must cost. Still another repository of anger in the novel is Lawrence Boythorn. Thus the healthily expressed rage on this side or that side of Jarndyce echoes the satiric heart cries of the present-tense narrative of *Bleak House* rather than Summerson's cautious record. She wins the trophy for secret aggression, if you will, and he for repressed anger.

The two characters are closely associated in the futile effort to save Richard Carstone from himself, from Jarndyce and Jarndyce, and from the jaws of Vholes. The issues of vocation and personal application become very obvious in the novel, as they were in *David Copperfield* with happier result. Carstone is undoubtedly his own worst enemy, and long ago George H. Ford argued convincingly that the Victorian passion for earnestness is as important a theme in *Bleak House* as Chancery itself.[6] Even the eccentric Mr. and Mrs. Bayham Badger register how little Carstone is prepared to learn medicine, and there are plenty of witnesses to his failure in each of the other professions open to a gentleman: so much so that readers can have little patience with him.[7] Though no one in the little circle surrounding Jarndyce is any more closely related to him than "cousin" implies, he and Esther are very much in loco parentis—or as father and sister perhaps—to dear Rick. So feckless is the youth that one suspects some little anger must mix with their increasing sorrow and tendency to keen for the son and brother before he is dead; and of course, such circumstances of family life permit no easy response.

Richard Carstone will be followed in the Dickens canon by the likes of James Harthouse, Tip Dorrit, Pip Pirrip, and Eugene Wrayburn, in a sequence that shows the novelist increasingly patient and even concerned for the species. It seems more than a coincidence that during the writing of *Bleak House* Dickens was worried about the prospects in life of his oldest son Charley and began to chafe at what seemed to him the boy's own attitude.[8] In the novel, of course, there is also a "Charley," of stunning dedication quite the opposite of Carstone's. Her real name is Charlotte Neckett, and Esther and her guardian encounter her in the same tenement in which Gridley lectures them that it is not the system but the individuals who ought to be held to account. Charley—the uncertain gender of the name is immediately noted—is taking in washing and caring for her two younger siblings, after both parents have died.

> We were looking at one another, and at these two children, when there came into the room a very little girl. . . . Her fingers were white and wrinkled with washing, and the soap suds were yet smoking which she wiped off her arms. But for this she might have been a child, playing at washing, and imitating a poor working-woman with a quick observation of the truth. . . .
>
> "Is it possible," whispered my Guardian, as we put a chair for the little creature, and got her to sit down with [the youngest]: the boy keeping close to her, holding on to her apron, "that this child works for the rest? Look at this! For God's sake look at this!" (15.188)

Readers are justly moved by this scene, even though much standard class condescension is evident—and more of the same when Jarndyce later makes "a present" of Charley to Esther (23.299) or Esther teaches her maid to read and write. That domestic service is the solution for the girl's plight says something of Jarndyce's personal style, perhaps, but far more of opportunities available in the culture at large.

This time Jarndyce has sallied forth in search of those in need, for he has heard of the children's situation. Neckett, their father, was the debt collector who regularly pursued Harold Skimpole and whom readers have already encountered as "Coavinses"—the name of the lock-up he works out of—in the second number of *Bleak House*. The news of his death, in fact, elicits from Jarndyce an unusual statement and near-reproof of Skimpole, in defense of Neckett's unpopular calling: "The man was necessary. . . . If we make such men necessary by our faults and follies, or by our want of worldly knowledge, or by our misfortunes, we must not revenge ourselves upon them. There was no harm in his trade. He maintained his children. One would like to know more about this" (15.186). The revenge hereby reproved is implicit in Skimpole's casual breaking of the news a moment before, though Jarndyce is kind enough to identify it with the attitude any of us is liable to take against such functionaries. Mainly he expresses anger and distress in this scene, as elsewhere, by head rubbing and pacing to and fro (Summerson recalling these signs for us as usual). But there are also these few words of rare direct discourse.

"There was no harm in his trade": this disclaimer would seem to be extendable to the entire system of accountability and enforcement of contracts in the modern political economy. "He maintained his children": Neckett participated in that system from motives that are assumed to operate in every family unit, the aggregate of which units comprises the economy. Here Jarndyce takes into consideration first the system and then the responsible individual—always conceived as the wage earner of the family, within which motives other than the strictly economic still apply. His general position need not contradict his opinion that part of the system, Chancery practice, is rotten; nor does his support for the responsible Neckett necessarily conflict with Gridley's belief that individuals ought to be held accountable. His alluding to "this monstrous system" of Chancery a few pages later (15.193—that phrase is offered in indirect discourse by Summerson) expresses his condolence with Gridley, not a final difference in opinion. Still, Jarndyce's dire consciousness of systemic wrongs together with his acceptance of the global system—that which is "necessary"—may be finally harder to sustain than Gridley's cries for vengeance. The pain as well as anger that Jarndyce experiences when the east wind blows is apparently endemic, and this pain can only be alleviated by solitude or small forays against the injustice of things that do not alter the larger picture.

Moreover, as the rest of the novel shows, Jarndyce's expressed grounds for charitable intervention cannot be fully determinate. The disgusting Vholes is another individual who practices his trade and supports his family: should we therefore conclude that "this man was necessary"? The obvious recourse is to apply the second test, whether there is any harm in his trade, and find that indeed there was. But immediately some determination is called for, and harm will seem to be a matter of degree. "*No* harm in his trade" may be a standard too high to fit Neckett or any unit in the functioning economy. It would seem that a fine casuistry, such as George Eliot might entertain, is the only recourse here. More certain to influence us, in novels and in life, is the style of the individual in question. In this respect, we can be sure, Dickens will not let the reader be at a loss. His lawyer Vholes stirs up trade at others' expense and unctuously parades his family's needs: "With my three daughters, Emma, Jane, and Caroline—and my aged father—I cannot afford to be selfish," etc., etc. (37.471). A little exposure to Vholes confirms that he is a very different customer from the late Neckett; and

Dickens's imagination—not only in *Bleak House*—frequently embraces positive and negative configurations of similar sentiments. We also know that he was developing a complicated sense of unpleasing functions that are apparently necessary to society, because he went on to invent a more positive, eccentric, and magical part to play for Pancks, the rent collector in *Little Dorrit*.

Given that Jarndyce's thoughts are mostly hidden from us and that his position, when stated, is both depressive and difficult, it is a wonder that readers are confident that they can see into his heart. We tend to accept Summerson's guidance, of course, and her experience is colored by gratitude; but still Jarndyce looms larger in the novel than the record seems actually to warrant. The reason is Harold Skimpole, a character before whom Jarndyce is generally helpless and whose antithetical principles thereby define him. Skimpole is one of the two characters in *Bleak House* modeled on well-known personalities: he is modeled on Leigh Hunt, and Lawrence Boythorn on Walter Savage Landor.[9] Summerson, in fact, links and contrasts the two, "Mr. Boythorn attaching so much importance to many things, and Mr. Skimpole caring so little for anything" (15.185). I have suggested that Boythorn, along with Gridley, serves to displace some of the anger that is just visible but repressed in Jarndyce. Skimpole, however, is the intellectual foil for Jarndyce, the character whose verbal fencing makes the issues as clear as they are ever likely to be. Since Jarndyce seems hardly at all aware of this relation, we have a dialogue in which the lightweight does most of the talking.

So necessary is Skimpole for defining Jarndyce, apparently, that at the end of the novel he leaves behind a diary in which is written, "Jarndyce, in common with most other men I have known, is the Incarnation of Selfishness" (61.729). By then, of course, the reader is expected to understand this remark as incontrovertible testimony to the opposite truth, even though this particular bit of outrageousness is uncharacteristic of Skimpole's true style and more indicative of Dickens and Summerson's effort to stop his voice for good (it is the last we hear of him).[10] Skimpole is present from the first, in the very chapters in which Summerson and hence the reader get to meet Jarndyce. He is present throughout the encounters with Gridley and Charley in Bell Yard, though one scarcely realizes this until he speaks "for the first time since our arrival, in his usual gay strain" (15.194). After this point, appearances of Jarndyce and Skimpole together are less frequent and less revelatory. Esther Summerson, who is present in all the scenes and in her naive way has been skeptical of Skimpole from the start, takes over most of the damage control.

Harold Skimpole is very much a part of Esther's first acquaintance with her guardian. She realizes that Jarndyce, now "nearer sixty than fifty," was the gentleman she confusedly met in the stagecoach six years earlier on the way to Greenleaf School, but her arrival at Bleak House in the company of Ada and Richard provides her first opportunity to study the man and his ways, "at once so whimsical and so loveable" (6.60–61). That afternoon Skimpole is already present, and more of Summerson's chapter is devoted to his talk, in direct discourse and free indirect style, than is devoted to Jarndyce; and since his speeches are "playful, yet always fully meaning what they expressed," we are expected to attend to them. We also hear more of his background than we ever hear of Jarndyce's. Two qualities make Skimpole an especially welcome guest at Bleak House. First, Skimpole does not embarrass his host by showing gratitude; he announces to the newcomers, in fact, "I don't feel any vulgar gratitude to you. I almost feel as if *you* ought to be grateful to *me,* for giving you the opportunity of enjoying the luxury of generosity" (6.67). Unquestionably, the title of the chapter, "Quite at Home," refers as much to Harold as it does to Esther, Ada, and Richard. Second, in the host's words, this guest is "the finest creature upon earth—a child" (6.64). Skimpole both is introduced as a child on this occasion and speaks of himself as a child; and throughout the novel, especially when he gives trouble, Jarndyce prefers to think of him as a child. The child thus helps define Jarndyce as a volunteer father—a guardian, in truth—and only as a father, perhaps, can he bestow freely of his charity without regard for its potentially damaging effects, since both Puritanism and Victorian political economy were wary of the effects of charity on the recipients.[11] Harold Skimpole is closer to Richard Carstone than to the guest who has just been handed the housekeeping keys. After Summerson brilliantly mimics his confessions of inadequacy in the management of time and money, she gives in direct discourse his advice to the world on choosing a profession: "Go your several ways in peace! Wear red coats, blue coats, lawn sleeves, put pens behind your ears, wear aprons; go after glory, holiness, commerce, trade, any object you prefer; only—let Harold Skimpole live!" (6.66). Thus he enumerates and rejects some of the professions Carstone will later run through. He also engages with Ada Clare in such a way as to indicate why Jarndyce must be a parent to her also. "I almost loved him," Summerson reports, for the way he spoke of Ada:

> "She is like the morning," he said. "With that golden hair, those blue eyes, and that fresh bloom on her cheek, she is like the summer morning. The birds here will mistake her for it. We will not call such a lovely young creature as that, who is a joy to all mankind, an orphan. She is the child of the universe."

Mr. Jarndyce, I found, was standing near us, with his hands behind him, and an attentive smile upon his face.

"The universe," he observed, "makes rather an indifferent parent, I'm afraid."

"O! I don't know!" cried Mr. Skimpole, buoyantly.

"I think I do know," said Mr. Jarndyce. (6.68)

On a second reading of *Bleak House*, this conversation weighs a little ominously because of the fate in store for Ada, in which Skimpole plays an unattractive if small part. His verbal ability to play opposite Jarndyce in the novel, often without the necessity for the latter to speak at all, is impressive. Hours later that evening Skimpole is taken—arrested for debt—by Neckett, and again the dialogue provides a foretaste of what is to come. "Don't be ruffled by your occupation," Skimpole tells him. "We can separate you from your office; we can separate the individual from the pursuit." As the pursued, Skimpole does not quite want to say "this man was necessary," but mentally he is already abreast of Jarndyce's position. "The butterflies are free," he protests. "Mankind will surely not deny to Harold Skimpole what it concedes to the butterflies!" (6.71). Painter and musician (formerly a doctor), he is nothing if not an escape artist (and logician).

The next day at breakfast Skimpole expounds his "Drone philosophy," which Summerson again ingeniously develops in the free indirect style, with just a touch of her acerbic, or what would be acerbic, commentary: "—always supposing the Drone to be willing to be on good terms with the Bee" (8.87). There is no indication that Jarndyce is even present at this breakfast, but immediately afterward in her account, he introduces her to the Growlery, to the story of his uncle Tom Jarndyce, and to his inheritance of Bleak House and the slum property in London that has also become entangled in the court. Skimpole does not appear again until the morning in London when he casually lets drop the news of Coavinses's death. Appropriately, the conversation that morning has first turned to the drone's habit of meaning to pay his bills rather than handing over money, as in this parable of the lamb and the butcher:

> "But, suppose," said my Guardian, laughing, "he had meant the meat in the bill, instead of providing it?"
>
> "My dear Jarndyce," he returned, "you surprise me. You take the butcher's position. A butcher I once dealt with occupied that very ground. Says he, 'Sir, why did you eat spring lamb at eighteen-pence a pound?' 'Why did I eat spring lamb at eighteen-pence a pound, my honest friend?' said I, naturally amazed by the question, 'I like spring lamb!' This was so far convincing. 'Well, sir,' says he, 'I wish I had meant the lamb as you mean the money!' 'My good fellow,' said I, 'pray let us reason like intellectual beings. How could that be? It was impossible. You *had* got the lamb, and I have *not* got the money. You couldn't really mean the lamb without sending it in, whereas I can, and do, really mean the money without paying it!' He had not a word. There was an end of the subject."
>
> "Did he take no legal proceedings?" inquired my guardian.
>
> "Yes, he took legal proceedings," said Mr. Skimpole. "But, in that, he was influenced by passion; not by reason. Passion reminds me of Boythorn." (15.184–85)

Skimpole's claim to reason is not an idle boast. His surprise at Jarndyce's question is not surprise that his patron does not immediately take sides with him, but surprise that he does not take the point—just as it is amazing that the butcher could ask why one would eat spring lamb. "I like spring lamb," and the butcher has a supply: given these conditions, the question is what distribution of lamb is appropriate. Do the lessons of political economy depend any less on good intentions than Skimpole's alternative? Do not tit-for-tat exchanges take into account the respective strengths of the two parties? There is almost always some truth in what Skimpole says. The distributions he advocates also resemble those of Jesus in the Gospels, such as the parable of laborers in the vineyard.[12] That the teller of Skimpole's parable is the one who benefits may give the story a bad taste but need not invalidate it. Jarndyce, like the butcher in the story, has not a word: his view of legal proceedings, after all, has much in common with the Drone's. Furthermore, Jarndyce is not engaged in commerce but in charity, so his interlocutor's affinity for Christian thinking cannot be amiss. Skimpole's role, in part, is to make plain in words the quixotic nature of charitable deeds. He is Jarndyce's sounding board, even though his quality of talk makes the dialogue seem to originate with him. He earns his keep in the novel, certainly, if not in Dickens's overt notions of political economy.

The voluble Skimpole has in common with Jarndyce a profound awareness of the interdependency of human society. His numerous illustrations of this connectedness, therefore, help fill in what Jarndyce means when he says of Neckett, "The man was necessary." Their attitudes about the matter differ greatly, as charity and idleness differ, or compassion and carelessness. For Jarndyce the modern consciousness that humanity is bound together in self-regulating systems is painful, because little can be done to change anything. For Skimpole the same consciousness of relatedness justifies his existence without the need to do anything, and the pained moral view is replaced by aesthetic enjoyment. On that first afternoon at Bleak House he expresses satisfaction with his new acquaintances as follows: "For anything I can tell, I may have come into the world expressly for the purpose of increasing your stock of happiness. I may have been born to be a benefactor to you, by sometimes giving you an opportunity of assisting me in my little perplexities" (6.67). On the return from the visit to Neckett's children and the encounter with Gridley, Skimpole finds his tongue again in time to reflect on how Chancery seems to have been designed for Gridley to work out his feelings on, as he himself has been of use to Neckett. "He had found Coavinses in his way. He could have dispensed with Coavinses. . . . But what turned out to be the case? That, all that time, he had been giving employment to a most deserving man . . . enabling Coavinses to bring up these charming children in this agreeable way, developing these social virtues!" In this conversation, Skimpole locates "purpose" and "principle" in all such connectedness (15.194–95), in a kind of parody of nineteenth-century political economy.[13]

What Skimpole says of Neckett is more or less true and echoes Jarndyce's sentiments in the foregoing scene. He also anticipates Summerson's growing suspicion that he lacks what *she* thinks of as principle and purpose—an "airy dispensing with all principle and purpose" that offends the mistress of responsibility and would-be protector of Carstone (37.460). Of course, Skimpole has her number, too:

> "Now when you mention responsibility," he resumed, "I am disposed to say, that I never had the happiness of knowing any one whom I should consider so refreshingly responsible as yourself. You appear to me to be the very touchstone of responsi-

bility. When I see you, my dear Miss Summerson,
intent upon the perfect working of the whole little
orderly system of which you are the centre, I feel
inclined to say to myself—in fact I do say to myself,
very often—*that's* responsibility!" (37.467–68)

Summerson can hardly refrain from repeating this bit of imper-
tinence, for it is what she and Jarndyce have felt all along. Note
how Skimpole injects the word "system" with his praise. Their
intellectual difference concerns whether purpose and principle
reside in the system already or whether they have to be willed;
their moral difference is too great for words.

"Is there such a thing as principle, Mr. Harold Skimpole?"
This direct challenge comes from Boythorn, in an attempt to
get past Skimpole's easy adherence to "the social system . . .
a system of harmony." The two have begun to differ over the
likes of Sir Leicester Dedlock, that "mighty potentate" whose
patronage Skimpole would appreciate and whom Boythorn de-
spises (18.226). Much later, when Skimpole is introduced to Sir
Leicester, Summerson wryly observes that the potentate rather
approves of this artist who characterizes himself as "perfectly
idle" and "a mere amateur" (43.530). Throughout the novel,
thanks to Summerson's watchful eyes and quick ears, we note
how prepared Skimpole is to tilt the harmonious system his way
if opportunity should present itself. At the same time, the vision
of the man is quite extraordinary and, as verbalized, surpasses
that of any other character. The vision necessarily encompasses
both good and evil, as Skimpole makes clear when he graciously
extends it to cover Esther's illness:

He was charmed to see me; said he had been shed-
ding delicious tears of joy and sympathy, at intervals for six weeks, on my account; had never been so
happy as in hearing of my progress; began to under-

stand the mixture of good and evil in the world
now; felt that he appreciated health the more, when
somebody else was ill; didn't know but it might
be in the scheme of things that A should squint
to make B happier in looking straight; or that C
should carry a wooden leg, to make D better satisfied with his flesh and blood in a silk stocking.
(37.459–60)

Skimpole's selfishness is contemptible, and his taking advantage of those who cannot defend themselves is wrong. But despite his carelessness about the feelings of A and C and Esther,
and the lives of Jo and Richard, his disarming argument is
harder to fault. His aesthetic overview of Summerson's illness
does not differ entirely from the assimilation of the illness by
her own narrative, nor his poetry from Dickens's poetic justice.

The harmonious system smoothly replicates a Christian acceptance of good and evil. Skimpole practices little good in the
world; for petty gain he consciously betrays at least two persons; but his theology is sound, so to speak—he never denies
the existence of evil. Perhaps his most notorious illustration of
how good may nevertheless flow from evil is one that he himself
presents as "an extreme case." "Take the case of the Slaves on
American plantations. I dare say they are worked hard, I dare
say that they don't altogether like it, I dare say theirs is an un-
pleasant experience on the whole; but they people the landscape
for me, they give it poetry for me, and perhaps that is one of the
pleasanter objects of their existence" (18.227). The dispropor-
tion of evil to good in the illustration is indeed so extreme that
it is scarcely laughable; it's sick. The joke darkly contends that
any quality or quantity of evil in the world can be contemplated
serenely as long as it fits my scheme of things. The mono-
maniacal equation here is between Skimpole and God, whom

theology credits for understanding the purpose of evil when we do not. Thus Skimpole's aesthetic view of the universe cannot be divorced from the great Chadband's strained theology. For Chadband—that other acrobat of words and stealer of scenes in *Bleak House*—conceives of misery and sin as existing in the world to provide an object for his pleasing discourse. "O glorious to be a human boy!" he caws at the cornered Jo. "And why glorious, my young friend? Because you are capable of receiving the lessons of wisdom, because you are capable of profiting by this discourse, which I now deliver for your good" (19.242).

The "mixture of good and evil in the world" that Skimpole meets with artless cheerfulness and Chadband with hilarious preaching weighs differently upon John Jarndyce, who tends to fall silent before suffering or euphemistically invokes the east wind. The interconnectedness of human lots that ostensibly buoys Skimpole's spirits depresses Jarndyce, because private acts of charity become lost in this world, much as he and Summerson watch Charley "melt into the city's strife and sound, like a dewdrop in an ocean" (15.195). The case is hard for Jarndyce, since Skimpole's charm has long entertained and distracted him, and this pleasure must draw to an end—though mercifully Summerson never details how her guardian endures his disillusionment. She has preserved her distance all along: "I thought I could understand how such a nature as my guardian's . . . found an immense relief in Mr. Skimpole's avowal of his weakness and display of guileless candour; but I could not satisfy myself that it was as artless as it seemed" (37.460). Among her many credits, Summerson gets credit for resisting Skimpole's charm. She has never been in need of Bucket's friendly warning that when someone pretends to be a child, "that person is only a crying off from being held accountable, and that you have got that person's number, and it's Number One" (57.682). It is fair to add that she could never comprehend a Drone philosophy even if the philosopher were quite selfless, since she has always been, in her husband's words, a "busy bee" (67.770).

Also on the last page of "The Close of Esther's Narrative"— last paragraph—in a tableau of all the faces dear to her, Jarndyce makes his last appearance between her husband's "handsome" face and the wistful allusion to her own with which the novel breaks off. She is sure, she writes, "that my guardian has the brightest and most benevolent face that ever was seen" (67.770). Mr. Jarndyce probably deserves to be known as second in benevolence only to Mr. Pickwick among the characters of Dickens. Only less obviously than Pickwick, he has a soft spot for women: the erotic component of his charitable impulse is so gentle, however, as to enhance his guardianship. Surely Dickens identifies not a little with Jarndyce and thereby invites the reader, as well, to imagine the represented world of *Bleak House* from his presumed point of view. We know that Dickens could be aggrieved by the receipt of begging letters, for example, and one of the first things we learn about Jarndyce is that he is besieged by such letters: "It seemed to Ada and me that everybody knew him, who wanted to do anything with anybody else's money" (8.92).[14] Happily, Jarndyce's plight coupled with his freedom from resentment are attractive—if only because readers do not know much more about him. Traditionally, the words of the dying can be taken for truth, and thus Gridley's testimony ought to count: "You are a good man, superior to injustice, and God knows I honour you" (24.313). The respect for John Jarndyce that is offered the reader even serves as a check on insistent identification with Esther Summerson.

.

6

The Novel's Satire

The spare title of Dickens's novel covers a lot of ground. As we have seen, one alternative or associated title, "Tom-all-Alone's," survived through nine different slips in Dickens's hand before his eye and ear were satisfied that "Bleak House" would encompass his intentions. By contrast, "Chancery" in these slips appears just five times, each time in a subordinate clause as a form of subtitle.

Tom-all-Alone's is first mentioned by Jarndyce at the beginning of number 3—some "property of ours, meaning of the Suit's," in London (8.89). A true introduction to this property has to await the end of number 5, because it depends on the novelist's construction for the reader of the very interconnectedness of the world of *Bleak House* that will stymie Jarndyce's charitable will and stimulate Skimpole's bent for getting on. Dickens needed to have in place Jo, the principal itinerant and go-between of the novel, and to acquaint the reader with Chesney Wold, the estate of the Dedlocks in Lincolnshire—and with a good many other loci of his satire—before he could spring the key question: "What connexion can there be, between the place in Lincolnshire, the house in town, the Mercury in powder, and the whereabout of Jo the outlaw with the broom, who had that distant ray of light upon him when he swept the churchyard step?" (16.197).

The rhetorical question is followed by another still more portentous, probing the relation of the "many people in the innumerable histories of this world" who have been "curiously brought together." A similar question will be posed in the first number of *Little Dorrit:* one of the providential tasks of the novelist in his grand inventions is to bring home the connectedness of not a few characters. The rhetoric is also satiric, in the dire voice that leaves such questions unanswered, or answered only in part. Connections are to be proved with the reader at hand and lose none of their ominousness in the telling. Here the connection is made with, and by, Jo and the street he inhabits:

> Jo lives—that is to say, Jo has not yet died—in a ruinous place known to the like of him by the name of Tom-all-Alone's. It is a black, dilapidated street, avoided by all decent people; where the crazy houses were seized upon, when their decay was far advanced, by some bold vagrants, who, after establishing their own possession, took to letting them out in lodgings. Now, these tumbling tenements contain, by night, a swarm of misery. As, on the ruined human wretch, vermin parasites appear, so these ruined shelters have bred a crowd of foul existence that crawls in and out of gaps in walls and boards; and coils itself to sleep, in maggot numbers, where the rain drips in; and comes and goes, fetching and carrying fever, and sowing more evil in its every footprint than Lord Coodle, and Sir Thomas Doodle, and the Duke of Foodle, and all the fine gentlemen in office, down to Zoodle, shall set right in five hundred years—though born expressly to do it.

As in *Little Dorrit,* too, houses are prone to collapse with "a crash and a cloud of dust," though the inhabitants of Tom-all-Alone's regularly adapt themselves to the ruins and rubbish. Dickens does not fail to repeat what Jarndyce has told Summerson earlier: "This desirable property is in Chancery, of course"

(16.197–98). The law's delay and costs have effectively destroyed responsible private ownership, hence the urban saga of squatters and corrupt advantage.

The narrator professes not to know "whether 'Tom' is the popular representative of the original plaintiff or defendant in Jarndyce and Jarndyce; or whether Tom lived here when the suit laid the street waste, all alone, until other settlers came to join him" (16.198). Predictably, we are never to know all the connections but to be made uneasy by the possibility of more. The inspiration for the name of the place scarcely stops with Tom Jarndyce, the victim of Chancery who blew his brains out. The name Tom, the itinerant clad in rags, the vermin and foul beings, and the rain that penetrates "these ruined shelters" of the urban landscape Shakespeare had offered for Dickens's taking, in the heath scenes of *King Lear:*

> Poor naked wretches, whereso'er you are,
> That bide the pelting of this pitiless storm,
> How shall your houseless heads and unfed sides,
> Your loop'd and window'd raggedness, defend you
> From seasons such as these? O, I have ta'en
> Too little care of this! Take physic, pomp,
> Expose thyself to feel what wretches feel,
> That thou mayst shake the superflux to them,
> And show the heavens more just.[1]

In his extremity Shakespeare's Lear has glimpsed a connection between pomp and what wretches feel. Dickens rings so many changes on the connection—between Sir Leicester at the place in Lincolnshire and Nemo in his muddy grave, between the powdered footmen and the crossing sweeper with his broom, and so on—that this particular inspiration might be missed. Yet the sheer power of the play for Dickens is evident in much of his work, and perhaps the charity that Lear and Gloucester learn from their tragic suffering has found its way to the quixotic Jarndyce, metonymically wounded by the life he finds around him. This speech of Lear's is the cue for poor Tom's emergence from the hovel that the king needs to share. In the heath scene that follows, poor Tom comments on his experience as a betrayed child: "Who alone suffers, suffers most in the mind."[2] In the passage from *Bleak House,* the narrator speculates on the loneliness of the illiterate Jo and others like him in the modern world of print: "It must be a strange state, not merely to be told that I am scarcely human . . . but to feel it of my own knowledge all my life!" (16.198). Tom-all-Alone's is Jo's habitation when he has one; he is the "human wretch" to whom the place is compared. Poor Jo, houseless and windowed only in rags, is Dickens's figure for the minimal humanity that attaches to us all.

Certainly this passage in number 5 speaks proleptically to the role Jo will have in fetching and carrying fever to Charley Neckett and Esther Summerson in number 10. That infectious disease can attack individuals across class lines is the novel's principal symbol not just of medical or political failure but of the connectedness that behooves compassion, awareness of a common humanity, and reform of our ways. Not until Jo's death in number 15 does the satirist pull out all the stops: "Dead, your Majesty. Dead, my lords and gentleman. Dead, right Reverends and Wrong Reverends of every order. Dead, men and women, born with Heavenly compassion in your hearts. And dying thus around us every day" (47.572). The last rites for Jo have nevertheless focused on the boy himself: penitent, and comforted by Snagsby and Woodcourt at George's shooting gallery. Their instruction and his faltering recitation of the Lord's Prayer, slight as they are, signify his accommodation to a common faith. (A parallel will be afforded later by Richard Carstone's last moments.) With irony at once heavy and mischievous, the chapter that ends the previous number and that prepares for the death bears the title "Stop Him!" Therein Woodcourt and the reader discover the direct link between Jo's wretched existence and Esther's illness and near death.

This chapter, resolving a main line of suspense in the novel, also begins with Tom-all-Alone's: "Darkness rests upon Tom-all-Alone's. Dilating and dilating since the sun went down last night, it has gradually swelled until it fills every void in the place." The darkness provides a respite and a space for the satirist to work his personifications. Just as blatantly as Edgar in *King Lear* invents for himself the role of poor Tom the Bedlam beggar, so Dickens personifies the locus of contemporary social problems and their interconnection:

> Much mighty speech-making there has been, both in and out of Parliament, concerning Tom, and much wrathful disputation how Tom shall be got right. Whether he shall be put into the main road by constables, or by beadles, or by bell-ringing, or by force of figures, or by correct principles of taste, or by high church, or by low church, or by no church. . . . And in the hopeful meantime, Tom goes to perdition head foremost in his old determined spirit.

> But he has his revenge. Even the winds are his messengers, and they serve him in these hours of darkness. There is not a drop of Tom's corrupted blood but propagates infection and contagion somewhere. It shall pollute, this very night, the choice stream (in which chemists on analysis would find the genuine nobility) of a Norman house, and his Grace shall not be able to say Nay to the infamous alliance. There is not an atom of Tom's slime, not a cubic inch of any pestilential gas in

which he lives, not one obscenity or degradation about him, not an ignorance, not a wickedness, not a brutality of his committing, but shall work its retribution, through every order of society, up to the proudest of the proud, and to the highest of high. Verily, what with tainting, plundering, and spoiling, Tom has his revenge. (46.551–53).

The changes Dickens has been able to ring on Tom, from infection and pollution to misalliance, for example, or from ignorance to wickedness and brutality, work themselves out from one end of the novel to the other and are aptly figured in Jo and the homeless in the streets. Summerson's first impression of London in the daylight is marked by wonder at "the extraordinary creatures in rags, secretly groping among the swept-out rubbish for pins and other refuse" (5.47). Note the "secretly," as if this humblest seeking for a living were fraught with real or projected shame. At the nadir of the novel's principal story of the proudest of the proud, when "of all men upon earth, Sir Leicester seems fallen from his high estate to place his sole trust and reliance" upon the detective Bucket, the latter's first thought to himself is how he will be able to find the fleeing Lady Dedlock among those secretive homeless ones: "Many solitary figures he perceives, creeping through the streets; many solitary figures out on heaths, and roads, and lying under haystacks" (56.669,673). The repetition of "solitary figures" signals guilt and alienation as much as despair. Like these scions of an underclass, both Captain Hawdon and Lady Dedlock die alone.

The satiric charge of *Bleak House* is so comprehensive that readers are bound to differ about its true symbolic center. Because of the powerful opening of the novel, Jarndyce's pointed antipathy, Flite's caged birds, Krook's wild parody, and the eventual send-up of Jarndyce and Jarndyce in tears and laughter, many have read the Court of Chancery as that center. Dickens's sarcasm at least conveys a unified theory of the practice of law:

> The one great principle of the English law is, to make business for itself. There is no other principle distinctly, certainly, and consistently maintained through all its narrow turnings. Viewed by this light it becomes a coherent scheme, and not the monstrous maze the laity are apt to think it. Let them but once clearly perceive that its grand principle is to make business for itself at their expense, and surely they will cease to grumble. (39.482)

And the theory embraces a wide range of instances, from the truly devouring Vholes to the complacent, personally quite modest Kenge: "This is a very great country, a very great country," and—or because—"its system of equity is a very great system, a very great system" (62.740). This same system, obviously, touches on numerous specifically rendered lives in the novel: because of the false hopes held out, it is partly responsible for Carstone's failure of earnestness and vocation; it has brought grief and despair to Gridley, madness to Miss Flite; it is the legal foundation, apparently, of the material condition of Tom-all-Alone's.[3]

Between the filth and disease of Tom-all-Alone's and the Court of Chancery lies the shadow of the mock–Lord Chancellor Krook and his rag-and-bottle shop. Krook rents a room there to Nemo, who ekes out a living by copying law papers yet has befriended Jo, and another room to the crazed hanger-on of the court, Miss Flite. But his own means of living corresponds to the street trades represented by the crossing sweeper and the scavengers glimpsed by Summerson in the London morning and charted by the remarkable journalism of Dickens's contemporary Henry Mayhew.[4] The strange shop lies in the neigh-borhood of the law—close by the wall of Lincoln's Inn—and the main salvage accumulating there would seem to be paper. If Snagsby, the law stationer, supplies fresh paper, Krook buys up all the used paper he can put his hands on. Summerson observantly notes that "everything seemed to be bought, and nothing to be sold there" and that the shop has "the air of being . . . a dirty hanger-on and disowned relation of the law," even before Flite announces to her that Krook "is called among the neighbours the Lord Chancellor" and his shop "the Court of Chancery" (5.48–50). Everything in and nothing out: the perfect model of the equity system, according to Dickens, and not wholly different from the Circumlocution Office of *Little Dorrit* in that respect. This Lord Chancellor has another pecu-liarity, which he shares with Jo: his illiteracy. All that script and print accumulating in the shop is as meaningless to the "Court of Chancery" as it is to the crossing sweeper. While Esther and Ada are present with Miss Flite Krook nonethe-less weirdly demonstrates his half-understanding of the written word by chalking on the wall, one letter at a time and each time rubbing it out, the words "Jarndyce" and "Bleak House" (5.55). This brush of near-illiteracy with the court, and with the main action of the novel as narrated by Summerson, is both ignorant and uncanny, or mad and mischievous.

Chancery has only an oblique relation to another target of satire in *Bleak House,* the political establishment. The two insti-tutions have in common traditional ways and selfish inertia but no very direct link that is examined in the novel. Implicitly, the political establishment's wealth and property will be affected by the equity system from time to time, but Dickens is far more concerned for the people who are trapped by the system and ruined. Both the court and Parliament are to blame by default, nevertheless, for permitting the conditions prevalent in Tom-all-Alone's. The root cause of stagnation in government is the monopoly of office: the cabinet ministers, the power brokers in the counties are all drawn from the same set of people. Just as in *Little Dorrit* Dickens would insist that all officials of government belonged to the Barnacle or Stiltstalking families, in *Bleak House* the ministers of state run an alphabetic gamut of sameness from Boodle to Zoodle (not omitting Noodle) and members of Parliament from the Right Honourable William Buffy, M.P., to a capricious Puffy. "Boodle and Buffy, their followers and families, their heirs, executors, administrators, and assigns, are the born first-actors, managers, and leaders, and no others can appear upon the scene for ever and ever" (12.146). But whereas the emphasis in *Little Dorrit* will fall upon obfuscating bureaucracy and the science of How Not To Do It, in *Bleak House* it falls on the dying aristocracy and the decay of the art of governing. This establishment, in its playacting, is bringing on its own demise: "dandyism" is the problem, a notion borrowed from Thomas Carlyle.[5] "Dandyism?" The narrator pretends to catch himself: "There is no King George the Fourth now . . . ; there are no clear-starched, jack-towel neckcloths, no short-waisted coats, no false calves, no stays." Instead he discerns "Dandyism of a more mischievous sort, that has got below the surface and is doing less harmless things than jack-toweling itself and stopping its own digestion." In religion, this dandyism manifests a "lackadaisical want of emotion," and in fashionable circles, it puts "a smooth glaze on the world." Dandyism is determined "not to be disturbed by ideas," and "not to be in earnest, or to receive any impress from the moving age" (12.144–45). If Dickens contributes his own word to this critique, it is "Dedlock." He weighs the ideas of Rouncewell, the ironmaster from the North and son of Sir Leicester's housekeeper, against "the Dedlock mind," as fearful of educating people beyond their station as of "obliterating the landmarks, and opening the flood gates, and all the rest of it" (28.354). We get little idea of how the ironmaster addresses the future other than by educating young Rosa to be a fit match for his son Watt, but the play of the novel on the deadlocked political establishment is relentless. Sir Leicester himself is less dandified than his houseguests, perhaps, though he can be charmed by Skimpole's self-identification as "a perfectly idle man" and "mere amateur" (43.530)—the very opposite character, even if we knew nothing else of Skimpole, from the Carlylean captain of industry.[6]

Numbers 13 and 15 of *Bleak House* have no chapters from Summerson's pen. A chapter in the former called "National and Domestic" begins, "England has been in a dreadful state for some weeks." The narrator's deadpan story tells of a crisis in government owing to a quarrel between Lord Coodle and Sir Thomas Doodle; there are no other persons who can possibly serve in their stead. A "stupendous national calamity" is thus averted when the two make up, but Doodle finds "that he must throw himself upon the country—chiefly in the form of sovereigns and beer" (50.495–96). Though all this nonsense drips with sarcasm, it might be argued that Dickens gives us a livelier account of bribery and corruption in the Eatanswill election (read: eat and swill) in *Pickwick*. The weight of the satire in *Bleak House,* apart from the monopoly of office among an incompetent few, is on the decline and fall of a once ruling class, who are met with again at Chesney Wold in the "Domestic" half of the chapter. The opening paragraph of the novel has conceived, from the mud and fog pervading Lincoln's Inn and Holborn Hill in the city of London, "the death of the sun" (1.5); now we are to understand that "the fire of the sun is dying" in the home of the Dedlocks (50.498) and presumably in other such estates across the land. The paragraphs gather the darkness upon Chesney Wold as they previously had upon Tom-all-Alone's: not for the purpose of exhibiting it in a crueler light of the dawn, however, but to mark the end of its days. Primarily, the collapse of Sir Leicester and the Dedlock pride is to be conveyed by the exposure of a sexual secret, that of Lady Dedlock's premarital affair. That prospect renders the plot all the more mysterious for today's readers; the affair asks to be read as a serious fall and a symptom, and in context a sign of waning power. Vaguely, at his noblest, Sir Leicester is brought into the modern world—or returned to a still older world of kindness—by the stroke he suffers on learning the truth; but possibly the novelist too finds it easier to forgive Honoria once she has been vanquished and put down.

Many other things wrong with the world according to *Bleak House,* and insisted upon by its stark yet capacious title, have little to do with the Court of Chancery or similarly antiquated institutions of a doomed national leadership. Most memorable, because of the sheer persistence of Mrs. Jellyby's monomania, is the case of "telescopic philanthropy" introduced in the first number. Summerson's narrative is the medium here, and as with her first acquaintance with Harold Skimpole, an irony of understatement renders the phenomenon all the more startling. Esther is too inexperienced to know just how surprised she should be; her interlocutors are left to do the talking. The swift mobilization of Caddy Jellyby—"I wish Africa was dead" and "I wish we were all dead" (4.43–44)—contributes much to the effect. Dickens's point is that the tremendous burden of correspondence and organization that Mrs. Jellyby shoulders on behalf of the natives of Borrioboola-Gha must be at the expense of charities nearer to home: the neglect of Caddy, Peepy, and the other Jellyby children, for a start. When he seconds this false philanthropy with the antics of another mother of small children, Mrs. Pardiggle, he pursues the theme home and complements the satire with a different slant: Mrs. Pardiggle's forays into brickmakers' cottages are downright aggressive, accusatory, and uncharitable—as reflected still more pointedly in the unchristian resentment of her own children, those little ones named Egbert, Oswald, Francis, and Alfred and trained early in hypocrisy, whom Esther meets the day after her arrival at Bleak House. These introductions, too, are necessary to prepare for the death of the crossing sweeper: "He is not one of Mrs. Pardiggle's Tockahoopo Indians; he is not one of Mrs. Jellyby's lambs, being wholly unconnected with Borrioboola-Gha; he is not softened by distance and unfamiliarity; he is not a genuine foreign-grown savage; he is the ordinary home-made article." Today's knowing anticolonialists need not shiver at the wrong being done here to Borrioboola-Gha or to the Tockahoopo. True, Dickens's make-believe nations are linguistically stereotyped as African or North American Indian, but even if they were real places one wouldn't wish upon them the attentions of Jellyby and Pardiggle. He protests against the condition of the home product of imperial England: "Dirty, ugly, disagreeable to the senses," as the passage continues. "Homely filth begrimes him, homely parasites devour him, homely sores are in him, homely rags are on him: native ignorance, the growth of English soil and climate, sinks his immortal nature lower than the beasts that perish" (47.564). So-called philanthropy, Dickens charges, is motivated not by compassion or the perception of need but by self-interest and idle entertainment; the so-called philanthropists look away from nearby wrongs, which are painful even to the self-righteous. Private charity is as neglectful of Tom-all-Alone's as the court and government are.

One role of the great Chadband in the novel is to dramatize religion's neglect—and worse—of the poor. The disagreeable Chadband has a hilarious voice; he might be said to be all voice.[7] He is not quite a match for the incomparable Pecksniff of *Martin Chuzzlewit*, but in his first appearance at Snagsby's he seizes the opportunity to say grace, and performs this remarkable speech with an originality equal to Pecksniff's grace after meat. Chadband's address begins, "My friends . . . what is this which we now behold as being spread before us? Refreshment" and segues to "Why can we not fly, my friends?" before salivating more and more freely over the bread, butter, eggs, ham, tongue, sausage, and "such like" that have been laid before him (19.237). This splendid preacher preaches for no particular congregation; if anything, his is the Victorian equivalent of a T.V. ministry, attaching itself to fame or notoriety as it can but mainly regardful, the style suggests, of being fed. There is a wonderfully renewable emptiness in his catechizing and apparent logic. Repeatedly, his improvising is directed at Jo of Tom-all-Alone's, as the lowest of the low, because he can be confident that every one of his listeners looks down at Jo. His Christian ministry is but another attack, a scapegoating, or at best an exploitation of the poor. As the dying Jo recalls, "Mr. Chadbands he wos a prayin wunst at Mr. Sangsby's and I heerd him, but he sounded as if he wos a speakin' to hisself, and not to me. He prayed a lot, but *I* couldn't make out nothink on it" (47.571).

Amid the range and abundance of Dickens's satire it is still possible to generalize, I believe, about his intentions. The principal kinds of offense displayed in *Bleak House* can be thought of as forms of parasitism, a relation that subtends institutions as well as practicing individuals. Harold Skimpole is but one of many parasites; his unique function is daringly to articulate the drone philosophy, and his very articulation of it preys shamelessly on the Gospels and exchange economics. Tulkinghorn carves out a living from the great estates of the land and preys on their secrets, storing them for his own use rather than for any evident need. Lesser blackmailers such as the Chadbands, Smallweed, and Mrs. Snagsby go for quicker profits to be made from other people's secrets. Sir Leicester himself and his relations thrive only on the wealth of their ancestors. But the great institutions of the Chancery court and Parliament, since they operate at others' expense and contribute nothing but pain, have also become parasitical, bleeding both individual hosts and the nation. These actions are not just lightly worrisome to the satirist. In a sense, all are parasites who receive more than they contribute to the vast social interrelatedness of which both Jarndyce and Skimpole are sensitively aware.

The two unmistakable parasites, let us say, are Skimpole and Chadband. Never at a loss for words, they stop at nothing; and thus they prey on the poorest of the poor, even though they are attracted to bigger game. They never meet in the novel, but they both betray Jo. Skimpole turns Jo over to Bucket for a five pound note, and the supposed man of God uses Jo for his own purposes instead of teaching him the gospel.

> "My young friend," says Chadband, "you are to us a pearl, you are to us a diamond, you are to us a gem, you are to us a jewel. And why, my young friend?"
>
> "*I* don't know," replies Jo. "I don't know nothink."
>
> "My young friend," says Chadband, "it is because you know nothing that you are to us a gem and jewel. For what are you, my young friend? Are you a beast of the field? No. A bird of the air? No. A fish of the sea or river? No. You are a human boy, my young friend. A human boy. O glorious to be a human boy! And why glorious, my young friend?" (19.242)

But notoriously the only value of the human boy that the preacher can conceive of is that of someone to preach at—a gem or jewel to be seized upon by Chadband. He teaches the boy not a thing, not even to pray; his discourse is empty; he returns nothing for the jewel he finds. These vile usages figuratively join the parasites, also, to Tom-all-Alone's, where humanity "crawls in and out of gaps in walls and boards; and coils itself to sleep in maggot numbers."

The satire of false philanthropy and self-aggrandizing religion is memorable because of the single-mindedness Dickens grants to malpractitioners like Jellyby, Pardiggle, and Chadband, and because their selfish aims are so diametrically opposed or deaf to the claims of Christianity. Yet it is true that a dim view of life colors other aspects of the two narratives of *Bleak House*—possibly because the writing of the novel is suffused with mourning.[8] The suppressed anger of John Jarndyce, the suppressed disappointment of Esther Summerson, the frustration of many, and the absence of kindness in others have a cumulative effect as powerful as that of the satire. The harboring of suspicion and the maneuvering with secrets of other people's lives are not confined to Tulkinghorn and the rabble of petty blackmailers but attach to Inspector Bucket's profession as well. When Dickens's detective practices deceit in the arrest of George, for example, it leaves such a bad taste that some readers may be put off by his treatment of Hortense as well. It is fair to say that not only charity but erotic love lives under a cloud in *Bleak House*. The love of Richard and Ada becomes more and more one-sided until it resembles nothing other than the doomed devotion of a woman to her man. Jarndyce keeps his love so well in hand that his loss of Esther to Woodcourt causes him no great pain; Woodcourt himself never longs for the heroine. The doctor would court but his love is also deeply convenient, of a piece with his near-demonic powers over death. Esther's excessive modesty tends to deprive her love of direction; and Lady Dedlock's fixation on the grave of Nemo signals guilt more than a return to the great passion of her life. That leaves Rosa's chance for happiness with Watt Rouncewell—if she can bear up under the necessary lessons from her prospective father-in-law. It is all too easy to confine oneself to the Growlery when thinking about *Bleak House*.

Caddy Jellyby's father has a bit of advice for his daughter on learning that she plans to get married. Unless she makes a home for her husband, she "had better murder him than marry him." A full sense of Mrs. Jellyby's failure in this line prompts him to remark further, of his younger children, that "the best thing that could happen to them was, their being all Tomahawked together" (30.369). Even English novels that happily celebrate courtship and marriage are likely to draw existing marriages with an amused or satiric pen: Jane Austen's novels, for example. In *Bleak House* nearly all the married couples (and the exceptions, the Chadbands and the elderly Smallweeds, are not reassuring) are dominated by the female partner. This circumstance cannot be attributed to enlightened feminism; what Dickens thinks of feminism can be deduced from the brief appearance of the unmarried Miss Wisk and her program for "the emancipation of Woman from the thraldom of her Tyrant, Man" (30.375).[9] On the contrary, the marriages in the novel, which range from the utter neglect of her family by Jellyby to the modus vivendi of the Bagnets (she providing all the thinking and he pretending to maintain discipline), evidence more of what is wrong with the world: for if the benign examples are merely amusing, what is there to be amused about? Male sovereignty has been abridged. The Pardiggles are in as bad shape as the Jellybys, except that they deserve each other. The Snagsbys live in fixed opposition to one another, he forced to keep secret his compassion for Jo, she persuaded that the secret is more treacherous. The satisfaction Mr. Bayham Badger takes in Mrs. Badger's former husbands, Captain Swosser and Professor Dingo, is fine for him; yet she has the staying power, and it may be that her third husband will not be the last. One never imagines Lady Dedlock managing Sir Leicester in any such fashion as these wives have adopted: she is far too adroit at the manners of the class she has aspired to. But she too has married to advantage, as they say. She knows how to wear the clothes and jewels, and she has the ambition, the hauteur, and sex appeal to carry it off. Even poor Caddy and poor Ada prove stronger than their husbands.[10]

The frustration or lovelessness of so many relationships undoubtedly helps to make the novel bleak. As if differences between partners were not enough, indeed, the two narratives tell of illness and death. Besides the deaths that Ruskin felt were brutalizing and extreme, there are Sir Leicester Dedlock's gout and the stroke he suffers, Lady Dedlock's terrible fatigue, Richard Carstone's waning away, Guster's fits and Caddy's deaf and dumb child, the fever that attacks Jo, Charley, and Esther, and the temporary blindness suffered by Esther and then by the dying Jo.[11] Though sickness, near-death, death itself are commonplace in romance as well as satire, *Bleak House* measures out more than its share of sadness, perhaps, by joining these two genres. One critic calls it the most brilliant novel in English yet "the most upsetting" by Dickens.[12] "What connexion can there be?" The connectedness may be the trouble. The modern conviction—the Enlightenment conviction, if you will—is that our local efforts, our laws and institutions as well, are ours to shape as we will and know best. Connectedness is a given, and the effort required a constant. We must keep doing in order to hold up our end. It is almost tempting to become ill and die; as Esther in the delirium of her fever wishes "to be taken off from the rest" and die (35.432). Or if we take it easy and still manage to thrive, we are parasites and drones. Dickens's next major protagonist, Arthur Clennam, pronounces in the first number of *Little Dorrit,* "I have no will."[13] That projection of middle age comes oddly from a writer as active day by day as Dickens was. Yet *Bleak House* is already haunted by a lack of will, perhaps, or by a sense of undeserved achievement. Esther Summerson, who wills so strongly to help others but gets more than she gives in the end, is troubled also. Busy bee, be busy: the business for its own sake seems a distraction.

It should not be overlooked that the success of *Bleak House* as satire depends on small hopes and decencies as well as the exposure of great wrongs. Because it is a satire as well as romance, there needs to be an imbalance between the pervasive wrongs—malfunctioning institutions and outrageous practice, astounding parasites and underlying sadness—and the few signs of redemption. Sometimes the sign comes from an unexpected source. "Full forgiveness. Find———": that from the stricken Sir Leicester (56.669). That hope is small and decency nearly overwhelmed makes the satiric point. Think of how scarred by life are the handful of agents of good in the novel: Charley, for example, and Caddy. Esther herself was meant to be partly of this type, had the wish fulfillment of romance not carried the day; her separate narrative is a gesture in this direction. Jarndyce, surely, is to be understood as deeply scarred before the action commences, even though his face is "brightest and most benevolent" at the end (67.770). But the best illustration of the use Dickens makes of this principle is trooper George's shooting gallery and its inhabitants: as marginal a place and pair of characters as only Dickens or Shakespeare might imagine.

George's shooting gallery is shelter for the dispossessed and dying, no less marvelous than a hovel on a stormy heath for sheltering a fool, a madman, and a king. It corresponds to other shelters in Dickens, like the instrument maker's shop in *Dombey and Son,* but is more minimal and grotesque: after all, the one outright murder in *Bleak House* is by pistol at close range. The gallery serves as a hospice, regardless of its powder and shot, for the dying Gridley and then for the dying Jo. Nursing the dying are two very weak lights indeed, George the ex-soldier and his familiar Phil Squod. The former is utterly in debt for the purchase of the business but is almost ennobled by this fact; for unlike Skimpole or Carstone he accepts, quite simply, his responsibility to pay. Similarly, he will accede to his arrest for a murder he has nothing to do with. His entire outlook is self-abnegating and chargeable to the penitence with which he views his failing of his mother—who, unknown to George, loves him more than she does his brother, the ironmaster Rouncewell. Phil Squod is the grotesque extreme of the scarred goodness in Charley, Caddy, and Esther. His ugly countenance has been burned, if we can believe him, by his trade as a tinker, by "larking" with other workers at a forge, by an "accident at a gas-works," and by an explosion that blew him out the window at a "firework business." Consequently, he too has been stripped of self-interest: "If a mark's wanted, or if it will improve the business, let the customers take aim at me. They can't spoil *my* beauty. *I'*m all right. Come on! If they want a man to box at, let 'em box at me. Let 'em knock me well about the head. *I* don't mind." A character who defies anyone to spoil his beauty is a standout in this novel. Phil's very way of moving about the gallery confirms his history: "I have been throwed, all sorts of styles, all my life!" (26.327–28).

Such are the marginal but dependable beings to whose care Gridley and Jo can be entrusted when dying: those who have lost their lives shall save others. Gridley, the mortal victim of the court, and Jo, the object of all neglect, themselves join in the saving remnant. Their poverty and insignificance finally count in this satire. A "Joful and woful experience," as the narrator proclaims it earlier with Joycean aplomb (19.239), has been rendered accessible to view.

7

The Novel's Judgment

Miss Flight is expecting a judgment. She is the crazy but politely deferential woman who imagines that she has an interest in the case of Jarndyce and Jarndyce and attends the court day by day in expectation. She is the mad prophet whose sayings and symbols bode ill even when she means well. Flite is not completely crazy, of course. She keeps a good many birds in cages, to be released when the judgment is given. "They die in prison, though. Their lives, poor silly things, are so short in comparison with Chancery proceedings, that, one by one, the whole collection has died over and over again. I doubt, do you know, whether one of these, though they are all young, will live to be free!" (5.53). No character in *Bleak House* has a more fixed, emblematic role; and no character is more closely associated with the court, or with Jarndyce and Jarndyce, about which she may know as much as anyone. Pointedly, she appears in the first chapter's impersonal narrative but then again more fully in the third chapter, which is Summerson's first. She is last heard from at the close of the third chapter from the end, in which Summerson narrates the death of Richard Carstone and the end of the suit. "When all was still, at a late hour, poor crazed Miss Flite came weeping to me, and told me she had given her birds their liberty." Flite becomes, in effect, sane; the court itself has been judged. The release of the birds commemorates the freedom of Richard from the thralldom of Jarndyce and Jarndyce, as well as the departure of his soul for "the world that sets this right" (66.763).

The judgment, however one reads it, is remarkably understated. The notorious case of Jarndyce and Jarndyce comes to naught when the inheritances at stake have been entirely consumed by costs and lawyers' fees; no lawyer will touch it now. Miss Flite must release her birds willy-nilly, and when she does so, some truth has come home to her. All that is left are perspectives on the case that roughly correspond to the two narratives of *Bleak House*. For one, the victims of Chancery will die "over and over again" and not even the young "will live to be free." For the other, on familiar terms with one poor victim, the sacrifice is of someone we know—in the foreground, in human time, burdened with moral understanding and relieved by faith in the next world.

> Evening had come on, when I lifted up my eyes, and saw my guardian standing in the little hall. "Who is that, Dame Durden?" Richard asked me. The door was behind him, but he had observed in my face that some one was there.
>
> I looked to Allan for advice, and as he nodded "Yes," bent over Richard and told him. My guardian saw what passed, came softly by me in a moment, and laid his hand on Richard's. "O sir," said Richard, "you are a good man, you are a good man!" and burst into tears for the first time.
>
> My guardian, the picture of a good man, sat down in my place, keeping his hand on Richard's.
>
> "My dear Rick," said he, "the clouds have cleared away, and it is bright now. We can see now. We were all bewildered, Rick, more or less. What matters! And how are you, my dear boy?"
>
> "I am very weak, sir, but I hope I shall be stronger. I have to begin the world." (65.761–62)

Never mind that the scene begins, "when I lifted up my eyes," in language reminiscent of the Twenty-third Psalm, with "my guardian" in the role of the Lord: it really is of consequence for the interpretation of *Bleak House* that the end of the famous Chancery suit is narrated almost casually by Esther Summerson and that she requires more space to tell of this single casualty, who is her friend and Ada's husband. How could it be otherwise? In that other, impersonal narrative in the present tense, nothing is ever over with—not even Jo, who goes right on "dying thus around us every day."

Interpretation must rely on the double narrative. Perspectives are gained, lost, and restored throughout *Bleak House* by the distribution of the two sorts of chapters—impersonal present, personal past. Though Dickens does not impose a fixed pattern—strict alternation or equal-length segments, say—certain rules obviously apply. Both narratives adhere to the same chronology of events, both are reliably demarcated by chapter division, both are internally consistent as to the person and tense of the verbs. The result is an impressive work of montage, which ought by now to have earned Dickens the reputation of composing in 1852–53 a distinctly modernist text. Like most modernist experiments, it poses problems of interpretation that further engage serious readers. More than most Victorian novels, it calls attention to its own design; it presents itself both as a representation of life and as a self-conscious construction. This is *Bleak House*—"the less substantial Edifice" that Dickens compared to Tavistock House, in which it would be written.[1]

Probably no one has ever tried to work out all of the possible effects of the juxtaposition of the two narratives, though Judith Wilt has given a good idea of how it might be done. For example, Summerson, in her mode of constructing this edifice, notices the simple beauty of the Lord Chancellor's gold lace, the "courtly and kind" manner, the "affable and polite" sensitivity that accompanies his "searching look" and brisk dismissal, the casual but accurate understanding of Richard's need to be spoken to, standing man to man, "as if he still knew, though he *was* Lord Chancellor, how to go straight to the candour of a boy" (3.31–32). This sound and solid human being is the same man that another observer in another mode, or the same observer in another mode, earlier descried sitting "with a foggy glory round his head, softly fenced in with crimson cloth and curtains," carrying on the traditional jokes about Jarndyce and Jarndyce, and "dexterously" vanishing when addressed by the ruined man from Shropshire about whose existence the Chancellor must affect to be "legally ignorant . . . after making it desolate for a quarter of a century" (1.6,10,7).

At a minimum the two modes force the reader to ask which description is the more revealing. Wilt speculates that both narrators may be the same not merely because they both originate with Dickens but because the investment in a female protagonist commits the novelist to "the wider anxieties of the Self-Other relationship," as opposed to "the simple narcissism of his male avatars." As I have tried to make clear, I believe that narcissism, male or female, still very much underlies this heroine's text. Wilt daringly suggests that Esther's anxiety, in the form of concern for others, affects the impersonal narrative as well, though she does not finally attempt to prove this: "Dickens's Esther Summerson shows him a new kind of horizon, and in so doing, liberates in the book's other, sister, voice, the most profoundly direct address to the aggregate Other, 'ladies and gentlemen born with Heavenly compassion in your hearts,' that he was ever to make."[2]

Some broad differences between the two narratives are so evident that they are not in need of proof. Wilt's main purpose is to bring out the contrast between the essential confusion and tentativeness of Summerson's state of knowledge and the pronounced certainties of the satiric overvoice. "Esther is certain of nothing," and for that reason perhaps is more noticing. In contrast, the other narrative not only protests the fog but often comes right out and tells us what to think, even when it cannot know for sure: thus, "the one great principle of the English law is, to make business for itself" (39.482).[3] And tentativeness, I might add, is reflected by that other authority of the personal narrative, Jarndyce—as in "We were all bewildered, Rick, more or less." Summerson's account of things *is* personal. The people and things and actions she encounters are experienced and reported up close; hence sympathy or discomfort can be registered. Everything she reports is constrained by her opportunities to observe, and thus a class difference appears in the substance of things narrated in the novel. At first Esther is acquainted solely with people of her own class. Only gradually does she meet with the poor or homeless and the people of fashion, and when she does widen her acquaintance, the new experience may be temporary. She never has a second interview with Lady Dedlock after the latter has confessed their relationship. The other narrative is immediately at home with high society or, as it hovers above the streets, the law courts and the poor. This is the voice that asks what connections there can be.

Certain important differences are functions of the tenses of the two narratives. The initial narrative, which confines itself throughout to the present tense, is overarching and primarily visual. It possesses what would soon become cinematic capabilities of panning in and out of scenes, of cutting from Chancery Lane to Lincolnshire and back again. Summerson's model is the long-tested biographical method for composing novels. It begins with her earliest memories and closes "full seven happy years" after the events related (67.767), which have also become memories. The missing epochal event, her unknown birth, is slowly reconstructed from the very sorts of evidence that the would-be blackmailers seek; her marriage and complete assurance of the future erase even that mystery, which no longer signifies. Because the temporal dimension of events is Summerson's concern, her narrative provides the main continuity of the novel. The narratives belong to distinctly different literary modes. Summerson's opening upon the past and future has the shape of new comedy, with its marriage plot and temporary dip in the protagonist's fortunes. Jarndyce, if he can be thought of as a traditional senex, is a rather charming blocking agent, who changes course of his own accord. The comedy plot necessarily unfolds over time, as does all romance of wish fulfillment: wishes can never be fulfilled without a before and after.[4] But satire, the mode of the other narrative, is in one sense timeless. Satire does not propose reforms, it just angrily shows things for what they are. Even topical satire is not precise as to the history of the faults it finds. It slashes away at human foibles and social conditions, some of which may be under repair and others irreparable. It keeps foreseeing the worst but mainly consists of outbursts and ironies that provide their own satisfaction; its scorn and laughter are delectable enough. Whereas comedy achieves a happy ending, satire often just leaves off. And so in *Bleak House:* already in number 18, as well as in the last double number, the satirical present-tense voice relents and relinquishes its authority to comedy. From an overall view of the novel, the satire itself can be thought of as a blocking agent that finally gives way.

The division of multiplot novels into equal-length monthly installments, once scoffed at by art-of-the-novel critics as dictated merely by sales, created an arbitrary formal structure itself suggestive of some modernism. Thus even a text as complicated as *Bleak House* may have an exact center, around which a turning in both narratives is constructed. While the novel's original readers awaited the new year of 1853 and the publication of number 11 in order to learn the outcome of Esther Summerson's illness (she remained unconscious all that time), they also awaited clarification of the smoky and spooky disappearance of Mr. Krook by spontaneous combustion. Both turnings sound false alarms but in different registers: Esther's pathetic and Krook's prophetic. Her illness and near-death are the low from which her fortunes will rise; his combustion (real enough according to Dickens) is a warning to the actual Lord Chancellor and to Chancery of their deserved fate, which no more comes to pass than Esther's threatened death. In the former case Dickens was manipulating a fiction entirely of his own making and narrated by his heroine; in the latter he was constrained to cope symbolically with an institution not of his making or within his power directly to explode.[5] But the overlay of the two actions is surely purposeful. Increasingly Dickens chose to feature the center point of his twenty-number productions. In *David Copperfield* this tendency is already evident, and his remaining novels of the same length are similarly divided: *Little Dorrit* into two equal parts entitled "Poverty" and "Riches," and *Our Mutual Friend* into four, thereby preserving the same center point.[6] The coincidence of Esther's low point and Krook's demise in *Bleak House* foretells the contrast in the last number between her marriage and advance to the new Bleak House and the dissolution, in cynical laughter and an accompanying death, of Jarndyce and Jarndyce. The arithmetical position of the double turning, in its arbitrariness, attests for today's readers to the modernist leaning of the novel. The fiction of *Bleak House* does not merely pose as a representation of mid-nineteenth-century life; it shows off not a little its own design, which is that of a careful montage of two narratives.

Strictly as a matter of representation, Dickens wrote himself into difficulty with the dramatic end he determined for the shadow chancellor Krook. To be sure, he was exercising his satirical license by declaring at the close of number 10 that his character had "died the death of all Lord Chancellors in all Courts, and of all authorities in all places under all names soever, where false pretences are made, and where injustice is done. . . . Spontaneous Combustion, and none other of all the deaths that can be died" (32.403). Yet when questions were raised—by the knowledgeable George Henry Lewes, among others—Dickens dug in his heels and held that people can and occasionally do burn up after consuming too much alcohol.[7] This claim was not only weaker but in a different mode from the blow up of all authorities whatsoever who are guilty of false pretenses. Dickens divided his preface to the completed novel between assertions that "everything set forth in these pages concerning the Court of Chancery is substantially true" and mentions of "about thirty cases on record" of spontaneous combustion, thereby nearly forgetting that Krook was never anything but a mock chancellor and his fate a symbolic threat to the court. Not that his readers showed much more imagination in this regard. At least some of their objections came to hand before number 11 went to press, for in a long passage added to the manuscript Dickens had already cited some of his research and sarcastically remarked "the late Mr. Krook's obstinacy, in going out of the world by any such byeway," as if the obstinacy were the character's own (33.413-14).[8]

How much better Dickens could justify his idea when not ill-advisedly defending himself on the facts can be seen from the opening of the same number and chapter—midway in the novel—where he parrots the language of the journalists who have arrived in Chancery Lane to report the astonishing demise of the rag-and-bottle dealer:

> Now do these two gentlemen not very neat about the cuffs and buttons who attended the last Coroner's Inquest at the Sol's Arms, reappear in the precincts with surprising swiftness . . . and institute prequisitions through the court, and dive into the Sol's parlour, and write with ravenous little pens on tissue-paper. Now do they note down, in the watches of the night, how the neighbourhood of Chancery Lane was yesterday, at about midnight, thrown into a state of the most intense agitation and excitement by the following alarming and horrible discovery. Now do they set forth how it will doubtless be remembered, that some time back a painful sensation was created in the public mind, by a case of mysterious death from opium occurring in the first floor of the house occupied as a rag, bottle, and general marine store shop, by an eccentric individual of intemperate habits, far advanced in life, named Krook.

Thus the second half of *Bleak House* commences, after a month's interlude, with a production of supposed newspaper accounts that function *as* the narrative of the sensational event. With each repetition of "Now do those two gentlemen . . . reappear," "Now do they note down," "Now do they set forth," the present time of the general narrative notches forward, even as the news account being produced according to form harks back to the previous night, anticipates its readers' recollections of the earlier death on the premises, recurs to that time to refresh the public record, before it goes on to summarize the reporters' interviews with one "Mr. Swills, a comic vocalist, professionally engaged by Mr. J. G. Bogsby," respectable landlord of Sol's Arms, and with "two intelligent married females residing in the same court, and known respectively by the names of Mrs. Piper and Mrs. Perkins," about the peculiar smell and "impure state of the atmosphere" on the present occasion—the very effects experienced with alarm by Guppy and Tony Jobling at the end of *Bleak House* number 10. The opening paragraph of the new number (of which I have extracted about a third) keeps losing itself in production of the unnamed journalists' writing, which is assimilated in turn by their product, the resulting news story. But the satirist also keeps reasserting his authority by exaggeration, jokes, and asides: "Now do they show (in as many words as possible), how during some hours of yesterday evening . . ." (33.403–4). Journalism too, is being sent up, with due attention to its catering to local businesses, its language and pretensions. All this while the portentous (and highly unusual) event of spontaneous combustion is played down as well as up, while the present all-important state of Esther's consciousness is simply a negative, a cessation of consciousness and break in the Summersonian account of itself.

In his preface Dickens would huffily observe ("I have no need to observe") that he does not "wilfully or negligently mislead my readers." But who would not applaud him if he had simply invented the idea of spontaneous combustion and turned it to ironic account in this false catastrophe? The preface, not the novel, is mistaken and unfortunate in tone. His responsible attitude—or the attitude of his day—toward the making of representations could not keep abreast with his creative design, which was becoming more modernist than Victorian. *Our Mutual Friend,* the last completed novel, is better known for its contribution to modernism because of its prominence in T. S.

Eliot's early drafts of *The Waste Land*.[9] But it may be that *Bleak House* deserves as much credit as any prose work of its time for a modernist initiative, notwithstanding its commitment to a strong representation of the facts and proof of the heroine's innocence.[10] Not only does Dickens experiment with Joycean adaptations of the style to what is represented, such as in the reportage of Krook's combustion, but his recourse to incantation and distancing himself from the very voices he invokes may remind one of Eliot.

The preface would never lead anyone to expect more than one narrative. "In Bleak House," it temperately concludes, "I have purposely dwelt upon the romantic side of familiar things" —a locution expressive of the whole project of romantic realism in the nineteenth century.[11] By the time Dickens has finished the novel and addressed the public in this preface, Summerson has been dispensed with; or, better, Dickens is entirely comfortable with the fracture of the novel as written. On Summerson's side, it might be said that she has no responsibility for the difficulties addressed in the first four paragraphs of the preface; as to spontaneous combustion in particular, she was neither present nor awake at the time and could have nothing to add. Just because Dickens never alludes to the fracture and rebonding of *Bleak House*, that feature of it seems the most off-handedly modernist. "I have a great deal of difficulty in beginning to write my portion of these pages": that casual opening of the third chapter is all the reader has to go on, and the explanatory clause—"for I know I am not clever"—merely points to Summerson's modesty as the reason for mentioning the difficulty at all (3.17). The novel just starts over again with a different voice. The only other overt reference on Summerson's part to the writing of her share is the opening paragraph of the last chapter: "Full seven happy years I have been the mistress of Bleak House. The few words that I have to add to what I have written, are soon penned: then I, and the unknown friend to whom I write, will part for ever. Not without much dear remembrance on my side. Not without some, I hope, on his or hers" (67.767). And here she applies two conventions for bringing self-narrated stories to a close: she gives a measure of the interval, seven years, between the main action and the writing, and she graciously takes farewell of the reader. Again the burden of her words is modestly self-aggrandizing. The phrase "mistress of Bleak House," formerly the code for marriage to Jarndyce, now boasts of her marriage to Allan Woodcourt; and she endorses the fiction that she remembers her reader in order to be remembered in turn. That she, a fictional person, is in any way acquainted with the readership helps assimilate her authorship to Dickens's. The coyness and unaccustomed care with the gender of pronouns suggest that this might be a new romance from the pen of Dame Trot Copperfield or the autobiography of a Dickens in drag.

I have finally to disagree with the readings of *Bleak House* that see this work of montage not as a modernist but as a postmodernist text. The original reading of this kind is by J. Hillis Miller, in a wide-ranging and influential introduction to the novel that construes the narratives as two incompatible visions of supposed representations: Summerson's is a providential vision, whereas the other narrator's is dark and nihilistic. Miller too enlists Tom-all-Alone's as the primary object of the latter vision; but he does not perceive a generic division between comedic and satiric modes. His observation about the (secularized) providential cast of Summerson's narrative situates that portion of the novel, at least, in mainline British fiction; but he finally bears down upon an almost Manichaean difference between the two narratives. His key paragraph concludes, "Though the happy ending of *Bleak House* may beguile the reader into accepting Esther's view as the true one, the novel does not resolve the incompatibility between her vision and what the other narrator sees. The meaning of the novel lies in this irresolution."[12]

For Miller to concede that the ending may beguile the reader shows what he judges an unforced reading of *Bleak House* to be like. The choice of "beguile" is a compliment, no doubt, to Summerson's narrative voice. At the same time it scants the powerful actions of the novel that make up her story. The mother of the supposed-to-be dead child dies; the menacing lawyer who learns the secret of their relationship dies; the young husband of the beautiful Ada Clare dies; a crossing sweeper, the emblem of social neglect and carrier of disease, dies; even Caddy Turveydrop, called Jellyby, fares poorly. Certainly some of these actions, the death of Jo especially, weigh heavily in the satire of Chancery and the condition recognized as Tom-all-Alone's. But in that case they are overdetermined by their inclusion in Esther Summerson's progress. Even time works for the heroine, and the fate *she* tells for Jarndyce and Jarndyce is in the past tense. The last joke about Jarndyce and Jarndyce undercuts all the exaggerated rhetoric devoted to it earlier in the present tense; the interminable lawsuit is terminable after all. This is satire for satire, with Summerson winding it all up like a ball of yarn. The suit that baffled experts is now understandable by anyone, even a woman.

Miller would like to think of Jarndyce and Jarndyce as undecidable and the mirror of language. He states right away that "*Bleak House* is a document about the interpretation of documents. Like many great works of literature it raises questions about its own status as a text. . . . The situation of the characters within the novel corresponds to the situation of its reader or author."[13] It goes without saying that interpretation is a part of life, and interpretation of documents a function of literacy.

A novel that purports to be a representation of life could well contain pages about documents. Still, *Bleak House* never affords its readers a chance to look over the shoulder of a lawyer interpreting a difficult page or two. The documents in Jarndyce and Jarndyce are voluminous but figured from the start as worthless, like the litter in Flite's reticule, "which she calls her documents; principally consisting of paper matches and dry lavender" (1.7). Much more is made of who will get possession of certain letters; and far from there being a problem in interpreting these letters, it soon emerges—without their ever being read—that they are relics of a love affair between one Nemo and the present Lady Dedlock.

Bleak House does not notably question itself as writing or as interpretation. As for its author, when challenged on spontaneous combustion, he claims that his fiction is true. Rather, it is Miller who insists on this uncertainty, in order to compliment Dickens's novel for postmodern insight into language and society. To make his point he even dramatizes interpretation— which is inescapable—as evil:

> The sombre suggestion toward which many elements of the novel lead, like pointers converging from different directions on a single spot, is that the guilty party is not any person or persons, not correctable evil in any institution. The villain is the act of interpretation itself, the naming which assimilates the particular into a system, giving it a definition and a value, incorporating it into a whole. If this is the case, then in spite of Dickens's generous rage against injustice, selfishness and procrastination, the evil he so brilliantly identifies is irremediable. It is inseparable from language and from the organization of men into society.[14]

Miller expands on his theme as if he were a novelist himself, if not a romancer; his hero Dickens strives against evil like a knight errant, but in the Manichaean wilderness good may not overcome evil. He is too expert a reader not to note that Gridley, in *Bleak House,* protests that it is not the system that has doomed him but the failure of anyone to take charge of things. "The system!" Gridley exclaims with bitter irony. "I am told, on all hands, it's the system. I mustn't look to individuals. It's the system" (15.193). That Gridley's disgust is akin to Dickens's own is apparent from the more truly systematic institution satirized in *Little Dorrit.* Chancery is an archaic court of law, the Circumlocution Office a modern bureaucracy, but in both the trouble lies in the greed, incompetence, or refusal to take responsibility of the individuals involved. "Come, responsible Somebody; accountable Blockhead, come!" the exasperated author would demand in a piece for *Household Words.*[15] But of course it is possible that Dickens had the wrong explanation or that the novels he wrote convey a different idea. Miller believes that "the whole bent of *Bleak House* is toward indicating that it is in fact the systematic quality of organized society which causes Gridley's suffering—not a bad system of law, but any system, not a bad representative government, but the institution itself, not the special evil of aristocratic pride, but any social organization based on membership in a family." Miller does not merely address the postmodern *condition:* old institutions or new, it makes no difference. He is as conservative in this respect as the satirist in Dickens. He argues ahistorically that "system" deprives individuals of their own histories. "As soon as a man becomes in one way or another part of such a system, born into it or made a party to it, he enters into a strange kind of time," with no "present self or present satisfaction," nor "any possibility of ever going back to find the origin of his personal plight."[16] Yet the selfhood thus lost, one wishes to reply, is very like that promised by Esther Summerson's progress and her narrative, which traces her origins and effectively sorts them out. The key difference of interpretation here depends on whether the reader feels that the two narratives are still on equal terms at the end of the novel.

There is a frisson to Miller's reading, which I have characterized as Manichaean. The "evil" that *Bleak House* addresses is both irremediable and ubiquitous, a concomitant of language and of social life. The "irresolution" of the narratives confirms this state of being, whether for the characters or the author and readers. All must endure "the violence exercised over the individual by language and other social institutions." Yet Miller and *his* readers are not filled with despair at the human condition; on the contrary, there is a kind of elation in our powerlessness. Interpretation is evil but unavoidable, and everyone goes right on interpreting away. An evil that puts everyone in the same fix is not so bad after all (and not so simpleminded as the happiness Summerson proposes for herself). And there is still that dire thought: a novel is composed of language and constitutes a system. Thus "*Bleak House* itself has exactly the same structure as the society it exposes. It too assimilates everything it touches into a system of meaning." And "it too is made up of an incessant movement of reference in which each element leads to other elements in a constant displacement of meaning." Each and every metaphor contributes to this movement and displacement. For example, those "Mercuries" who are the Dedlock footmen repose "like overblown sunflowers" at Chesney Wold (48.573). In such case, the metaphors "remind the reader that there are no real footmen in the novel."[17] Surely only the postmodern faithful need this reassurance. A better test would be to ask whether Dickens could not use the same metaphors in an article on Queen Victoria's real footmen without impugning the latter's existence.

These two arguments, that the system is evil and the novel partakes of the system, are the starting place for a second post-modernist reading of *Bleak House*. D. A. Miller is explicitly critical of J. Hillis Miller's reading and wittily distances himself from both Marxist and deconstructive criticism.[18] He catches the frisson of inescapable system but argues much more tightly and then hermetically than the first Miller. The atmosphere of his *Bleak House* is claustrophobic, or as he would say, "carceral," and the ubiquity of power distinctly Foucauldian.[19] Miller pays little heed to the double narrative. Instead he concentrates on the two practices of power that the novel evokes most blatantly: the Court of Chancery and the detective police under Inspector Bucket. He boldly argues that the latter practice answers to the frustration of the former but then is frustrated in turn, when a third institution ("the novel") struggles in vain for a satisfactory solution. The substitution of the one practice for the other makes intuitive sense, since Dickens first takes up and makes amply clear the frustrations of the court and subsequently introduces the police action; that the two institutions are not involved with the same case and that the murder of Tulkinghorn is solved before Jarndyce and Jarndyce dissolves in costs do not seem to matter. "One consequence of a system that, as it engenders an interpretative project, deprives it of all the requirements for its accomplishment is the desire for an interpretative project that would *not* be so balked." Once that is said, the critic can fairly predict that a detective practice will be called for. "What such a desire calls for . . . is the detective story."[20] This explanation, or story of the story, of *Bleak House* is facilitated by the absence of any author. The said desire hovers close about the text and "effectively" seeks a detective story because that is what *Bleak House* delivers.

The novel, in sum, seeks to achieve closure by resorting to murder and its successful detection. But then Inspector

Bucket's relatively swift apprehension of Hortense is also unsatisfactory. Here D. A. Miller has to rely heavily upon Hortense's defiance of Bucket after her arrest in number 17. She is a killer whose spirits cannot be kept down, and she turns upon the detective with three arresting questions of her own as to Tulkinghorn, Lady Dedlock, and Sir Leicester: "But can you restore him back to life? . . . Can you make a honourable lady of Her? . . . Or a haughty gentleman of *Him?*" (54.652–53). As Miller appreciatively notes, "the various existential problems" raised by Hortense trump the detective's solution of the crime.[21] But what is Hortense? Of the three look-alikes, Lady Dedlock, her daughter, and Hortense, the chief suspect and foremost guilty party is the first—or so Summerson has feared and the other narrative will promptly confirm in the long passage beginning "Her enemy he was, and she has often, often, often, wished him dead" (55.666). Not only has Lady Dedlock wished Tulkinghorn dead, but she and her daughter are better off with him dead. Miller never asks why the crime was committed or what the arrest and fixing of the blame on Hortense accomplishes. For the "desire" frustrated by the equity court and the calling for the police, *any* murder would serve just as well. As to the "various existential problems" that Hortense throws in the face of the arresting officer, only the first—shooting the man—can be said to be her achievement. The other two are mere taunts, for she has *not* brought disgrace on the Dedlocks. If anything, putting away Tulkinghorn for them has temporarily checked the scandal. Her boasting of the act is merely her angry confession, something which has become pro forma for detective stories ever since.

D. A. Miller's other evidence of the frustration of the detective turn of the novel is Bucket's failure to catch up with Lady Dedlock alive. A refutation of his idea will depend upon my reader's acceptance of the earlier judgment that Dickens, his culture, his heroine, and most readers allow that she is better off dead. If in truth the ostensibly charitable purpose of Inspector Bucket had been successful and he had caught up with the lady in time, that particular phase of the novel's closure would have been weakened, not strengthened. Like the first Miller, this Miller contends that "the novel" wishes to achieve closure but cannot quite do this; it wishes to distinguish itself from the practices that it reproves but cannot quite do that. Is Jarndyce and Jarndyce a very protracted suit, seemingly never to end and finally inconclusive? Just so *Bleak House* is a very long novel and "is driven to admit the *inadequacy* of this closure" (the capture of Hortense and failure to save Lady Dedlock). Obviously, neither Miller regards seriously Summerson's narrative or the plot of the novel as it involves its protagonist. The later Miller merely upstages the earlier; his reading is diachronic and his Foucauldian inspiration makes the system to which the novel is subject more ominous. Notoriously, *Bleak House*—and by extension any long Victorian novel—constitutes "a drill in the rhythms of bourgeois industrial culture."[22] Pity readers of the still longer novels of pre-industrial Europe and China.

The cause of Miller and Miller, like that of Jarndyce and Jarndyce, thrives upon a presumed need for certainty. But whose need? D. A. Miller sums up the position well when he states that every "opposition" that *Bleak House* seeks to establish "is accompanied by the possibility that it may be, or have been, nullified."[23] Notice how guarded and minimal an assertion this is. "Nullified" is a strong word, itself heavily invested in opposition and the law of the excluded middle. Yet when all is said and done, nullification is only a "possibility," and that hedged by the mood of the verb. The oppositions that the novel seeks to establish may or may not be nullified—or latterly, deconstructed. This reading of the novel begins to sound alarmingly like a brief for Jarndyce and Jarndyce. I do not believe that all works of literature (or other texts) turn in upon themselves, or that *Bleak House* is a peculiarly postmodernist work. Its two narratives, and some lesser features, do anticipate modernism. This unexpected and unapologetic division does call attention to itself. Once it has our attention, the question to ask is what happens to the two perspectives thus provided.

What happens is this. After all the formidable buildup of the Court of Chancery, the enveloping fog, stupendous obscurity, and voracious delays told of in the impersonal narrative, Summerson tells us in passing of the day on which Jarndyce and Jarndyce was "over for good." What one voice pronounced with accents of apocalyptic doom dissolves in shallow laughter and sacks of documents—paperwork provided at high cost that is now so much waste. In her very brief account (so much that is more urgent is now being related that there is little space for it), Summerson remarks on the laughter of the lawyers no fewer than six times; the fate of Jarndyce and Jarndyce is thus to be told in a disbelieving moment by the female narrator. Compare the understated triumph of Esther Summerson as narrated also by herself: whereas the suit that seemed to go on forever is finished, the heroine will live happily ever after in form. For Carstone, too, a future is in store, and therefore the chapter is entitled "Beginning the World," with reference to his passing on, its principal subject. Formally, as well, the present-tense narrative has yielded to that with a past and future, Summerson's story.

Number 17 of *Bleak House* is entirely narrated in the third person, yet already the main objects of satire have been left behind. This number is devoted to the activities of Inspector Bucket—checking the lesser blackmailers, arresting Hortense for the murder, preparing to search for Lady Dedlock—and to the last direct information about that lady alive, including the extraordinary advisory on her mental state as if *she* were the murderess (55.665–67). The suspense really picks up in number 18, when the tracking down of her mother is narrated by Summerson, not, as we would expect, by the impersonal narrative through which so many matters are first introduced. Lady Dedlock herself has been chiefly an object of that narrative, as has Bucket. It is not only the last word on Jarndyce and Jarndyce that falls to Summerson's pen; each of the major lines of suspense are now hers to trace, and that is why she can turn off the Chancery business so lightly. At the end of number 17, Bucket "mounts a high tower in his mind" (56.673)—as he might metaphorically see his way in a late novel of Henry James—but the work of this all-seeing detective is narrated in number 18 by two chapters that are both titled "Esther's Narrative." Sandwiched between is a chapter from the other narrative devoted to George's arrival at the Dedlock town house to join his mother and care for Sir Leicester: except for an excursus on rumor (58.690–91), there is scarcely any satiric matter; rather, the tone is elegiac. The last double number of the novel is still largely in Summerson's capable hands—six of the eight chapters in all. The other two are again devoted to George, first on a visit to his brother the ironmaster in the North and finally to Chesney Wold, where all is quiet.

The question of when this novel begins to draw to a close is a study in itself. As I have suggested, a case can be made for a turning or beginning of the end precisely midway through *Bleak House,* with the illness of Esther and the combustion of Krook. The scenes throughout are more carefully sequenced than those of any Victorian multiplot novel I can think of; it is so well crafted that it has an implicit self-awareness like the explicit self-awareness of Fielding's *Tom Jones.* Only the death of Jo competes emotively with Esther's happiness, and that is carefully placed just three-quarters of the way through, in number 15. The murder of Tulkinghorn and arrest of Hortense are put out of the way before the death of Lady Dedlock, which closes the next-to-last number. Esther takes leave of Skimpole and accepts Woodcourt, along with the new Bleak House, before the closing of Jarndyce and Jarndyce kills Carstone. Intervening before "The Close of Esther's Narrative" falls the last chapter on Chesney Wold. Fittingly, this narrative itself has become much subdued and is now impersonal only in form. All the indignation and savage scorn, the prophecies of dire things to come, have gone. One of the satire's principal themes, the delineation of a deadlocked aristocracy, gives over to the reconciliation of George with his mother, the housekeeper, and a chastened Sir Leicester. To be sure, Dickens seems to believe discipline is a good thing: "George makes his military bow. 'As far as that goes, Sir Leicester, I have done my duty under discipline, and it was the least I could do.'" And contrary to what Hortense hoped, the baronet rises superior to the scandal of his wife's old affair: "His noble earnestness, his fidelity, his gallant shielding of her, his generous conquest of his own wrong and his own pride for her sake, are simply honourable, manly, and true" (58.696,698). Dickens seizes the opportunity to remind his readers that such qualities transcend class, though pointedly Sir Leicester and Lady Dedlock have no issue, whereas the housekeeper's sons between them divide the tasks of caring for her at Chesney Wold and caring for the nation in the factories of the North.

Conceivably Dickens might have concluded his satire with an apocalyptic scene as thoroughgoing as that of Pope's *Dunciad*. In the first place, however, he did not construct an allegory such as Pope's fiction but pretended to represent the Court of

Chancery just as it was. Thus he was constrained by the court's real continuing existence and confined his allegory to Krook's extraordinary blowup. Still more pertinent, a catastrophe like that of the *Dunciad* would have made his protagonist's survival irrelevant. Such a catastrophe *would* have rendered the two narratives incompatible. Instead, he eased off the satire, sacrificed only Richard Carstone, and let Summerson's more conventional novel ending have its way. The convention appealed to is too popular—then and now—to dismiss just because it is rather like a fairy tale. The business of getting married and living happily ever after in a Victorian novel, especially, could stand for the proper end of life, as in *David Copperfield*.[24] The convention even holds forth its kernel of positive apocalyptic lore, the promise of a new beginning for a few. The ghost of Richard, in the next world, may well envy those privileged to begin over again in the new Bleak House.

Readers may judge differently as to whether the rewards of this denouement, which is deeply wishful, are finally justified by everything that has gone before. The ascendancy of Summerson's story asks us to place great store in her individual salvation, while the world struggles on as best it can. Wilt finds the egocentricity of the design more satisfying than that of *Copperfield* and even *Great Expectations*—more earned, as it were.

> Since [Esther's] purpose is the full telling of a story larger than herself and her own past to an audience wider than herself and her own present or future, her feats of memory, her insights into other minds, her happy presence at the crucial scenes of so many other lives are more credible than David's or Pip's. For her purpose in the writing is different from theirs. The story that is larger than her own is more

real to her, hence has more body than the larger stories in *David Copperfield* and *Great Expectations* have to their narrators.[25]

It will be evident that I find Esther more self-aggrandizing and even dangerous to her friends. If anything, however, Dickens's strong identification with his protagonist tends to increase his readers' identification with her as well; and since this particular happy ending stands over against the wrongs of the world, a good case can be made for sympathizing with her triumph. *Bleak House,* as Wilt intimates, concerns more issues than the other two novels in autobiographical form. Each of them has something to say about archaic, dubious, or destructive practices of the law, but *Bleak House* speaks also of parliamentary failure, monopoly of public office, uncomprehending inertia, ignorance in high places, hateful philanthropy, illiteracy, infectious disease, unsanitary housing for both the living and the dead, homelessness itself, selfish comportment, absence of earnestness, free-loading dependency, complacency and dandyism, persecution by preaching, manipulation of secrets, harboring of suspicion, grief and madness. So perhaps we should trust to our identification with Esther Summerson, her divorcement from those things, and her survival in a new Bleak House so named as a reminder of where she has been and the things she has seen.

Bleak House is certainly the product of its author's ambition to move beyond "the ignorant Copperfieldian present." The protagonist is a woman and perhaps does possess something of Lady Macbeth's drive to live for the future, as that phrase suggests.[26] Miss Summerson cannot very well marry an angel such as Copperfield's Agnes, appreciative of her writing and pointing upward at the end of life. Yet Dame Trot may have the advantage of Trotwood all the same if she can be her own witch.

It is remarkable how utterly she has vanished when Dickens turns about to write his preface to the book; and I know of no occasion in which he afterward recalls this narrator-protagonist as a stand-in for himself, as he does with Copperfield.[27] Being a woman, and not being associated with real property, she is more nearly mortal than your average male hero of a nineteenth-century British novel. Woman or witch, she presumes to win her readers' love.

On the other hand, this triumph in the super-Copperfieldian mode may have led Dickens to experiment in *Hard Times* with a narrative that is the least egocentric, whether told in the first person or not, since *Pickwick*. The next book is the closest Dickens comes to writing a novel without a hero—nor has it room for any such quixotic character as Mr. Pickwick or "my guardian," John Jarndyce. How *Hard Times* works, or whether it works at all, is something of a puzzle.

8

Dickens in Coketown

To the extent that Dickens's working notes preserve the order and sequence of his thinking about his next novel, the name uppermost in his mind was that of the character Gradgrind. As proposed titles, he began with "Stubborn Things" and "Fact," followed by "Thomas Gradgrind's facts" and "Hard-headed Gradgrind." The character's name then suggested "The Grindstone" and variations, before Dickens hit upon "Hard Times," which he first struck out and then repeated a couple of times in the midst of a dozen more possible titles such as "Prove it!" or "Rust and Dust." The two monosyllables that survive this competition, *Hard Times,* echo *Bleak House* well enough except that they promise history, an account of the times rather than a significant place. In the same working notes, *Bleak House* is very much present as a control for the composition of the shorter novel, the only one to be designed by Dickens himself for the weekly pages of *Household Words.* He uses the measure of the former novel's monthly numbers to estimate the manuscript pages he will need, because he counts on the discipline he has achieved in writing at that pace: "Mem. Write and calculate the story in the old monthly Nos."[1]

Because of the new novel's timeliness, its setting made history of sorts. The scene is not London with an associated countryside but a northern industrial place: "a great town— called Coketown in the present faithful guidebook" (1.3.13).[2] Dickens introduces this name as if he were substituting it for the known name of a recognizable place.[3] At the beginning of his second installment he struck Coketown as "the keynote" of *Hard Times:*

> It was a town of red brick, or of brick that would have been red if the smoke and ashes had allowed it; but as matters stood it was a town of unnatural red and black like the painted face of a savage. It was a town of machinery and tall chimneys, out of which interminable serpents of smoke trailed themselves for ever and ever, and never got uncoiled. It had a black canal in it, and a river that ran purple with ill-smelling dye, and vast piles of building full of windows where there was a rattling and a trembling all day long, and where the piston of the steam-engine worked monotonously up and down like the head of an elephant in a state of melancholy madness. It contained several large streets all very like one another, and many small streets still more like one another, inhabited by people equally like one another, who all went in and out at the same hours, with the same sound upon the same pavements, to do the same work, and to whom every day was the same as yesterday and to-morrow, and every year the counterpart of the last and the next. (1.5.22)

Most often, in literary histories, the real name of this town is said to be Preston, since Dickens was concerned about the Preston strike and lockout at the end of 1853 and traveled there in January in preparation for writing his novel.[4] But in truth Coketown has made history as a generic rather than a disguised place, most notably when the name was borrowed by Lewis Mumford to characterize nineteenth-century industrial cities generally, whether in Europe or America.[5]

Though *Hard Times* commences with Gradgrindian "fact" in the schoolroom and the Gradgrindian home called Stone Lodge—which if it were not rigidly square might have been called Grindstone—there can be little doubt that the keynote assured the novel's fame and notoriety. That Dickens's attack on Coketown was ultimately more aesthetic than moral added to its impact. Ruskin, allowing that "Mr. Bounderby is a dramatic monster . . . and Stephen Blackpool a dramatic perfection," declared this novel the greatest Dickens had written.[6] George Bernard Shaw contrasted the industrial town with Tom-all-Alone's in *Bleak House* and remarked that whereas the slum in London could be and had been "cleared away," such towns were still very much part of the twentieth-century landscape: "Coketown is the whole place," according to Shaw, and "*Hard Times* was written to make you feel uncomfortable."[7] According to Mumford, "In a greater or lesser degree, every city in the Western World was stamped with the archetypal characteristics of Coketown. Industrialism, the main creative force of the nineteenth century, produced the most degraded urban environment the world had yet seen."[8] The unrelieved sameness of Coketown is a disgrace deeper than poverty and even less redeemable than the disharmony of its social classes, which Dickens has little enough idea of how to put right.

Hard Times was championed by F. R. Leavis in 1948 as "a moral fable." Leavis actually followed Shaw quite closely in assessing the novel but without some of Shaw's reservations and with a few absurdities of his own authoritarian style, such as the claim that Flaubert "never wrote anything approaching" Mr. Sleary's philosophy "in subtlety of achieved art." In truth Leavis's essay would never have achieved the prominence it has enjoyed were it not for the bald assertion at the beginning of his book that Dickens could not be admitted to the august company of George Eliot, James, and Conrad because except for *Hard Times,* he had never presented any "challenge to an unusual and sustained seriousness." After such presumption—only a little less than that of Mr. Bounderby in the novel—it was not hard to score with praise of *Hard Times* as "a completely serious work of art," in which a "profoundly serious intention is in control."[9] Leavis never quite says, apart from long quotations from the proprietor of the horse-riding, what the moral of the story is, though he seems to prefer Sleary's wisdom to Stephen Blackpool's conviction that the relations of owners to workers and the conditions of industrial life generally are all a muddle.

Still, it is easy to grasp how *Hard Times* differs from *Bleak House* and other Dickens productions, which Leavis dismissed as sentimental entertainments rather than serious works of art. And the difference is important: for the first time since *Pickwick,* Dickens conceived of a plot that is not importantly driven by wish fulfillment. It is as if the conspicuous selfhood of the Copperfield narrative and the still more modest, no less aggrandizing Summerson narrative, in their close identification with the author, had temporarily exhausted the egocentric design of Dickens's typical plots (or the plots of most British novels of the nineteenth century, similarly devoted to courtship and marriage, if not always as triumphantly as these two). Short as it is, *Hard Times* is also a multiplot novel, and it is not easy to locate the affective center or to name with confidence the protagonist. Thomas Gradgrind might be one choice, in that his action closely involves that of his daughter Louisa as well. Another choice, offset by his working-class status—which tends to bar identification with author or an imagined reader—is Stephen Blackpool. The actions of both are tragic, however, even if the second has been judged bathetic. To these could be added, for satiric accompaniment, the fall of Josiah Bounderby, "the Bully of humility" (1.4.17), and the removal and death of Sissy Jupe's father. One reason *Hard Times* does not succumb to wish fulfillment is that it is, in most of these registers, tragic. By the same token it is "serious": Leavis handily pontificates about the artistry of the novel without pausing to consider what kind of actions it represents.

Some critics have been goaded by Leavis's unguarded praise —or his contention that elsewhere Dickens accomplished little —to point out simplifications and failures of tone in *Hard Times* and, above all, the lack of a coherent program for the improvement of either education or industrial relations. Even earlier, Humphry House had written of the novel's limitations and his personal distaste for it.[10] Raymond Williams also had severe things to say:

> There are no social alternatives to Bounderby and Gradgrind: not the time-serving aristocrat Harthouse; not the decayed gentlewoman Mrs. Sparsit; nowhere, in fact, any active Hero. . . . *Hard Times,* in tone and structure, is the work of a man who has "seen through" society, who has found them all out. The only reservation is for the passive and the suffering, for the meek who shall inherit the earth but not Coketown, not industrial society. This primitive feeling, when joined with the aggressive conviction of having found everyone else out, is the retained position of an adolescent. The innocence shames the adult world, but also essentially rejects it.[11]

For Williams the novel is like a children's book; apparently if it boasted an identifiable hero, it would be less so. Yet still other readers continue to be charmed by the novel's anti-utilitarian sentiments and surrender to it wholeheartedly. Martha Nussbaum's chapters are only the most recent of public attempts to expropriate the lessons of *Hard Times.*[12]

One explanation of this difference of opinion is that the novel is incomplete, that it does not quite stand by itself. We know that as a practical matter, Dickens undertook the work as a means of boosting the sales of *Household Words:* "There is such a fixed idea on the part of my printers and copartners in Household Words, that a story by me . . . would make some unheard-of-effect with it, that I am going to write one."[13] Joseph Butwin has contended that *Hard Times* thereby became a fictionalization of the very sorts of topical issues in which the journal hoped to interest its readers. If the novel seems sketchy or incomplete to later readers, it would have seemed much less so to those who met it surrounded by the usual weekly fare. "The emergent meaning of the fiction is always validated by the constant possibility of fact. The journalist stands behind the novelist, and the power of the press is brought to bear on a novel whose purpose is 'the general improvement of our social condition.'"[14] In her *Companion* to the novel, Margaret Simpson demonstrates that insofar as anonymous contributions to *Household Words* ("Conducted by Charles Dickens") can be said to fill out or supplement the weekly installments of *Hard Times,* they do so amply, for many of these articles are on themes touched upon in the fiction.[15]

Yet this short novel, especially as published in book form in 1854 and available ever since, has still seemed awkward to many, inconsistent or unfinished rather than incomplete in this sense. Thus David Lodge acknowledges that Dickens's rhetoric may be affected by the proximity of the journalism—whether his own articles or articles by those under his direction—but finds the results very mixed all the same. Apropos of Williams's comment that the positions taken in *Hard Times* are not fully adult (and it is a text frequently read in schools), Lodge has acute things to say about its deployment of fairy-tale materials. Not only does Dickens make a case for treating children to fairy tales, but his actors, motifs, and language now appear to shape themselves from such material. He suggests that *Hard Times,* since its actions do not end happily, may be thought of as an ironic fairy tale; but such a "morally-simplified, non-social, and non-historical view of human life and conduct" cannot do what is required of it. In sum, "where Dickens invokes the world of fairy-tale ironically, to dramatize the drabness, greed, spite and injustice which characterize a society dominated by materialism, it is a highly effective rhetorical device; but where he relies on the simplifications of the fairy-tale to suggest means of redemption, we remain unconvinced."[16]

A more strictly rhetorical explanation of why the novel provokes extreme assessments one way or the other is the heavy use of repetition. Dickens seems determined to imitate, in the writing, the very repetitiousness that he finds so inane and stultifying in M'Choakumchild's school or in the lives of Coketown's "hands." Thus in the first paragraph of *Hard Times* an unspecified voice is heard calling on the school children for "Facts" five times over; but in the second paragraph as well, which is of description rather than direct discourse, four sentences in succession begin, "The emphasis was helped by," with changes rung on the prepositional phrase alone. Or in the initial description of Coketown, already cited, the opening clause, "It was a town," recurs three times, and the remaining two sentences begin with the pronoun "It," as if to support the monotony of the elephantine engines and the sameness of everything: the sameness of the streets, the inhabitants, the hours, the pavements, the work, the days, and the years in the redoubtable industrial town.

The repetition is conceived as repellent. Thomas Gradgrind introduces himself over and over again in free indirect style; he insists on the name as he insists to the children on the importance of naming things and getting the facts. The description of Josiah Bounderby in the anonymous narrator's voice is still more repetitious:

> He was a rich man: banker, merchant, manufacturer, and what not. A big, loud man, with a stare, and a metallic laugh. A man made out of a coarse material, which seemed to have been stretched to make so much of him. A man with a great puffed head and forehead, swelled veins in his temples, and such a strained skin to his face that it seemed to hold his eyes open, and lift his eyebrows up. A man with a pervading appearance on him of being inflated like a balloon, and ready to start. A man who could never sufficiently vaunt himself a self-made man. A man who was always proclaiming, through that brassy speaking-trumpet of a voice of his, his old ignorance and his old poverty. A man who was the Bully of humility. (1.4.16–17)

Again, the very metaphor and reach of the description, lively enough in themselves, are reduced to noise by a syntactical stutter and compulsive repetition of "man" (eight times). The prose, in short, strives to outdo Bounderby's own style, which treats listeners as if they were deaf or had never heard him before. He is said, for example, "only to be satisfied by three sonorous repetitions" of his typical boast of how he was knocked about and forced to run away as a child, becoming a mere vagabond (1.4.18). Later Dickens nicely discriminates between his two boastful men by allowing Gradgrind to fall silent while Bounderby repeats himself as loudly as before. Though Gradgrind once emphatically repeated his own name to all who were constrained to listen, now Bounderby is left to speak both names. After Louisa has fled from James Harthouse and taken refuge in her father's home, her husband charges in and opens up in the same old way:

> Now, look you here, Tom Gradgrind. . . . You have said your say; I am going to say mine. I am a Coketown man. I am Josiah Bounderby of Coketown. I know the bricks of this town, and I know the works of this town, and I know the chimneys of this town, and I know the smoke of this town, and I know the Hands of this town. I know 'em all pretty well. They're real. When a man tells me anything about imaginative qualities, I always tell that man, whoever he is, that I know what he means. He means turtle soup and venison, with a gold spoon, and that he wants to set up with a coach and six. That's what your daughter wants. Since you are of opinion that she ought to have what she wants, I recommend you to provide it for her. Because, Tom Gradgrind, she will never have it from me. (3.3.179)

Bounderby's cleverest line, about the turtle soup and the rest, has been repeated in the novel ad nauseam. The point of the repetition, obviously, is that he is inordinately pleased with himself but that his cleverness is severely limited. A novelist or dramatist who gives such prominence to a boring voice thereby risks boring the reader or audience. When Dickens, especially in the early chapters of *Hard Times*, replicates this manner of speaking in his descriptions of character or of Coketown, he redoubles the risk. This, I believe, is another principal reason for the widely varying assessments of his achievement. Some readers love the mockery, never tire of the ruthless imitation of sameness; but others react to it as mere sameness, and then the method defeats itself. The putdown intended by the narrative style becomes as simpleminded as that of the dunces, and in a few places the style has proved contagious even when no putdown or mockery is intended. Thus Louisa, in the late-night interview that represents the height of her unselfish and unrequited love for her brother, addresses young Tom with three successive sentences beginning "You may be certain that" (2.8.142). She purposes, no doubt, the same sort of emphasis as her husband Bounderby employs, but the scene affords no ironic distancing. Tom, needless to say, is unmoved.

Bounderby himself most readers find highly entertaining. The Bully of humility is the boldest hypocrite in Dickens after Pecksniff in *Martin Chuzzlewit,* and both owe something to Molière's Tartuffe—chiefly in putting on an act that is simply not available to more straightforward persons. If Signor Jupe, Sissy's runaway father, is never allowed to perform for us, Coketown's very own clown puts on his act again and again. Of course, Bounderby is not a smooth hypocrite, like the sanctimonious Pecksniff or Tartuffe; he is roughhewn and seemingly without guile. They are on the make, whereas he only wants a cover for having made it as "banker, merchant, manufacturer, and what not." They carefully refine, to their advantage, Christian humility and the lessons of the Sermon on the Mount; he adopts the humility of the self-made man, or the capitalist myth that the poor shall be exalted. Unlike *Bleak House,* this industrial novel undertakes no satire of Christian ministry; instead of religiosity the arena is that of snobbery, more in keeping with the study of that phenomenon in Thackeray's *Book of Snobs.* Beautifully, Dickens pairs Mr. Bounderby with Mrs. Sparsit, two snobs who assiduously flatter and deceive one another. The former affects to have no family and to look up to hers even as he boasts that he keeps a gentlewoman on salary. The relict of Mr. Sparsit, who on his mother's side was "a Powler," etc. (1.7.37), addresses Bounderby as "Sir" and is worth every penny of her pay.

The extraordinary thing is that if one looks for a figure for the author in *Hard Times*—in the absence of any projective design of wish fulfillment—that figure is Bounderby. The resemblance may not be altogether surprising: almost certainly the great Pecksniff also owes something to Dickens's own self-knowledge.[17] Before writing *Martin Chuzzlewit*, Dickens had been accused by a few American newspapers of traveling to the United States to lobby for the cause of international copyright, from which he stood to profit hugely. His novel about the self and selfishness in its many guises, however it came about, produced the smooth hypocrite Pecksniff. In the ten years since that novel, he had countered selfishness with the dream visions of the Christmas books, examined pride in *Dombey and Son*, and above all translated his unforgettable experience as a middle-class child forced to labor in a blacking warehouse in *David Copperfield*. The autobiographical novel, especially, helped put to rest some of the self-questioning that led to it. Certainly, as we have seen, it triggered his ambition to accomplish still greater things, the first of which was *Bleak House;* and though that novel also adopted an egocentric design—deflected upon a female protagonist—both it and *Hard Times* are much more concerned with public issues than was *Copperfield*. In all this deserving success and in the progress of his life and work, Dickens was undeniably the self-made man. Moreover, the effect of writing of his origins and treating the shameful blacking-warehouse time as young Copperfield's excruciating experience below stairs in Murdstone and Grinby's wine business was to publicize, even to boast, of the difficulties that "worked together to make me what I am." Dickens did not need to identify with Bounderby (who would?) in order to exorcise the boast that Bounderby stood for. He understood the satisfaction attainable from hardship and humble beginnings that one has far surpassed. He had personal experience of the complicated—potentially self-contradictory—snobbery of belonging to a certain class while at the same time claiming credit for rising to that class. Bounderby has made a monster of his mother, pretending that she abandoned him, and asserted that his grandmother—who died before he was born—drunkenly neglected him, so that he had to run away. Dickens bitterly blamed his mother for wanting to abandon him to the blacking warehouse when his father was willing to send him back to school: "I never afterwards forgot, I never shall forget, I never can forget, that my mother was warm for my being sent back."[18] Though Dickens had more schooling than the lying Bounderby admits to, he had less than any other novelist of his stature. Moreover, one of Dickens's parents was now dead, and he could reflect on his fictional treatment of them both. Even earlier, he knew that he had not invented the Murdstones (wicked stepparents) or the Micawbers (magnificent travesties) without implicitly telling lies about John and Elizabeth Dickens. He had turned to success the fictitious as well as the real plight of these parents, who loved him in their fashion, even if they never could love him enough.

Another clue suggests why Dickens could do the Bounderby clown so well: the man is fond of the word "vagabond." "Then I became a young vagabond," Bounderby boasts, "and instead of one old woman knocking me about and starving me, everybody of all ages knocked me about and starved me." Quite carried away, he continues about himself in the third person:

> Vagabond, errand-boy, vagabond, labourer, porter, clerk, chief manager, small partner, Josiah Bounderby of Coketown. Those are the antecedents,

and the culmination. Josiah Bounderby of Coketown learnt his letters from the outsides of shops.
. . . Tell Josiah Bounderby of Coketown, of your
district schools and your model schools, and your
training-schools, and your whole kettle-of-fish of
schools; and Josiah Bounderby of Coketown, tells
you plainly, all right, all correct,—he hadn't such
advantages . . . and you may force him to swal-
low boiling fat, but you shall never force him to
suppress the facts of his life. (1.4.18)

That a little vagabond is what Dickens might have become
is told in his autobiographical fragment also, as published by
Forster in the *Life*. It is the last word of a paragraph whose
every sentence begins "I know," as if working up the kind of
emphasis by repetition featured in *Hard Times* and adopted
most loudly by Bounderby.

I know I do not exaggerate, unconsciously and un-
intentionally, the scantiness of my resources and
the difficulties of my life. I know that if a shilling
or so were given me by anyone, I spent it in a dinner or a tea. I know that I worked, from morning to
night, with common men and boys, a shabby child.
I know that I tried, but ineffectually, not to anticipate my money. . . . I know that I have lounged
about the streets, insufficiently and unsatisfactorily
fed. I know that, but for the mercy of God, I might
easily have been, for any care that was taken of me,
a little robber or a little vagabond.[19]

The usual explanation of Dickens's need to write of his early
life in the fragment and in *Copperfield* is that he both blamed his
parents and felt guilty on that account (it would make no sense

to tell a story of which he was simply and utterly ashamed). Because he was proud, he also wished to explain where he had come from to become what he was; as with Bounderby, he could never be forced "to suppress the facts of his life," at least not altogether. The Bounderby who emerges in *Hard Times* is testimony not just to the maturity of Dickens but to his formidable dramatic gift. Since Bounderby is the villain of the melodrama and the dunce of the satire, there is no danger of overt identification with him. Yet the character's energy and outrageousness are telling; introspection of some kind has been turned to laughter.

Also remote from the kind of authorial identification represented by David Copperfield or Esther Summerson is Stephen Blackpool, the martyr of the saint's story in *Hard Times*. Still, however ennobled and dignified he is, this lonely working-class man exhibits some of his author's penchant for feeling sorry for himself. A loose association with Dickens is evident in two respects: Stephen's concern with divorce and his role as spokesman on social issues. Though there is obviously no resemblance between the factory-worker's wretched alcoholic wife and Catherine Dickens, the novelist did nevertheless separate from his wife a few years later and had persuaded himself by then that his marriage was intolerable. His forty-second birthday, 7 February 1854, was celebrated as the writing of *Hard Times* got under way; Stephen is described as forty when the novel begins and is about forty-four when he meets his death. Like Dickens also, he has been married for eighteen years and was married at Eastertime.[20] No intrinsic demand of his role as a spokesman on social issues necessitated that he be trapped in a miserable marriage or come to love the much better woman, Rachel. Pointedly, Stephen's early marriage has been to a woman as unsuitable in temperament as Josiah Bounderby and Louisa Gradgrind are unsuitably matched in age. Comparison of the two marriages in the novel is inescapable. When Stephen initially appeals to Bounderby for help, he is sternly reminded that he married his wife "for better or worse"; but he has read "i' th' papers that great fok . . . are not bonded together for better for worst so fast, but that they can be set free fro' *their* misfortnet marriages, an' marry ower agen" (1.11.59). Much later, when Louisa has run away from Harthouse and Bounderby both, her father attempts to remind the husband of his marriage vow, and the narrator comments, "Mr. Bounderby may have been annoyed by the repetition of his own words to Stephen Blackpool" (3.3.180). Annulment of marriage by Parliament was not a practical alternative for either working-class or middle-class individuals, and Dickens carefully informed himself of the ins and outs of the marriage laws at this time.[21]

"Of the whole Coketown question" (2.2.96), needless to say, Stephen's views are closer to Dickens's than to Bounderby's. In truth Bounderby, when he is not prating of turtle soup, Turkish carpets, and other niceties demanded by the Hands, provides a soundingboard for the position Dickens adopts through Stephen. Just as the protest against the marriage laws takes place with the workingman on his feet before the master, so are Dickens's principal thoughts about industrial differences aired in front of Bounderby. If these thoughts are less than incisive, that is because Dickens carefully avoids taking a position on any of the economic issues, such as what portion of profits in textiles should accrue to the owners and what portion to the workers, or how much surplus ought to be reinvested. Stephen speaks only in general terms, and in a glancing way, of the material conditions of the workers' lives. He gestures mainly toward quality-of-life issues. In reply to Bounderby's question, "What . . . do you people, in a general way, complain of?" (Bounderby impressively folds his arms, but even he doesn't wish to talk in figures or concrete measures), Stephen replies:

'Deed we are in a muddle, Sir. Look round town—
so rich as 'tis—and see the numbers o' people as
has been broughten into bein heer, fur to weave, an'
to card, an' to piece out a livin', aw the same one
way, somehows, twixt their cradles and their graves.
Look how we live, an' wheer we live, an' in what
numbers, an' by what chances, and wi' what sameness; and look how the mills is awlus a goin, and
how they never works us no nigher to onny dis'ant
object—ceptin awlus, Death. (2.5.113)

Every "how," "wheer," and "what" clause, obviously, fails
to render the complaint specific. Stephen's own experience is
not invoked; instead, like Betty Higden's appeal in *Our Mutual
Friend,* his seems to originate in large part from what he has
read in newspapers. The speech continues, "Look how you considers of us, and writes of us, and talks of us, and goes up wi' yor
deputations to Secretaries o' State 'bout us." In the same interview, Stephen rehearses those measures in industrial disputes
that Dickens believes will not work: strong-arming, gloating,
claiming the right exclusively for one side, failing to be kind
and patient, treating people like machines. "Nor yet lettin alone
will never do 't. Let thousands upon thousands alone, aw leading the like lives and aw faw'en into the like muddle, and they
will be as one, and yo will be as another, wi' a black unpass-
able world betwixt yo, just as long or short a time as sitch-like
misery can last" (2.5.113,114). Because Stephen stands outside
the conflict alongside his author, he need not be a representative workingman. He has been summoned to this interview
by Bounderby just because he has been ostracized by his fellow workers; and he is dismissed by Bounderby without his job.
Dickens could hardly be more emphatic about the man being
a loner. Stephen's differences from his fellows are scarcely ar-

ticulated, either by the character or by the narrator: something to do with a promise, which Louisa later guesses to have been a promise to Rachel. That his relations are with women rather than men—with Rachel, Louisa, his unwanted wife, and even Bounderby's mother, as it turns out—confirms his apartness. Dickens is not of the workers either, nor of the owners: he enlists a spokesman who stands apart, distressed by what he feels and seeks to understand.

Readers who can accept Bounderby as a lively caricature still have trouble with Stephen Blackpool, who is also a bit unreal. Yet few readers forget him, either. Dickens insists further on the character's apartness by turning him into a wanted criminal after he is set up by Tom Gradgrind as someone likely to take the rap for his own robbing of Bounderby's bank. The practical motive of Tom "the whelp" is evident, as is the low meanness; yet he is but one of a crowd. Slackbridge and the men of the trade union, Bounderby and the manufacturers also need to find a scapegoat for their own failings; and this scapegoat the novelist will raise up in order to shame all those who have scorned him—and the readers of the novel as well—into reconcilement of their differences. When Stephen is pulled from the abandoned mine shaft, therefore, he has survived long enough to unite the community in the effort to rescue him and to speak one more time with authority.

> I ha' fell into th' pit, my dear, as have cost wi'in the knowledge o' old fok now livin, hundreds and hundreds o' men's lives—fathers, sons, brothers, dear to thousands an' thousands, an' keeping 'em fro' want and hunger. I ha' fell into a pit that ha' been wi' th' Fire-damp crueller than battle. I ha' read on 't in the public petition, as onny one may read, fro' the men that works in pits, in which they ha' pray'n

and pray'n the lawmakers for Christ's sake not to let their work be murder to 'em, but to spare 'em for th' wives and children that they loves as well as gentlefok loves theirs. When it were in work, it killed wi'out need; when 'tis let alone, it kills wi'out need. See how we die an' no need, one way an' another—in a muddle—every day!

Furthermore, "He faintly said it, without any anger against any one. Merely as the truth" (3.6.200). By thus meditating on others' suffering rather than his own, Stephen the martyr earns the privilege of glimpsing the Christmas star before he dies. The language recalls the death of Jo in *Bleak House*—"And dying thus around us every day"—except that this literate workingman calls directly for the amelioration of such conditions—"See how we die an' no need . . . every day."[22]

Stephen, to be sure, speaks more softly than the satirist's warnings of the previous novel. One advantage gained by the divided narrative of *Bleak House* is that Dickens could let loose with one voice while the temperate, supposedly naive voice of Summerson preserved a balance. On the whole, the much shorter *Hard Times* mounts a fiercer, less compromising attack on contemporary Britain. The treatment of Parliament, for example, though brief and glancing, is harsher. In *Bleak House* the accounts of Coodle, Doodle, and their fellows are almost leisurely, suggestive of the parasitism of the monopoly of office. The view of the same institution in *Hard Times* is more contemptuous. Mr. Gradgrind becomes a member of Parliament and is generally away in London in the middle part of the novel. At the time Louisa is summoned to Stone Lodge because of her mother's last illness, "her father was usually sifting and sifting at his parliamentary cinder-heap in London (without being observed to turn up many precious articles among the rubbish), and was still hard at it in the national dust-yard" (2.9.147). If the idea of Parliament as a dust yard, with the members sifting by hand through the ashes and detritus of the nation, requires illustration for today's readers, there is a familiar sketch of a dust yard in Henry Mayhew's *London Labour and the London Poor,* which suggests that it was mainly women who did such sifting.[23] Dickens keeps the figure brief, dismissive, but returns to it again: "Mr. Gradgrind, apprised of his wife's decease, made an expedition from London, and buried her in a business-like manner. He then returned to the national cinder-heap, and resumed his sifting for the odds and ends he wanted, and his throwing of the dust about into the eyes of other people who wanted other odds and ends—in fact resumed his parliamentary duties" (2.11.154).

In general, the parasitism remarked everywhere in *Bleak House* and the system at work in Chancery were not such intractable problems as the conflict arising in the industrial North, for which—Dickens suggests—what goes on in London is little more than an abstraction. Historically, the court was in the process of reform, as was the civil service, whereas the struggles of manufacturers with the trade unions were just getting started. As Robin Gilmour writes, "The social evils of *Hard Times* are no longer the legacy of the past but the creation of the new men of mid-Victorian England—bankers, industrialists, trade unionists, utilitarians."[24] *Hard Times* makes it clear that its author was opposed to collective action: it is not merely the Slackbridges who are the problem, but the danger of many men moving as one and what they will do. Dickens is fair enough to observe that the owners have their own association and are prepared to lock out the workers. He also ridicules some folklore popular with that class in Coketown: "Any capitalist there, who had made sixty thousand pounds out of sixpence, always professed to wonder why the sixty thousand nearest Hands didn't each make sixty thousand pounds out of sixpence, and more or less reproached them every one for not accomplishing the little feat" (2.1.90). Even if *Hard Times* proffers no solution to economic distress other than consideration and patience, it manages to expose foolishness, stubbornness, and blind partisanship.[25]

But mainly the attack upon Coketown is conducted on aesthetic grounds. Dickens and his friend Stephen Blackpool are obsessed with two things: numbers and sameness. It is the multiplier effect implicit in "fact, fact, fact" that threatens and fails to credit individuals. As Stephen exclaims at the last, "thousands upon thousands" of people have pressed into towns like this one, and they are all leading "the like lives" and falling into "the like muddle." The same two factors dominate the "key-note" of the novel. In the rapid growth of Coketown,

> all the public inscriptions in the town were painted alike, in severe characters of black and white. The jail might have been the infirmary, the infirmary might have been the jail, the town-hall might have been either, or both, or anything else, for anything that appeared to the contrary in the graces of their construction. Fact, fact, fact, everywhere in the material aspect of the town; fact, fact, fact, everywhere in the immaterial . . . and what you couldn't state in figures, or show to be purchaseable in the cheapest market and saleable in the dearest, was not, and never should be, world without end, Amen. (1.5.22–23)

Even the echo of the prayer book could be said to make an aesthetic rather than a moral point: the creation of Coketown has been a travesty of the Creation. *Hard Times* is about the appearance—in both senses of the word—of the nineteenth-century industrial city, which manmade creation was fundamental to its time and remains with us. A reaction to the numbers and sameness of people and things in Coketown is not of itself less important than social or economic analysis. This is an environment protested against by other prophets, from Ruskin to Mumford, because it is an environment for which humanity is responsible.

9

Louisa Gradgrind's Role

In the chapter called "Father and Daughter," Thomas Grad-grind begins their appointed interview in his study with the words "Louisa, my dear, you are the subject of a proposal of marriage that has been made to me." That is an odd way of putting the matter, some may think, though formal and true enough. The daughter's waiting, expectant silences leave the father less "collected" than she is, and it takes a few moments before he names the proposer, Mr. Bounderby.

> Silence between them. The deadly statistical clock very hollow. The distant smoke very black and heavy.
>
> "Father," said Louisa, "do you think I love Mr. Bounderby?"
>
> Mr. Gradgrind was extremely discomfited by this unexpected question. "Well, my child," he returned, "I—really—cannot take upon myself to say."
>
> "Father," pursued Louisa in exactly the same voice as before, "do you ask me to love Mr. Bounderby?"
>
> "My dear Louisa, no. No. I ask nothing."
>
> "Father," she still pursued, "does Mr. Bounderby ask me to love him?"
>
> "Really, my dear," said Mr. Gradgrind, "it is difficult to answer your question—"

"Difficult to answer it, Yes or No, father?" (1.15.75–76)

This colloquy, which effectively draws both Louisa's childhood and book 1 of *Hard Times* to an end, becomes one of the most powerful in Dickens. It has been anticipated, to be sure, by the dialogue between little Paul and his father in *Dombey and Son* that began, "Papa! what's money?" and quickly put the older man on the defensive; but that scene was shorter and productive of nervous laughter rather than distress and tragic overtones.[1] This colloquy is like the first scene of *King Lear* with Cordelia asking the questions, and it is fraught with disaster. As Gradgrind is forced to answer or evade his daughter's questions, his speeches become longer and more foolish. In view of his role in the first third of the novel, in fact, they have to be perceived as comic, whereas her words are deadly serious and spoken with ample knowledge of the man in front of her. He suggests that her "expression" may be "misplaced"; and the word "love" is not used again. She asks what he would "advise . . . in its stead." He arrives at "Fact" and thence is properly launched on a review of marriage statistics for England and Wales, India, China, and Tartary, to show that the disparity in age between his daughter and his friend "almost ceases to be disparity, and (virtually) all but disappears," when regarded statistically. It is not his faulty logic but the entirely different register of the two voices that makes the colloquy at once absurd and ominous. Again she asks what she "should substitute for the term I used just now? For the misplaced expression?" Their talk continues, then dies into silence once more before Louisa supplies, figuratively and obliquely, her own precocious answer.

> Removing her eyes from him, she sat so long looking silently towards the town, that he said, at

length: "Are you consulting the chimneys of the Coketown works, Louisa?"

"There seems to be nothing there but languid and monotonous smoke. Yet when the night comes, Fire bursts out, father!" she answered, turning quickly. (1.15.76–78)[2]

Though Gradgrind claims not to "see the application of the remark," much later it will come home to him—as to the reader—when Louisa flees from the languid James Harthouse, the monotony of her married life with Bounderby, and her own feelings to recover and remain in her father's house. Her career is his tragedy, in the sense that the tragic recognition and over-throw of the Gradgrindian system are his. In this first of the two critical scenes between them, the daughter already intu-its emotions that he has neglected or possibly forgotten. She is present in many more scenes of the novel than he and is a far from usual Dickens heroine in two respects. One is the erotic strain, of which the metaphor "Fire bursts out" is only the most obvious indication. The other is that the narrative of *Hard Times* almost never directly gives away her thoughts. So far is Louisa from a conventionally understood heroine— let alone an Esther Summerson—that we glimpse her thoughts from the outside when we are privileged to understand them at all. In this scene, for example, as her father "bent his deep-set eyes upon her in his turn, perhaps he might have seen one wavering moment in her, when she was impelled to throw her-self upon his breast, and give him the pent-up confidences of her heart" (1.15.77). Even here, where Dickens is being more overt than elsewhere, he tells the reader no more than Louisa tells Gradgrind of what these confidences might be. The two respects in which Louisa is unusual as a heroine—the erotic strain and her hiddenness—are more characteristic of fast or loose women in the English novel. Commonly the reader is not privileged to know the thoughts of such prominent and, in part, sexually motivated women as Becky Sharp or Charlotte Stant. The Duessas, not Una, are concealed from view.[3]

Since readers do not immediately identify with Louisa Gradgrind and are forbidden to know her thoughts, her role as heroine depends on moments of suspense like this that excite sympathy and on certain subordinate but parallel actions. The earliest hint of any story development in *Hard Times* is provided by Gradgrind's question—"repeated at intervals" all the way home after he has caught Louisa and Tom peeping at the circus—"What would Mr. Bounderby say?" This topic is negatively charged by Louisa's "intense and searching" look at her father in answer, which he fails to notice (1.3.16). That the charge is erotic is made certain by the end of the short chapter following, which introduces Bounderby in person. While the fifteen- or sixteen-year-old Louisa's face is "ungraciously . . . turned away"—not for the first time, obviously—Mr. Bounderby kisses her cheek. When he is gone, she rubs at the spot with her handkerchief until her brother protests and she replies: "You may cut the piece out with your penknife if you like, Tom. I wouldn't cry!" (1.4.21). To the accompaniment of fact, fact, fact in the schoolroom, Dickens hints at a second form of child abuse and starts up a more anxious anticipation of the plot; nor can Louisa's physical revulsion here be forgotten when she so strangely agrees to marry the man at the end of book 1. A premise of this action is that Louisa is Gradgrind's favorite child, though this premise remains unspoken until the conclusion of the proposal scene:

> Mr. Gradgrind was quite moved by his success.
> . . . "My dear Louisa," said he, "you abundantly repay my care. Kiss me, my dear girl."

So, his daughter kissed him. Detaining her in his embrace, he said, "I may assure you now, my favourite child, that I am made happy by the sound decision at which you have arrived. Mr. Bounderby is a very remarkable man; and what little disparity can be said to exist between you—if any—is more than counterbalanced by the tone your mind has acquired. It has always been my object so to educate you, as that you might, while still in your early youth, be (if I may so express myself) almost any age. Kiss me once more, Louisa. Now, let us go and find your mother." (1.15.79)

With renewed meaning, when Louisa returns to him from Bounderby after her mother has died, Gradgrind uses the expression "my favourite child" twice more (3.1.165; 3.3.178).

The only other action to arouse suspense this early in the novel is the desertion of Sissy Jupe's father, both from his daughter and from Sleary's circus, or horse-riding as it is called. This painful parting, however (we never meet Signor Jupe in person), is clearly subordinate to what is happening in the Gradgrind family and ultimately positive in the parallel it constructs. Again, there is a daughter truer and wiser than her father, whose abdication creates another lopsided Lear situation.[4] That Jupe is a clown would not disqualify him for the role. Shakespeare's Lear is called fool often enough, and in the nineteenth century one grotesque offshoot of his play was Verdi's *Rigoletto*, based immediately on Hugo's *Le Roi s'amuse:* in both, the jester rather than the king or duke is father to the heroine. Catherine Gallagher suggests that the novel holds up a paternalist analogy between the family and society which it then departs from, since Gradgrind's family disintegrates as well as pulls together; also, when father and daughter do unite, they separate themselves from Coketown.[5] That the family model in question is distantly that of *King Lear* may qualify both points. The family bond is fragile, subject to searing misjudgments and selfishness. This family's experience is tragic; neither Shakespeare nor Dickens imagines a recovery from the experience that would permit living in the world in the accustomed family way. Yet Sissy's love for her father and Gradgrind's decision to befriend her (he seems to have no other motive in taking her into his home) are early signs of some redemptive turning. The true affective relations in *Hard Times* are those of two father-daughter pairs and one forbidden, and repressed, love between a man and woman. None of these relations is conceived as happy, though each is definitive for the individuals concerned.

Independent of such actions, the other important lines of suspense concern Stephen Blackpool. The latter's marital problem is introduced in book 1; he becomes a holdout from the trade union and is suspected of the robbery by the end of book 2; and the question of his whereabouts and his death occupy book 3. But his path also crosses with Louisa's in book 2, and upon her initiative. "For the first time in her life Louisa had come into one of the dwellings of the Coketown Hands; for the first time in her life she was face to face with anything like individuality in connexion with them" (2.6.119). That she tracks down Stephen in order to help him, after he has been discharged by Bounderby, is the strongest indication the novel gives of the compassion that survives under her habitual reserve in spite of her upbringing. That her brother Tom comes along and betrays Stephen testifies to the malicious effect of the same upbringing. In Stephen's dwelling place Louisa perceives his love for Rachel, whereas her brother sees an opportunity to cast suspicion on someone other than himself. We come to understand that Louisa also shares this workingman's hatred for a spouse; later she will implicitly be denied divorce, even as he has explicitly been informed that no law can help him.

As the eventual division of *Hard Times* into books shows, the main suspense continues to hang upon Louisa's story. She is married in the last chapter of book 1, and in the first chapter of book 2 James Harthouse comes to Coketown; she eludes Harthouse at the end of book 2, and Sissy persuades him to leave town at the beginning of book 3: all this, while Dickens refrains from narrating Louisa's immediate thoughts.[6] The idea for this complication of the plot—the idea of a would-be seducer—presented itself in the working notes for the novel with the query, "The man who by being utterly sensual and careless, comes to very much the same thing in the end as the Gradgrind school?" and the decision, "Not yet." That man resurfaces in the notes as Harthouse, and the novelist a second time queries himself: "To shew Louisa, how alike in their creeds, her father and Harthouse are?—How the two heartless things come to the same thing in the end? Yes. But almost imperceptibly."[7] Whether *Hard Times* quite achieves this demonstration may be doubted. In the chapters of book 2 devoted to Louisa's fall, Dickens may have intended to draw a connection between the Gradgrind philosophy and that of the amoral seducer who writes "languidly" to his brother about Coketown affairs and has "no energetic wickedness." The idea is that both philosophies omit feeling; yet one would have thought that the Gradgrindian pedagogy was energetic to a fault. The key passage in the novel does not argue imperceptibly, as Dickens hoped, but vaguely, unpersuasively. To be sure, it provides the most sustained account of Louisa Gradgrind's mental set at the time, but conjecturally, not as if the novelist knew her thoughts.

> It was even the worse for her at this pass, that
> in her mind—implanted there before her eminently

practical father began to form it—a struggling disposition to believe in a wider and nobler humanity
than she had ever heard of, constantly strove with
doubts and resentments. With doubts, because the
aspiration had been so laid waste in her youth.
With resentments, because of the wrong that had
been done her, if it were indeed a whisper of the
truth. Upon a nature long accustomed to self-
suppression, thus torn and divided, the Harthouse
philosophy came as a relief and justification. Everything being hollow and worthless, she had missed
nothing and sacrificed nothing. What did it matter,
she had said to her father, when he proposed her
husband. What did it matter, she said still. With a
scornful self-reliance, she asked herself, What did
anything matter—and went on.

Towards what? Step by step, onward and downward, towards some end, yet so gradually, that she
believed herself to remain motionless. (2.7.125–26)

Some of the vagueness is due to the turn away, "Towards
what?" Dickens is more devoted to the suspense of Louisa's
fall than he is to his theory. For the first time we are told of
her belief in "a wider and nobler humanity," but that has been
more finely shown by the previous chapter, which contained her
gesture of goodwill toward Stephen Blackpool. The proposed
argument was not that there is some good in everyone but that
Gradgrind's creed and Harthouse's come to "the same thing."

The argument would seem to depend on two unspoken
premises, not necessarily consistent with each other. The dire
premise—since Louisa is headed "downward"—is that everyone must have sensual propensities. Just as in the previous
chapter the narrator has warned that when "fancies and affec-

tions," and "romance," are absent from the Coketown workers' lives, "Reality will take a wolfish turn" (2.6.123), so when love is absent men and women will run off in all directions: aggression is the social danger, unchecked sexuality the domestic. The other, hopeful premise lies deeper and may be incoherent. If the "heartless" philosophies had hearts (the expression in Dickens's working notes), what then? The notion is that the heart contains moral force and direction, that heart may weigh against sexuality or aggression. So when children are free to enjoy the circus, for example, they are not likely to become overly sensual beings—even though, as Dickens mischievously points out, the women of Sleary's circus are "none of them . . . at all particular in respect of showing their legs" (1.6.32). There may be some truth in this idea, but it is not a truth that the novel examines very closely. Love is often thought to channel and direct sensuality, but why might not love prompt Louisa to run away with Harthouse? "If you ask me whether I have loved him, or do love him, I tell you plainly, father, that it may be so. I don't know!" Those are her words when she has returned to her father's house instead of eloping. Of course, she married without love. Would she have married with love if she had been differently brought up? Refused to marry Bounderby because fancies and affections would have been better developed? "Yet, father, if I had been stone blind; if I had groped my way by my sense of touch, and had been free, while I knew the shapes and surfaces of things, to exercise my fancy somewhat, in regard to them; I should have been a million times wiser, happier, more loving, more contented, more innocent and human in all good respects, than I am with the eyes I have" (2.12.163,162). Notice, in all *good* respects. This is the understood premise of Nussbaum's reading of *Hard Times*.[8] The assumption appears to be that fancy never leads to trouble or to crime but only to moral improvement. Dickens may be outlining a theory of repression in this novel, but if so he would seem to argue that repression is not just psychologically but morally bad for you.

Most often Louisa's thoughts have to be ascertained not from her words but from her face. Harthouse, initially attracted by that face and by her difference in age from her husband, becomes expert in watching her, notices her smile when her brother enters the room, and cultivates "the whelp" in order to gain the sister's confidence. Once the tempter achieves a degree of familiarity, his object's very reserve and apartness emit an erotic charge. The narrator, too, cannot know what "lay hidden in her own closed heart" (2.9.146). What Dickens brilliantly does is to dramatize this potent hiddenness of his heroine by use of Mrs. Sparsit, who also is constrained to watch from outside: "Mrs. Sparsit saw James Harthouse come and go; she heard of him here and there; she saw the changes in the face he had studied; she, too, remarked to a nicety how and when it clouded, how and when it cleared." She watches, in short, with the perspective that a reader also is forced to adopt, except that she is hoping for the worst — "she kept her black eyes wide open, with no touch of pity, with no touch of compunction, all absorbed in interest" (2.10.153). Dickens does not profess to know Mrs. Sparsit's thoughts directly, either; but he construes these thoughts for the reader under the figure of "Mrs. Sparsit's Staircase" (the chapter title). The intensity of her need "must have" acted upon her imagination:

> Now, Mrs. Sparsit was not a poetical woman; but she took an idea in the nature of an allegorical fancy, into her head. Much watching of Louisa, and much consequent observation of her im-penetrable demeanour, which keenly whetted and sharpened Mrs. Sparsit's edge, must have given her as it were a lift, in the way of inspiration. She

> erected in her mind a mighty Staircase, with a dark
> pit of shame and ruin at the bottom; and down
> those stairs, from day to day and hour to hour, she
> saw Louisa coming. (2.10.150–51)

Though the reader does not know Louisa's feelings, and the writer professes not to know them either, the two conspire in the expectation that the spiteful Sparsit will prove wrong. Dickens has early on started a comic development by hinting that the housekeeper is an amorous rival, whose black eyebrows have "contracted" at Bounderby's interest in the young girl (1.7.38). Pointedly, the housekeeper has to move out, to a flat above the bank, when Bounderby marries Louisa; just as pointedly, she is invited back when her "nerves have been acted upon" by the robbery (2.8.139)—a sure sign that, one way or another, husband and wife will be parting. It makes no difference that Mrs. Sparsit is falsely amorous; she knows she has a good thing going in the symbiosis of snobbery she enjoys with Mr. Bounderby. In a discovery scene that might have been scripted by Molière, she officiously collars the old woman Bounderby suspects of being in league with bank robbers, but who is actually his own mother. With the additional disclosure that Bounderby has lied all along about the character of this benign mother, "he could not have looked a Bully more shorn and forlorn, if he had had his ears cropped" (3.5.194). It is a joint comedown, of course, since Sparsit's role in it puts an end to her housekeeping for Josiah Bounderby of Coketown.

The discovery scene for Gradgrind is less happily done, for after the early chapters of the novel he is no longer a clownlike character. Unlike the mixture of comedy and tragic consequence in "Father and Daughter," the chapter in which Louisa's marriage is sealed, the chapter in which she returns to her father at the end of book 2, called "Down" from its position on Sparsit's staircase, falls flat upon foregone conclusions—notwithstanding the thunderstorm that announces it.[9] After bewildering Gradgrind with the news that she has never been happy and it is his fault, Louisa states that she has come to him "with another object" and outlines, without naming Harthouse, her current predicament. And in sum, "All that I know is, your philosophy and your teaching will not save me. Now, father, you have brought me to this. Save me by some other means!" (2.12.162,163). It is not immediately clear what other means she could have in mind. As for being received at Stone Lodge and thus physically separated from both her husband and her lover—this much she has achieved already. Remotely, "other means" might refer to divorce, like the one Stephen Blackpool asked for: Louisa is now face to face, after all, with her own member of Parliament. But most likely the means is love, a tall order for Gradgrind.

Hard Times provides a parallel to this relationship of father and daughter in Sissy Jupe's mourning for her father—a parallel that is obviously meant to be instructive. In book 1 Louisa is intrigued by Sissy's grieving for her lost father and her longing to hear from him, as if these emotions were touching but strange to Stone Lodge. But then, with a nice psychology, Dickens has his heroine sense the "wonder" and "pity," "sorrow" and "doubt" that Sissy must feel about her decision to marry Bounderby, with the result that "from that moment she was impassive, proud and cold—held Sissy at a distance—changed to her altogether" (1.15.80). This willful turning against her new friend is comprised of shame and resentment, envy and fear. The novelist follows suit and literally holds Sissy at a distance at that point: she is never mentioned in part 2, and the working notes record Dickens two or three times querying whether to bring her in and each time replying to himself "No," twice underlined.[10] At the beginning of book 3 Louisa is still hurt and resentful of Sissy, until she is won over by the child of the circus, and "the once deserted girl shone like a beautiful light upon the darkness of the other" (3.1.168). Sissy is absent from book 2 because the love for which she is the model is inconsistent with what has occurred there; but all the while at Stone Lodge she has effected a great improvement in Louisa's younger sister Jane. At the conclusion of *Hard Times,* unlike Louisa, she will marry and have children, confirming centuries of lore that faithful daughters make good wives and mothers. That is, daughters of their fathers: there is no Mrs. Jupe, and Dickens treats Mrs. Gradgrind as a joke, even in her death.

The elopement stopping short of adultery in *Hard Times* recalls the flight of Edith Dombey in *Dombey and Son.* The second Mrs. Dombey shows up in Dijon with the double purpose of ending her marriage and denouncing her would-be lover Carker. In each instance Dickens hedges on the sexual relationship, by effectively cuckolding the pompous husband but saving the wife from a conventionally irrevocable fall. But Mrs. Dombey is older than Mrs. Bounderby, far more experienced and proud. She has been married before, has married this time for money, and is shadowed by her look-alike, the prostitute Alice Marwood. In the absence of desire or a need for income, her relationship with the catlike Carker is finally unpersuasive. Like Louisa's, Edith's thought processes are concealed from the reader, while both faintly contemptuously marry as their families bid them. The catastrophe of the Bounderby marriage, however, is more moving because of Louisa's own evident bewilderment, and more convincing because of the underlying eroticism of her flight. Or it may be that the bored yet "amused and interested" James Harthouse (2.7.126) is a more likely catalyst than James Carker. Louisa also has the daughter's part to play, so that her role resembles that of Florence Dombey as well as Edith's. Again, though we know less about Louisa than about Florence, she may seem a more rounded character simply because she is more sexed and less good. In *Dombey and Son,* the unspoken evil is prostitution: the handsome Edith is prostituting herself in her second marriage to a wealthy man; the neglected daughter is exposed to prostitution when she is kidnapped by Alice Marwood's mother and when she is thrust a second time into the streets by her own father. In *Hard Times,* the evil is thwarted feeling and, by implication, thwarted desire.

Dickens makes it just possible that Louisa prostitutes herself —to Bounderby or to Harthouse—on account of her brother Tom. Louisa does not act for profit or under duress, but she has acceded to her father's teaching that love and other feelings should not enter into rational choice. Harthouse and Bounderby too—implicitly—recognize her affective ties to her brother and move to exploit them. Moreover, Tom urges her to marry Bounderby for his sake and subsequently contributes to her fall by bragging to Harthouse of his motives. In both events Louisa's attractiveness is an issue (though it is never remarked on by Bounderby), and her brother plays the pimp: certainly he should be thought of as prostituting his sister. Still more evidently, Louisa's love for her brother is unrequited. Not only does he continue in his selfish way, reckless of her interest, but he turns upon her at their final parting. "After all your love! . . . Pretty love that! You have regularly given me up. You never cared for me" (3.7.210). The facts, of course, are exactly the opposite: *Hard Times* is full of such flat-out ironies.

Dickens does seem to associate the unqualified devotion of a sister to her brother with incautious passion as well as generosity. He will tell a similar story of Lizzie Hexam and her brother Charley in *Our Mutual Friend.* Lizzie even stares into the fire and reads the pictures there as Louisa does, and Charley couldn't care less. Lizzie too flees from her seducer—and unmistakably falls in love with him. (Again the predator is languid and of a higher class.) In Bradley Headstone, at the same time, she contemplates a monster husband whom her brother expects her, for his own interest, to marry. How sisters and brothers can be so morally opposite to one another is another question, like the problem of the male siblings John and James Carker; but such differences are a given in Dickens's novel-making, as they are in fairy tales and in Calvinist tales of the elect.[11]

It has been argued that the Gradgrindian education is so unnatural that Dickens imagines it producing a perverted incestuous love in Louisa, though not in Tom. The unnaturalness of their childhood is certainly part of Dickens's point. Louisa herself wonders whether she has not pitied in her brother her own sad case: "Tom had been the subject of all the little tenderness of my life; perhaps he became so because I knew so well how to pity him" (2.12.162). But the scene that one critic cites as possibly revelatory of incestuous passion is far more pointedly homiletic.[12] When news comes of the robbery at the bank, Louisa is able to figure out that her brother is the criminal (the thought is never stated, but she later wordlessly shares it with Sissy). Having guessed this much, she puts on a robe and goes to him in the night, in the room that is kept for him at Bounderby's new country house.

> "My dear brother": she laid her head down on his pillow, and her hair flowed over him as if she would hide him from every one but herself: "is there nothing that you have to tell me? Is there nothing you can tell me if you will? You can tell me nothing that will change me. O Tom, tell me the truth!"
>
> "I don't know what you mean, Loo!"
>
> "As you lie here alone, my dear, in the melancholy night, so you must lie somewhere one night,

when even I, if I am living then, shall have left you. As I am here beside you, barefoot, unclothed, undistinguishable in darkness, so must I lie through all the night of my decay, until I am dust. In the name of that time, Tom, tell me the truth now!" (2.8.142)

This is indeed the climax of their relationship, and when Tom does not confide in his sister, he affirms their difference and, in effect, refuses his salvation along with her love. The scene may seem sexy, but it is truly fraught with death. That is why Dickens and Louisa emphasize the body: unselfish as always with her brother, she hints at his inevitable death and far more gravely stresses her own. Clothed or unclothed as she may be for sleep, she metaphorically gestures to her graveclothes. She would conceal her brother from others but with the idea that if he will confess to her, as to a priest, he may yet be penitent. The whole scene seems strained to us because of the Victorian homily on death; the scene's religion is so nonsectarian that it addresses but one incontrovertible fact—scarcely a matter of faith—that each of us must die. Death, just death, is the most powerful sanction Louisa can think of. If only Tom can return her trust, it will ease him. In the name of death, she urges, "tell me the truth now!" Dickens appeals to the same sanction when he generalizes the case to include himself and his readers in the closing words of *Hard Times:* "Dear reader! It rests with you and me, whether, in our two fields of action, similar things [similar to the lessons Louisa has learned and put into practice] shall be or not. Let them be! We shall sit with lighter bosoms on the hearth, to see the ashes of our fires turn grey and cold" (3.9.219). Most of us do not have hearthfires to gaze into any more, but the metaphorical meaning of these fires abides: let us repent and turn our acts to good before we die.

Louisa is not a Victorian angel like Florence Dombey or Agnes Copperfield; her passion and her loveless marriage tend to disqualify her. She is angel—neglected angel—to an unworthy brother only. Dickens informs us that she never remarries after Bounderby's death five years later, but she wins the love of Sissy's children and others, as well as learning to help the working people of Coketown. She cannot even be the Cordelia figure that Florence is for her broken father, because Gradgrind's tragedy is purely domestic. His daughter's plight has taught him that he was wrong to try to inculcate fact without feeling; his son's crime has, presumably, proved him wrong twice over. But *Hard Times* is another novel that, like *Bleak House*, explores the possibility of marriage by a young woman to a man old enough to be her father—this time negatively. Louisa's story begins with a shudder at the attentions of Bounderby, who is then three times her age. She doesn't shudder because she is in love with her younger brother Tom. Her life is oppressed and dominated by her father Tom, and well before she is old enough to marry she understands that Thomas Gradgrind has determined that she shall marry his friend Josiah Bounderby. The proposal scene—or Lear-like disposal scene—is conducted by her father on his friend's behalf. If there is an atmosphere of incest, it is of the overweening sort that bridges generations, both flattering and threatening to the young. Fortunately, it becomes quickly apparent to the reader that Gradgrind is not nearly as awful as Bounderby. The man is mostly confused, as well he might be, occupied by so many facts. Once Louisa has returned to him and blamed him outright, demanding that he admit his error, she can begin to return his love; and the reader can get along with him too. Gradgrind becomes remotely like John Jarndyce, though a far less cautious Jarndyce, who has rashly embraced facts and acted on a mistaken estimate of his friend Bounderby.

Dickens, too, is perhaps a little confused, in the sense that he still has not worked out "this one disparity" of age, with which he mocks Gradgrind and Bounderby (1.15.77). But he will work it out, with deep seriousness, in his next novel, *Little Dorrit*. There his hero is not strictly old enough to be the father of his "child," Amy Dorrit, since she is older than her small stature admits. Despite the achievement of *Hard Times* in doing without the egocentric design of Dickens's past novels, *Little Dorrit* once more fulfills wishes its protagonist scarcely acknowledges. What can be done for a forty-year-old hero who announces at the start that he has no will? Virtually the first thing Arthur Clennam has to say about himself or anything else is, "I have no will. . . . next to none that I can put into action. . . . Will, purpose, hope? All those lights were extinguished before I could sound the words."[13] His severe puritan upbringing is reminiscent of Esther Summerson's but uncannily, too, of Louisa Gradgrind's. "Fifteen or sixteen" when she enters the novel, one of the first things Louisa has to say is, "I was tired, father. I have been tired a long time" (1.3.15,16).

Little Dorrit is very much another father-and-daughter story as well. In William Dorrit, Dickens would create perhaps the most astonishing, if grotesque, Shakespearean figure of the nineteenth century, a King Lear of the Marshalsea. Then his protagonist would study closely the daughter in her Cordelia role and occupy the very space her father held in the debtor's prison, before realizing his love and hers. The example of Louisa Gradgrind for this larger achievement was not inconsiderable. Amy Dorrit may be the one Dickens heroine who is a convincingly passionate woman as well as an angel in the house, and the house is the Marshalsea prison.

10

The Novel and the Circus

When the novelist addresses his readers directly at the close of *Hard Times,* he purposefully distinguishes between "our two fields of action" (3.9.219). He cannot know which walk of life each reader occupies, but he intends that his own path—writing novels—should be regarded as a field of action like any other. He has gone to considerable lengths to celebrate his kind of work and its moral value, as represented by the horse-riding or traveling circus of the novel: an activity without much ostensible value other than entertainment. Although for industrial conflict Dickens and his spokesman Stephen Blackpool do not have a solution other than kindness and forbearance, the novel is rather more assertive about entertainment—and entertainment, variety, imagination may at least alleviate factory work and the conditions it brings with it.

The regard for imagination in *Bleak House* is very different. In that novel, the only spokesman for an aesthetic view of life and its enjoyment is the disarming Harold Skimpole. And Skimpole is undoubtedly the most eloquent and dangerous parasite to be exposed by the satire, since he skillfully plays to the charitable John Jarndyce. His Drone philosophy is immediately suspect in the eyes of Esther Summerson, who thereafter seldom misses a chance of quietly rebuking it. All Dame Trot's earnestness is lacking in *Hard Times* or else has been studiously redirected toward the need to let up. The medium of relief from all that Coketown signifies is Sleary's horse-riding, temporarily sited on the outskirts of the place; and the principle of relief is first stated by Sleary himself to Gradgrind: "People

mutht be amuthed, Thquire, thomehow. . . . They can't be alwayth a working, nor yet they can't be alwayth a learning."
Because the speaker is offering to "lay down the philothophy
of the thubject," this sentiment forthwith becomes "the Sleary
philosophy" (1.6.36). Thus Gradgrind's philosophy is directly
opposed by Sleary's, and Gradgrind's eventual fall and necessary recourse to the horse-riding to save young Tom from the
punishment he so richly deserves leave no question as to which
philosophy is superior.

Yet Dickens's novel is more puzzling than this ideologi-
cal opposition by itself implies. With its lack of an obvious
protagonist, shifting rhetoric and characterization, mixture of
hamming and pathos, childishness even, it may be thought of
as a kind of show, combining deliberate satire with improvi-
sation: thus Sleary's horse-riding is a circus within a circus.
In a second essay on *Hard Times,* Lodge compares its actions
to those of pantomime, a popular entertainment with which
Dickens was certainly familiar.[1] This perception, for one thing,
seems to make Lodge easier about the unevenness of the novel's
responses to social questions; and I would like to follow his
lead by thinking of it as a set of performances such as might be
managed by Sleary himself. The cast of characters and obvious-
ness of the jokes, the openness of the sentiments and satire to
different levels of interpretation, the attention to children as
well as adults, all remind one of a circus.

Children are of immediate interest in *Hard Times,* in the
schoolroom scenes and the initial encounter with the horse-
riding. Then Dickens has the tactlessness to pose in the same
chapters—in a rhetorical question, to be sure—an "analogy between the case of the Coketown population and the case of the
little Gradgrinds" (1.5.24). Childishness is distinctly a feature
not only of the would-be audience of the horse-riding but of
those who perform for it:

They all assumed to be mighty rakish and knowing, they were not very tidy in their private dresses, they were not at all orderly in their domestic arrangements, and the combined literature of the whole company would have produced but a poor letter on any subject. Yet there was a remarkable gentleness and childishness about these people, a special inaptitude for any kind of sharp practice, and an untiring readiness to help and pity one another, deserving often of as much respect, and always of as much generous construction, as the every-day virtues of any class of people in the world. (1.6.32)

Dickens is not disposed to laugh at Sleary's people any more than he is at the Coketown operatives, but he is prepared to laugh, and to invite us to laugh with him, at their supposed betters.

It is true that *Hard Times,* as a title, revisits the grim connotations of *Bleak House* and adds a sense of history, of urgency to these times. But there must be more to it than that. "Times" can mean episodes, adventures good and bad, anecdotal in the telling. The title, for example, might translate as hard knocks, adventures of a certain kind. Compare Charlie Chaplin's *Modern Times* (1936), a film that also has serious purposes but consists of comic fare; it may even borrow from the times of Dickens's novel. The film features industrial strife and the hardship of the workers. Management is personified by a single frightening figure, his giant image on a screen barking orders, much as management in the novel tends to be represented by a single comic figure, Bounderby. Like Stephen Blackpool, Chaplin is posed between the torturous system and the striking workers, with neither of which he is comfortable. Like Stephen, he is accused of crime, though he quickly adapts to his jail cell and later longs to return there as a refuge from the factory; he is the very abstract of hopeless but courageous love. Industrial accidents, the theme of Stephen's dying speech, are the principal stage for the physical clowning in *Modern Times,* which is nervously played out amid the grinding of huge gears and the shorting of electrical currents.

The only official clown in *Hard Times,* Signor Jupe, never appears in person but is only spoken of by his daughter and Sleary. But it is as if Jupe's absence had to be compensated for by amateurs. There are as many as six other clowns in the novel, all unconscious of their roles. Josiah Bounderby is clearly the greatest of them, along with his sycophant Mrs. Sparsit, either one of whom might be played by Molière himself. Those two obviously play a certain part, but their clowning exceeds their own awareness of it, and they are the funniest characters in the book. Of the same sort are Slackbridge and Harthouse, who are far less successful but are still brought on as absurd as well as wicked. One reason Slackbridge is such a poor show for Dickens is that no comedown is provided for him. He exhibits the fake sonorities of a Chadband, but nothing happens. Since these characters are clownish enough to be laughed at, they ought to experience a comedown, and perhaps even Harthouse's disappointment is treated too seriously.

Dickens does something quite fine with Thomas Gradgrind. A clown as tragic hero, Gradgrind not only comes down a long way but knows it. Sissy Jupe's embarrassed confession —"Father's a . . . a clown" (1.9.49)—should hint the truth to Louisa about her own father, who begins the novel very much like his friend Bounderby. Facts, Facts, Facts, Facts; the voice turns out to be that of Thomas Gradgrind, the name also repeated. To repeat lessons over and over in school implies that someone is stupid, but who? Pupils or master? The smart student concludes that it must be the master. Gradgrind thus begins as something of an automaton; surely he comes across at first as absurd, later as tragically mistaken. (Simpson locates two possible fictional models for the character in Bulwer-Lytton's *England and the English* of 1833, Samuel Square and Mr. Bluff. Both, of course, were already caricatures.)[2] By the end of book 1 of the novel, Gradgrind's silent daughter seems the wiser of the two; her return to Stone Lodge at the end of book 2 seals her father's education. Gradgrind thereafter is a changed man, but we are not allowed to forget his humiliation or his initial character. At the end of book 3, having resorted to the horse-riding to save his son, Tom, "Mr. Gradgrind sat down forlorn, on the Clown's performing chair in the middle of the ring" (3.7.208).

Sadness and defeat are scarcely unknown to clowns like Jupe, whose performing chair this presumably once was, or to Charlie Chaplin, Buster Keaton, and others whose film appearances made them famous clowns of the twentieth century. Dickens expects us to be moved by Gradgrind's comedown as we are not moved by Bounderby's, or by Gradgrind's either at first. The attraction of a clown like Bounderby is even more secret—something like envy of his stop-at-nothing invention of himself, which is held in check by higher-minded contempt for him and satisfaction at his downfall. Yet shared embarrassment is a factor in the sympathy extended to most circus clowns. Their very dress—showy, ragged, tramplike, ill-fitting, or wrong-sexed but always out of style and in the way—is an embarrassment. The circus appeals only because it both is and assuredly is not our world, and the horse-riding of *Hard Times* has to be understood in this double fashion. Dickens promotes the horse-riding and Sleary philosophy to the detriment of Gradgrindism, yet the punishment laid in store for Gradgrind is to have to sit forlorn in the clown's chair while he awaits help to save his son from the law.

A circus is still a circus: it can never be more than tolerated because it thrives, in its clowning and some of its other acts, on our worst fears. That the horse-riding remains alien and apart is still more evident from the punishment meted out to young Tom in the same scene. He is no clown—nothing but a nasty whelp—yet here he sits,

> in a preposterous coat, like a beadle's, with cuffs and flaps exaggerated to an unspeakable extent; in an immense waistcoat, knee-breeches, buckled shoes, and a mad cocked hat; with nothing fitting him, and everything of coarse material, moth-eaten and full of holes; with seams in his black face, where fear and heat had started through the greasy composition daubed all over it; anything so grimly, detestably, ridiculously shameful as the whelp in his comic livery . . . (3.7.208)

Thus a circus is both an asset to society, even a necessary entertainment according to Dickens, and a terror to find oneself in. Some members of Sleary's troop must regularly play this servant in blackface; the script in fact calls for two of them. But for the young criminal and his middle-class family the role is an exquisite torture—"grimly, detestably, ridiculously shameful."

At the other extreme from the whelp in *Hard Times* is the man he implicates in the robbery. Nothing of the clown in Stephen Blackpool, one may say, except that his position is most like that of Charlie Chaplin. Stephen is all victim—all martyr, even, since he speaks for the causes he is involved with and only suffers as a result. His downfall is all the way down, into the abandoned mine shaft to his death, the fault most directly of the whelp and those who fail to seal off mine shafts. Though clowns are sometimes almost purely victims, their own weakness must at least be partly responsible. Stephen's role is not played for laughs, just pathos. Yet he does appear weak, possibly effeminate, and somewhat caricatured by the strong northern dialect that he shares with no one in *Hard Times* save Rachel. And without being in a muddle he nevertheless repeatedly professes that "aw's a muddle." In a way his role, including his death, derives from Jo's in *Bleak House*. Stephen's muddle corresponds to Jo's nothink: "I don't know nothink." But whereas the illiterate Jo enjoys his author's implicit trust and occasionally utters an inadvertent witticism, the literate workingman discourses at length as Dickens's representative. The naive point of view so handy for the satirist has been exchanged for a spokesman clearly versed in the problems of Coketown and more. Since Dickens does not possess the answers to these problems, it becomes easier to attribute "aw's a muddle" to the character. In other words, he distances his spokesman from himself by emphasizing the strange tongue, the saintliness of the man, and the pathos of the case. Stephen is not exactly entertaining, but he is so helpless to begin with that his fall is something less than tragic.

Hard Times has clowns for every taste. Sleary himself, the eccentric spokesman for entertainment, is certainly one of them. In Gradgrind's first encounter with the horse-riding, even before he spies the truant Tom and Louisa there, he puts down circus folk as "vagabonds" (1.3.15). But Sleary is no more averse to that term than Bounderby was, since he employs it when parting from Gradgrind in the chapter called "Philosophical," the next-to-last of the novel: "Thquire, thake handth, firtht and latht! Don't be croth with uth poor vagabondth. People mutht be amuthed. They can't be alwayth a learning, nor yet they can't be alwayth a working, they an't made for it. You mutht have uth, Thquire. Do the withe thing and the kind thing too, and make the betht of uth; not the wurtht!" (3.8.215).

Like his author, Sleary appreciates that his field of action is not the same as most people's. Circuses are simply not the same as bread. They supply a different hunger, which is too often repressed in these hard times. Yet the reason for his emphasis—"You mutht have uth, Thquire"—is unclear.[3] "Must" if you hope to be amused? "Must" because unrelieved work and study are explosive ingredients in the social mix? Or "must" because we just will not go away? By means of the lisping, garrulous, brandy-drinking Sleary, Dickens again distances himself from an argument he does not fully know how to pursue.

Like Stephen's, Sleary's language is a nonstandard form of English. The choice of these two characters as spokesmen relies upon a tradition in the British novel that goes back through Scott to Shakespeare: the nonstandard as the demotic style. Thus Dickens also intends to speak through these voices for the people.[4] His proprietorship over both voices is nevertheless unmistakable, because sentiments similar to those of Stephen (on the sameness of lives in Coketown) and Sleary (on all work and no play) were expressed in the statement of purpose that accompanied the inaugural issue of *Household Words* four years earlier:

> To show to all, that in all familiar things, even in those which are repellant on the surface, there is Romance enough, if we will find it out:—to teach the hardest workers at this whirling wheel of toil, that their lot is not necessarily a moody brutal fact, excluded from the sympathies and graces of imagination; to bring the greater and the lesser in degree, together, upon that wide field, and mutually dispose them to a better acquaintance and a kinder understanding—is one main object of our Household Words.[5]

Each of these purposes is voiced anew in *Hard Times*, where their translation into dialect expresses the need to bring together "the greater and the lesser in degree." Sleary's strangeness cannot disguise that he is, like Dickens, a director and producer of shows who can also do his own act.

Another particularly telling voice originates with the horse-riding: that of Sissy Jupe, the daughter of a clown. Yet here Dickens seems less in command. Sleary and Stephen Blackpool speak with their own accents but only, one feels, as carefully coached by the author. Sissy Jupe begins in stunned silence as "Girl number twenty" (1.2.8), tends to employ a simple but antiquated language in giving her own story, and jumps out of voice and character altogether when dressing down James Harthouse in book 3. Actually, only one paragraph of the latter discourse—"Mr. Harthouse . . . the only reparation that remains with you," etc. (3.2.173)—is wholly incredible, for Dickens composes it as if he were writing a letter, with that primness of which he was quite capable when he felt he had the upper hand of his correspondent. Of course, Sissy Jupe is Dickens's creation, but in the part she plays in book 1 she is a more freewheeling and daring creation than either of his two more determinate spokespersons. Her otherwise inexplicable freedom from dialect—like Oliver's or Pip's—may be a sign that her words should be attended to even more carefully. When called upon in the school, she returns parable for parable, and she is later most closely associated in the novel with Louisa. Dickens relies upon the middle-class daughter as a potential holdout against Gradgrindism but endows the true clown's daughter with a voice. (Ironically, Gradgrind pities this second daughter for not getting over her love for that "unnatural vagabond," her father: 1.9.46.) One of the attractive things about *Hard Times* is that two young and otherwise unprivileged women appear to write their own scripts.

We can be sure that Sissy is on Dickens's side because in M'Choakumchild's classroom she proves so unteachable. "After eight weeks of induction into the elements of Political Economy," for example, "she had only yesterday been set right by a prattler three feet high, for returning to the question, 'What is the first principle of this science?' the absurd answer, 'To do unto others as I would that they should do unto me'" (1.9.46)— that is, the Golden Rule recommended by Jesus.[6] Most of what we hear about these school experiences is told by Sissy herself to Louisa, in their newfound intimacy before the latter's engagement to Bounderby. Rosemarie Bodenheimer has shown how important it is for Sissy to tell her story at this juncture of the novel, even though the chapter title, "Sissy's Progress," is ironic with respect to the school of facts.[7] Telling something of her life in the horse-riding and of her relation to her father admits of action over time, for one thing—the dimension that seems left out by the synchrony of names and definitions, the "nothing but Facts, Sir, nothing but Facts" (1.1.7) demanded of the schoolmaster by Gradgrind. Time will sort out the truth from error in the Gradgrindian system; truth, as the proverb has it, is the daughter of time.[8]

On this occasion Sissy speaks to Louisa of her former life but most memorably of another failure in her progress at school, when she is asked about statistics.

> "And I find (Mr. M'Choakumchild said) that in a given time a hundred thousand persons went to sea on long voyages, and only five hundred of them were drowned or burnt to death. What is the percentage? And I said, Miss"; here Sissy fairly sobbed as confessing with extreme contrition to her greatest error; "I said it was nothing."
>
> "Nothing, Sissy?"

"Nothing, Miss—to the relations and friends of the people who were killed. I shall never learn."
(1.9.48)

In that "nothing"—"I said it was nothing"—and the astonished echo, "Nothing, Sissy?" can be heard Cordelia and her father in the opening scene of *King Lear* again. Though Lear wanted nothing but flattery and M'Choakumchild nothing but facts, clearly both want only what they expect to hear, a form of flattery in itself. In each case a young woman's "nothing" quietly, determinedly rejects the predetermined answer demanded of her. The lesson in the novel is intended for the schoolmaster and for Louisa; yet, as often with fine parody, the interchange confers a critical insight into the original. At that anxious moment in Shakespeare's play, after the fulsome words of Goneril and Regan, just for an instant the audience may start with laughter at Cordelia's "Nothing." Lear and the schoolmaster are being told that they are on the wrong track if they genuinely seek the truth.

In this and one or two other ripostes, Sissy Jupe refuses to calculate percentages and creates breathing space for her sympathy with those who suffer, the individuals and families concealed behind statistics. She innocently turns the laugh upon her masters in the school, and she speaks movingly of the show people in the horse-riding, especially her father and his trained dog Merrylegs. At the end of the novel Sleary purposefully narrates to Gradgrind the last act of this dog and its undeniable loyalty. Here at his most philosophical, he draws two inferences: "one, that there ith a love in the world, not all Thelf-interetht after all, but thomething very different; t'other, that it hath a way of ith own of calculating or not calculating, whith thomehow or another ith at leatht ath hard to give a name to, ath the wayth of the dogth ith!" (3.8.215). The point is clear enough: even animals are capable of love, and animals are capable of finding their way without reference to the numbers. They do not go to school—or if they do, the school is a circus or a horse-riding. But Sleary's moral takes some of its force from Sissy's earlier story of Merrylegs and her father, which is also about love, though it begins with anger and despair. After a failed performance, Signor Jupe angrily started to retrain Merrylegs and the dog backed off.

> Everything of father's had gone wrong that night, and he hadn't pleased the public at all. He cried out that the very dog knew he was failing, and had no compassion on him. Then he beat the dog, and I was frightened, and said, "Father, father! Pray don't hurt the creature who is so fond of you! O Heaven forgive you, father, stop!" And he stopped, and the dog was bloody, and father lay down crying on the floor with the dog in his arms, and the dog licked his face. (1.9.49–50)

The story is a parable of the end of the clown's popularity and his very life, of his abandonment of Sissy and her continuing love. It is not less moving because the polysyndeton and short clauses recall the cadences of the Authorized Version of the Bible.

Say what one will about Dickens's sexism in other contexts, in *Hard Times* even the silences of the daughters tell against male superiority. In Sissy Jupe's first appearance in the novel, as girl number twenty, Gradgrind protests that "Sissy is not a name," then disparages her father's association with the horse-riding and insists on categorizing him as "a veterinary surgeon, a farrier, and horsebreaker." Condescendingly, he puts an easy question to her: "Give me your definition of a horse." Dickens gives Sissy's reaction as a sort of stage direction, in parentheses:

"(Sissy Jupe thrown into the greatest alarm by this demand.)" Her silence is Gradgrind's opportunity to pretend more surprise at her ignorance, and to fall back on male intelligence: "Some boy's definition of a horse. Bitzer, yours." And this talented boy's definition has wonderfully become famous:

> "Quadruped. Graminivorous. Forty teeth, namely twenty-four grinders, four eye-teeth, and twelve incisive. Sheds coat in the spring; in marshy countries, sheds hoofs, too. Hoofs hard, but requiring to be shod with iron. Age known by marks in mouth."
> Thus (and much more) Bitzer. (1.2.8–9)

The reader takes the point that Bitzer gets all the credit for knowing, in so many words, what Jupe must know much better by acquaintance, since she has until now lived among horses, their riders and trainers, in Sleary's horse-riding. Gradgrind has tried to set up Jupe, but the ironical presentation of the scene has set up Gradgrind and M'Choakumchild's star pupil: Bitzer's definition comes out as comical, pure fun. Yet this fun is not without its real-life historical basis. Dickens did not pull the definition out of thin air; he renders the definition ludicrous but expects his readers will find it familiar enough. Two authorities on Dickens and education, Philip Collins and K. J. Fielding, have shown that Bitzer's horse closely resembles definitions in teaching manuals of the time.[9] Collins offers in evidence a model lesson from a house journal called *The School and the Teacher* for 1857, on facts about a cat, that bears an uncanny resemblance to Bitzer's definition of a horse; Fielding demonstrates that children really were told about the grinders and other assorted teeth of ruminants. Some measure, therefore, needs to be taken of Dickens's satire in the famous schoolroom scene. Gradgrind's condescension and scorn for the young girl and everything associated with her are entirely uncalled for, and her innocence is far more evident than her ignorance. But the laughter elicited by Bitzer's horse springs from sudden recognition of how strange such words must be when isolated from their usual context and heard by someone of Sissy's experience. There is no more reason to suppose that Dickens condemns all such pedagogical efforts than to suppose that he is against all uses of that great nineteenth-century advance known as statistics. Rather, he is concerned for the abuse of the classroom and the abuse of statistics.[10]

Outwardly, Bitzer wins in the matter of horses; inwardly, Jupe wins. "Now, girl number twenty," Gradgrind can't help chortling, "you know what a horse is" (1.2.9); but the reader judges that she knows more about horses, together and apart, than Bitzer does, even though she never utters a word. Their mutual showdown displays the difference between knowledge by acquaintance (Jupe) and knowledge by description (Bitzer) that Bertrand Russell set forth in an important essay of 1912. Russell believed that acquaintance was primary; there was no such thing as understanding that did not ultimately depend on acquaintance. But the knowledge that comes by acquaintance cannot be conveyed without description.[11] The issues here can be more sharply drawn than the broad differences between the Gradgrind and Sleary philosophies. Dickens's fast and loose satire of the preaching of fact should not be allowed to obscure how close his thinking is to mainline Victorian philosophy, even that of utilitarianism. The moral claim that he makes for his own art, as for the art of the circus, is shared by that philosophy.

Often enough the uppermost moral of *Hard Times*, as fabled in the story of Gradgrind's family and lisped by Sleary (or applied more tenuously to industrial conflict by Stephen Blackpool), has been coupled with the most unforgettable portion of John Stuart Mill's *Autobiography*, published posthumously in 1873, nearly two decades after the novel. Of the principal crisis of his mental life, at age twenty, Mill wrote that "the habit of analysis has a tendency to wear away the feelings." He had been trained as a very young child to "the real connexions between Things, not dependent on our will and feelings; natural laws, by virtue of which, in many cases, one thing is inseparable from another in fact"; yet all this training suddenly failed him. Mill summarizes his conclusions at that time: "Analytic habits . . . are therefore (I thought) favourable to prudence and clear-sightedness, but a perpetual worm at the root both of the passions and of the virtues; and above all, fearfully undermine all desires, and pleasures, which are the effects of association."[12] Mr. Sleary himself could not say it better. And notice how readily Mill locates the pleasures of life and the virtues in the same camp. The recovery of feeling is construed as corrective in both texts; in neither the autobiography nor the novel is it certain why the exercise of feeling tends to the good. The Jupe-Bitzer dividing line, or the difference between knowledge by acquaintance and knowledge by description, is still more central in Mill's philosophy, specifically his logic, as long as one keeps in mind that neither kind of knowledge is adequate in itself.

Not the least circuslike act in *Hard Times* is its travesty of utilitarianism, but utilitarians never considered comprehension of the facts an end in itself. Mill's *A System of Logic Ratiocinative and Inductive* of 1843 (with two further editions published before Dickens's novel appeared in *Household Words*) was probably his single most influential book throughout the remaining decades of the century. The main thrust of the work is toward devising rules for induction, or the means by which science makes sense of the world, but then more aggressively toward the application of induction to the moral sciences, ethics and politics. The foundation built upon by both induction and deduction consists strictly of words—one may think of the emphasis on names and definition in the schoolroom of *Hard Times*. In names and definition, Mill argues at length, lie the real difficulties for clear thinking and communication. "When there is any obscurity, or difficulty," he writes, "it does not lie in the meaning of the proposition, but in the meaning of the names which compose it; in the extremely complicated connotation of many words; the immense multitude and prolonged series of facts which often constitute the phenomenon connoted by a name." (Mill uses "connotation" for the domain of a common noun, "denotation" for that of a proper name.) Accordingly, definition has much to answer for, and "the only adequate definition of a name is, as already remarked, one which declares the facts, and the whole of the facts, which the name involves in its signification."[13]

Recall Gradgrind's "Girl number twenty unable to define a horse! . . . Girl number twenty possessed of no facts in reference to one of the commonest of animals!" (1.2.9). No doubt Gradgrind and M'Choakumchild are possessed of some watered-down versions of Mill's imposing argument, such as might be found in *The School and the Teacher*. But if Mill is right that difficulty or lack of clear thinking is most likely to reside just here, then one can see the reason for the drill. He rehearses some of the same conditions again in the fourth book of *A System of Logic*, after his many pages on induction and before turning to the moral sciences. Here Mill is immediately concerned with scientific nomenclature, such as the classification of Linnaeus, and what he refers to as "Kinds."

> By a kind, it will be remembered, we mean one of those classes which are distinguished from all others not by one or a few definite properties, but by an unknown multitude of them: the combination of properties on which the class is grounded,

being a mere index to an indefinite number of other distinctive attributes. The class horse is a Kind, because the things which agree in possessing the characters by which we recognize a horse, agree in a great number of other properties, as we know, and, it cannot be doubted, in many more than we know.[14]

For the ongoing researches of zoology, even a Bitzer will have his work cut out for him, since the properties of species are not limited to their so-called defining characteristics. "Thus (and much more) Bitzer."

Yet Mill would insist just as firmly as Dickens that Jupe's acquaintance with actual horses is finally more important than Bitzer's graminivorous quadruped. Basic to Mill's entire project are dependable representations of a real world. Though his book has most importantly to do with induction, even the major and minor premises of deductive reasoning have no meaning for him except as they refer to sets of real objects. The bane of science—"one of the most fatal errors ever introduced into the philosophy of Logic"—is the notion "that what is of primary importance to the logician in a proposition, is the relation between two *ideas* corresponding to the subject and predicate," whereas what is truly primary is "the relation between the two *phenomena* which they respectively express." Words, descriptions, propositions are of course indispensable—the media of exchange, so to speak—in all reasoning and therefore of continual concern in *A System of Logic*. Yet words, according to Mill, "are always tending, like coins, to have their inscription worn off by passing from hand to hand; and the only possible mode of reviving it is to be ever stamping it afresh, by living in the habitual contemplation of the phenomena themselves, and not resting in our familiarity with the words that express them."[15] Words and definition, in short, are not the end of inquiry or the equivalent of experience.

Like David Hume's project in the eighteenth century, Mill's is most ambitiously aimed at securing grounds for moral reasoning; and like Hume's argument, Mill's softens as he approaches closer to that goal. It is not at all clear that he succeeds in extending the rules of induction to a naturalistic ethics, as he hopes and intends. The turn that he takes in the final chapter of *A System of Logic*—and for some this must seem a cop-out—is to art, or roughly the same solution to ethical and political dilemmas that Dickens proposes in *Hard Times*. In Mill's last chapter, morality, policy, and aesthetics are conjoined in what he calls "the general Method of Art, as distinguished from Science." For "though the reasonings which connect the end or purpose of every art with its means, belong to the domain of Science, the definition of the end itself belongs exclusively to Art, and forms its peculiar province."[16] This greatest of utilitarians thereby makes art more of a shibboleth than does the novelist, who in respect to Sleary's horse-riding, at least, is content to view it more or less as the entertainment business. Clearly the novelist and the philosopher share a great deal of common ground. Sissy Jupe supposedly shocks the younger children in M'Choakumchild's schoolroom by suggesting that the first principle of political economy is (or ought to be) the Golden Rule. But Mill is not shocked; he may even have been listening, for in the second chapter of *Utilitarianism* (1861), he wrote, "In the golden rule of Jesus of Nazareth, we read the complete spirit of the ethics of utility. To do as you would be done by, and to love your neighbor as yourself, constitute the ideal perfection of utilitarian morality."[17]

However one rates the conclusion of *A System of Logic*, the ending of *Hard Times* is surely a little disappointing. The problem is not the news that Tom Gradgrind will die penitent in

America, with his sister's name on his lips, or the decision not to allow Louisa to remarry and have children—and certainly not the last scene between Bounderby and Sparsit, which occupies most of the chapter—but the paragraphs telling what is in store for Louisa but speaking only obliquely of Sissy:

> Happy Sissy's happy children loving [Louisa]; all children loving her; she, grown learned in childish lore; thinking no innocent and pretty fancy ever to be despised; trying hard to know her humbler fellow-creatures, and to beautify their lives of machinery and reality with those imaginative graces and delights, without which the heart of infancy will wither up, the sturdiest manhood will be morally stark death, and the plainest national prosperity figures can show, will be the Writing on the Wall,—she holding this course as part of no fantastic vow, or bond, or brotherhood, or sisterhood, or pledge, or covenant, or fancy dress, or fancy fair; but simply as a duty to be done,—Did Louisa see these things of herself? These things were to be. (3.9.219)

Four words for Sissy Jupe seems a little thankless after her shrewd dissections of Gradgrindism; and the suppression of her marriage and the father of her happy children too like the lacunae of "The Close of Esther's Narrative" in *Bleak House*—even though the narrative of *Hard Times* is not designed around a self-aggrandizing heroine, as this paragraph shows. The identification of the working class with children that Dickens exposes satirically within the novel here spills out inadvertently again, along with an irritated insistence that whatever Louisa proceeds to do now, it had better not involve any sect, trade union, or fancy theory. Awkwardly, the novel's assumption that feeling and simple pleasures have a positive moral effect—the assumption in respect to passions and virtues apparent in Mill's *Autobiography* as well—comes out bluntly now as "duty to be done." That fostering of morality by imagination, and hence by the professional artist or writer, is nonetheless a central tenet of *Hard Times.*

Some unease or impatience seems to inhabit this novel. Since it is so openly concerned with the business as well as the need for entertainment, one would think that the novel would feel closer to the novelist who made it. For all the overt propaganda on behalf of art, Dickens—so committed to earnestness and the work ethic—remains distrustful, or very cautious about artists. *David Copperfield*, a much longer fiction ostensibly about a novelist, feels closer to the author because of its egocentric design: someone has arranged all the characters' roles, actions, and rewards in a satisfying relation to the hero. But novelist though he is, Copperfield tells us literally nothing about his profession except that he works very hard and that Agnes is wonderfully appreciative of his work. When in *Hard Times* Dickens extols fancy over fact and chooses the circus with its artist-manager to represent the cause, he proceeds to invent Sleary, with his brandy, his rolling and his fixed eye, and his obstinate lisp. In *Bleak House*, remember, Harold Skimpole was all for fancy and not much given to fact. Sleary sometimes asks for a "bethpeak," Skimpole always had his hand out. Sleary believes we cannot do without the circus, Skimpole fancied himself necessary to all his acquaintances. I am not suggesting that the two characters cannot be sharply distinguished, but that if Dickens tried in *Hard Times* to adopt a more positive line on the role of the artist, he was only partially successful. In *Little Dorrit*, the artist Henry Gowan reverts to something closer to the Skimpole type—similarly selfish and parasitic—but far more disagreeable.

Hard Times lacks any such figure of stability and respect as John Jarndyce. If not an artist, after all, Jarndyce is something of a magician, like Prospero.[18] He provides an education for a young girl and admires her himself but then arranges a marriage instead to a young man she admires and creates a new Bleak House for them to live in. If Jarndyce had been an impresario and performer like Wagner's Hans Sachs, he might have handed over Esther to Sleary's circus for marriage to a younger performer of her choice. Wagner seized the advantage of using his own art as propaganda for art in the opera he worked on from 1840 to 1864. Instead of setting up a M'Choakumchild, he staged a singing school for act 1 of *Die Meistersinger* and came out strongly for innovation rather than rote definition. The Bounderby-like match contemplated for Eva by her father Pogner comes to naught, while the music keeps making the case for more music. Dickens's medium tempted him to argument, an argument for which hyperbole and clowning were not wholly to the purpose. Still, he did not choose a medieval setting and he wrote about more than art. He took up the contemporaneous question of industrial relations, adopted his story to an unaccustomed tragic mode, and enjoyed a certain success. Ruskin, Shaw, Mumford, and many nameless readers have concurred that something needed to be done about Coketown; others have heartily agreed that life should not be all work or all study.

For all its clowns, *Hard Times* is darker in some respects than *Bleak House*. The failure of will and direction that is Richard Carstone, saved by death for "the world that sets this right," becomes the criminal case of Tom Gradgrind, whom the reader may care nothing about but about whose family it is possible to care. The well-meaning sexual interest of an older man, saved by his charity and better judgment, becomes Bounderby's marriage to an even younger woman, with all its lovelessness.

Dickens perhaps is afraid to become intellectually engaged with the problems of industrial relations, and the dedication of the book to Thomas Carlyle could hardly guarantee such engagement or resolve the problems. Similarly, though he might have been closer to John Stuart Mill on the relation of art to morality than either of them knew, in the theorizing of both writers the contribution of art remained more of a promise than a demonstration. The wide-ranging satire of the carefully built *Bleak House* cannot finally pretend to solve anything either, but it is deeply satisfying as satire: it makes us confident of what we do not like and what ought not to be, as long as we are reading or listening to it. The increasing authority of Summerson's narrative in any case assures us that anger can be given a rest for now; the griefs of Esther and Jarndyce both have quieted, as if a time of mourning were coming to an end. *Hard Times* is more fun, one might say, but less satisfying.

The shorter novel served as a check on the powerful egocentric designs of *David Copperfield* and *Bleak House*. With respect to inheritance or gain of property, all of Dickens's novels save for *Nicholas Nickleby* (1838-39) conclude modestly.[19] The new Bleak House, one assumes, is not nearly of the scale of the old one. *Little Dorrit* concludes most austerely, without even a hint as to the place Arthur Clennam and Amy Dorrit might live: "They went quietly down into the roaring streets, inseparable and blessed; and as they passed along in sunshine and shade, the noisy and the eager, and the arrogant and the froward and the vain, fretted and chafed, and made their usual uproar."[20] Compared to what wish fulfillment might achieve, after all, Dickens's coziest endings are subdued—equivalent in their way to the theme of renunciation in novels by George Eliot or Henry James. But all satisfactions of the self, from welcome flattery to delightful revenge, can be uncomfortable in the basically Christian ethos of Victorian times; Esther the abandoned child is on safer spiritual grounds than Esther who has won love at last, and won out over others. The novelist most wary of the pitfalls of wish fulfilliment in novels was William Makepeace Thackeray, whose *History of Pendennis* competed month by month with *David Copperfield*. In his finest contribution to nineteenth-century realism, *The Newcomes* (1853–55), Thackeray worked his way around to a happy ending for his younger hero, but after narrating the death of Colonel Newcome he placed the entire matter in the hands of his readers: if in some "Fable-land" wishes came true, well and good. In his great satiric novel *Vanity Fair* (1847–48) he worked out a second marriage for the better of his two heroines but then withdrew belief in it: "Which of us is happy in this world? Which of us has his desire? or, having it, is satisfied?—Come children, let us shut up the box and the puppets, for our play is played out."[21]

The moral at the end of *Hard Times* is addressed to the reader in a different key, but the novel itself is an appropriate epilogue to *Bleak House*. In calling upon himself and his reader to determine what things "shall be or not" (3.9.219), Dickens clearly looks to the future instead of to the past, the completed action of the previous novel. His featuring of children's pleasures and education in the short novel is quite different from Thackeray's admonishment of adults for dreaming and pretending the way children do, for it commits the novelist to future generations and appeals to the reader to share his concern. The reader is not invited to settle back and identify with a satiric voice, whether it be that of Thackeray in *Vanity Fair* or Dickens himself in *Bleak House;* nor can the reader easily identify with a center of desire, as in Summerson's narrative. Our laughter is invited, but identification is constrained by strange accents and worse antics. Clowning does not permit outright identification but rather a mixture of recognition and embarrassment. Above all, the action is openended, the future subject to harm as well as good. So also in the film *Modern Times* nothing is resolved forever. The gracefully hapless and asexual Charlie Chaplin tramps upon the open road, hand in hand with the girl known only as "the waif." Sleary's horse-riding may await the two on the margins of the next town, though not at the center or within any house.

NOTES

1. George H. Ford, *Dickens and His Readers: Aspects of Novel-Criticism since 1836* (Princeton: Princeton University Press, 1955), 100–108; Philip Collins, ed. *Dickens: The Critical Heritage* (London: Routledge, 1971), 11–15. See also Collins's headnotes on the reception of individual novels.

2. Facsimiles may be consulted in *Dickens' Working Notes for His Novels,* ed. Harry Stone (Chicago: University of Chicago Press, 1987), 186–205; a transcription is appended in the Norton Critical Edition of *Bleak House,* ed. George Ford and Sylvère Monod (New York: Norton, 1977), 773–99. As Stone points out (185), this order is not provably the order in which the slips were composed.

3. John Forster, *The Life of Charles Dickens,* 2 vols. (London: Everyman, 1950), 2:114.

4. Steven Marcus, *Dickens: From Pickwick to Dombey* (London: Chatto, 1965).

5. See Alexander Welsh, *From Copyright to Copperfield: The Identity of Dickens* (Cambridge: Harvard University Press, 1987).

6. To Mrs. Gaskell, 31 January 1850, *The Letters of Charles Dickens,* ed. Madeline House, Graham Storey, Kathleen Tillotson, et al. 10 vols. to date. (Oxford: Clarendon Press, 1965–), 6:22. Hereafter cited as *Letters.*

7. To Mrs. [Margaret] Howitt, 22 February 1850, *Letters,* 6:41.

8. To John Forster, [21 October 1850], *Letters,* 6:195; to Miss Burdett Coutts, 23 October 1850, *Letters,* 6:196.

9. To the Hon. Mrs. Richard Watson, 24 September 1850, *Letters,* 6:179.

10. Editors' note, *Letters,* 6:306n.

11. Edward Bulwer-Lytton, *Not So Bad As We Seem,* in *Dramatic Works,* Knebworth Edition, 2 vols. (London: Routledge, 1876), 1:288. Stanley Friedman, "*Bleak House* and Bulwer-Lytton's *Not So Bad As We Seem,*" *Dickens Quarterly* 9 (1992), 25–29, suggests some ways in which the novel may have been influenced by this play.

12. To Miss Burdett Coutts, 9 October 1851, *Letters,* 6:513.

13. To the Hon. Richard Watson, 31 October 1851, *Letters,* 6:532.

14. To the Hon. Spencer Lyttleton, 9 October 1851, *Letters,* 6:514.

15. To Mrs. Charles Dickens, 25 March 1851, *Letters,* 6:333; to Thomas Beard, 31 March 1851, *Letters,* 6:342.

16. Quoted by the editors, *Letters,* 6:333n.

17. To Mrs. Charles Dickens, 4 April 1851, *Letters,* 6:347-48.

18. To the Duke of Devonshire, 15 [April] 1851, *Letters,* 6:354. See also *Letters,* 6:656, 670.

19. To Mrs. Charles Dickens, 20 August and 21 August 1850, *Letters,* 6:152, 153.

20. To F. M. Evans, 17 April 1851, *Letters,* 6:355.

21. "Fiction, Fair and Foul" (1880), in *The Works of John Ruskin,* ed. E. T. Cook and Alexander Wedderburn, 39 vols. (London: Allen, 1903-12), 34:268-72.

22. Robert Newsom, *Dickens on the Romantic Side of Familiar Things: "Bleak House" and the Novel Tradition* (New York: Columbia University Press, 1977), 105-17.

23. "Lying Awake," from *Household Words* 6 (1852), 145-48; and "Night Walks," from *All the Year Round* 3 (1860), 348-52.

24. *The Journal of William Charles Macready, 1832-1851,* ed. J. C. Trewin (1967; rpt. Carbondale: Southern Illinois University Press, 1970), 289-92. For Macready's interpretation of Macbeth, see Alan S. Downer, *The Eminent Tragedian: William Charles Macready* (Cambridge: Harvard University Press, 1966), 318-38.

25. To Mrs. Gaskell [?13-14 March] 1852, *Letters,* 6:625. The allusion is to *Macbeth* 2.3.112.

26. Newsom, *Dickens on the Romantic Side of Familiar Things,* 111. Freud, incidentally, shared the old view that Dickens's later novels were inferior to *Copperfield:* see Ernest Jones, *The Life and Work of Sigmund Freud,* 3 vols. (New York: Basic, 1953), 1:174.

27. Alexander Welsh, *The City of Dickens* (1971; rpt. Cambridge: Harvard University Press, 1986), 107-16; Welsh, *From Copyright to Copperfield,* 165-72.

28. See especially Robert N. Watson, *Shakespeare and the Hazards of Ambition* (Cambridge: Harvard University Press, 1984), 83-141.

29. To Mary Boyle, 7 October 1850, *Letters,* 6:189.

30. *Macbeth,* 1.5.54-58. Quotations from Shakespeare are from *The Riverside Shakespeare,* ed. G. Blakemore Evans (Boston: Houghton Mifflin, 1974).

31. To Count Alfred D'Orsay, 1 October 1850, *Letters,* 6:184.
32. Quotations from the novel are cited parenthetically by chapter and page numbers from *Bleak House,* ed. Ford and Monod (note 2 above).

CHAPTER 2

Esther Summerson, Heroine

1. Forster, *Life of Charles Dickens,* 2:113–14.
2. Some older views are excerpted by Crawford Kilian, "In Defence of Esther Summerson," *Dalhousie Review* 54 (1974), 318–28.
3. Judith Wilt, "Confusion and Consciousness in Dickens's Esther," *Nineteenth-Century Fiction* 32 (1977), 285.
4. Forster, *Life of Charles Dickens,* 2:78.
5. Cf. E. D. H. Johnson, *Charles Dickens: An Introduction to His Novels* (New York: Random House, 1969), 23, 97; Ellen Moers, "*Bleak House:* The Agitating Women," *Dickensian* 69 (1973), 22; and Susan Shatto, *The Companion to "Bleak House"* (London: Unwin Hyman, 1988), 45–46, 47.
6. Robert Newsom, "*Villette* and *Bleak House:* Authorizing Women," *Nineteenth-Century Literature* 46 (1991), 54–81; Jean Frantz Blackall, "A Suggestive Book for Charlotte Brontë?" *Journal of English and Germanic Philology* 76 (1977), 363–83.
7. Martha Rosso, "Dickens and Esther," *Dickensian* 65 (1969), 91–94, makes a brief case for the heroine as an "alter-ego" for Dickens without any reference to Copperfield; see also Shatto, *Companion,* 7–8.
8. Charles Dickens, *David Copperfield,* ed. Nina Burgis (Oxford: Clarendon Press, 1981), 115.
9. Arthur A. Adrian, *Georgina Hogarth and the Dickens Circle* (London: Oxford University Press, 1957), 33–34.
10. Michael Slater, *Dickens and Women* (1983; rpt. London: Dent, 1986), 165–68.
11. Forster, *Life of Charles Dickens,* 1:32.
12. F. R. and Q. D. Leavis, *Dickens the Novelist* (London: Chatto and Windus, 1970), 156.
13. *David Copperfield,* 698. See Welsh, *From Copyright to Copperfield,* 114–15.
14. Cf. *David Copperfield,* 388. I refer to the opening paragraph of number 11, after Steerforth has eloped with Emily in number 10.
15. Newsom, *Dickens on the Romantic Side of Familiar Things,* 114–15.
16. Welsh, *From Copyright to Copperfield,* 48–54.
17. J. Hillis Miller, *Charles Dickens: The World of His Novels* (Cambridge:

Harvard University Press, 1958), 151; Garrett Stewart, *Dickens and the Trials of Imagination* (Cambridge: Harvard University Press, 1974), 136–42.

18. Forster, *Life of Charles Dickens*, 2:179.

19. See William Axton, "The Trouble with Esther," *Modern Language Quarterly* 26 (1965), 545–57; and Alex Zwerdling, "Esther Summerson Rehabilitated," *PMLA* 88 (1973), 429–39.

20. Timothy Peltason, "Esther's Will," *ELH* (1992), 671–91.

21. Northrop Frye, *Anatomy of Criticism* (Princeton: Princeton University Press, 1957), 33–67.

22. Audrey Jaffe, *Vanishing Points: Dickens, Narrative, and the Subject of Omniscience* (Berkeley: University of California Press, 1991), 151. See also 128–49.

CHAPTER 3
Ada Clare, Pride and Beauty

1. See Don Gifford, *"Ulysses" Annotated: Notes to James Joyce's "Ulysses,"* 2d ed. (Berkeley: University of California Press, 1988), 384n. The heroine of *The Lamplighter* (1854) was Gerty Flint.

2. Cf. W. J. Harvey, "Chance and Design in *Bleak House*," in *Dickens and the Twentieth Century*, ed. John Gross and Gabriel Pearson (London: Routledge, 1962), 149: "The curious thing is the feelings aroused by the Esther-Ada relationship seem more intense—and intensely rendered— than those aroused by the Esther-Lady Dedlock encounter."

3. Peltason, "Esther's Will," 683. Peltason pays fine tribute to Dickens's handling of his heroine's psychology, including the projection onto Ada "as a kind of alternative self" (682), though he doesn't pursue the hostility that I find in the unfolding action. His theme might be said to be the heroine's "progress in self-love" (673).

4. Cf. Lawrence Frank, *Charles Dickens and the Romantic Self* (Lincoln: University of Nebraska Press, 1984), 97–123.

5. Michael Steig, *Dickens and Phiz* (Bloomington: Indiana University Press, 1978), 148, points out that Phiz in the second half of the novel also no longer draws Lady Dedlock facing the viewer.

6. See Julian Moynahan, "The Hero's Guilt: The Case of *Great Expectations*," *Essays in Criticism* 10 (Jan. 1960), 60–79.

7. The pun in Woodcourt's name is noted by Taylor Stoehr, *Dickens: The Dreamer's Stance* (Ithaca: Cornell University Press, 1965), 146.

8. See Ford and Monod's textual note, *Bleak House*, 862.

9. William Axton, "Esther's Nicknames: A Study in Relevance," *Dickensian* 62 (1966), 159–60, notes the witchlike character of these names.

10. Lawrence Frank, *Charles Dickens and the Romantic Self*, 121.

CHAPTER 4
Honoria, Lady Dedlock

1. Richard Weisberg, *Poethics: And Other Strategies of Law and Literature* (New York: Columbia University Press, 1992), 67–73; Daniel H. Lowenstein, "The Failure of the Act: Conceptions of the Law in *The Merchant of Venice, Bleak House, Les Misèrables,* and Richard Weisberg's *Poethics,*" *Cardozo Law Review* 15 (1994), 1183–1221. Ross H. Dabney, *Love and Property in the Novels of Dickens* (London: Chatto, 1967), 82–87, writes on Tulkinghorn as a family lawyer. Shatto, *Companion to "Bleak House,"* 6–7, 41–42, nominates Hawthorne's Chillingworth and Jaffrey Pynchon as models for the character.

2. See Annabel Patterson, *Pastoral and Ideology: Virgil to Valéry* (Berkeley: University of California Press, 1987).

3. See Mike Hepworth, *Blackmail: Publicity and Secrecy in Everyday Life* (London: Routledge, 1975).

4. See W. H. D. Winder, "The Development of Blackmail," *Modern Law Review* 5 (1941), 21–50; and for a broader discussion, Alexander Welsh, *George Eliot and Blackmail* (Cambridge: Harvard University Press, 1985).

5. Steig, *Dickens and Phiz*, 152, and plates 99 and 100.

6. Stone, *Dickens' Working Notes for His Novels*, 215; see also J. Hillis Miller, Introduction, *Bleak House* (Harmondsworth: Penguin, 1971), 16–17.

7. John Kucich, *Repression in Victorian Fiction: Charlotte Brontë, George Eliot, and Charles Dickens* (Berkeley: University of California Press, 1987), 261–62.

8. George Orwell, "Raffles and Miss Blandish," *A Collection of Critical Essays* (New York: Anchor, 1954), 142n.

9. Ellen Moers is nonetheless able to include Hortense in the novel's cast of strong women; see *"Bleak House:* The Agitating Women," 21–22.

10. Cf. Stoehr, *Dickens: The Dreamer's Stance*, 165–67; Frank, *Charles Dickens and the Romantic Self*, 109, 118–19; and Susan K. Gillman and Robert L. Patten, "Dickens: Doubles:: Twain: Twins," *Nineteenth-Century Fiction* 39 (1985), 443–44.

11. Newsom, *Dickens on the Romantic Side of Familiar Things*, 88–90.

12. Frank, *Charles Dickens and the Romantic Self*, 114, 120. Robert Garis, *The Dickens Theatre: A Reassesment of the Novels* (Oxford: Clarendon, 1965),

138–41, attributes Lady Dedlock's punishment to her author's lack of moral imagination.

CHAPTER 5

Jarndyce and Skimpole

1. The refrains of an "undisciplined heart" and "unsuitability of mind and purpose" originate in chapter 45 of *David Copperfield*.
2. See Robert Louis Brannan, *Under the Management of Mr. Charles Dickens: His Production of "The Frozen Deep"* (Ithaca: Cornell University Press, 1966).
3. *David Copperfield*, 430.
4. Forster, *Life of Charles Dickens*, 2:197. See also *Letters*, 7:523n.
5. A letter of 1868, when Dostoevsky had begun *The Idiot*, associates his hero with both Don Quixote and Pickwick: *Selected Letters of Fyodor Dostoevsky*, ed. Joseph Frank and David I. Goldstein (New Brunswick, N.J.: Rutgers University Press, 1989), 270.
6. George H. Ford, "Self-Help and the Helpless in *Bleak House*," in *From Jane Austen to Joseph Conrad*, ed. Robert C. Rathburn and Martin Steinman, Jr. (Minneapolis: University of Minnesota Press, 1958), 92–105.
7. Cf. F. R. and Q. D. Leavis, *Dickens the Novelist*, 140–41.
8. Worries about Charley are well documented in the *Letters:* see the index to volumes 6 and 7, and especially To Miss Burdett Coutts, 20 September 1852, 6:763; To Hon. Mrs. Richard Watson, 22 November 1852, 6:808; To Miss Burdett Coutts, 14 January 1854, 7:244–46.
9. Forster, *Life of Charles Dickens*, 2:100–102; and Dickens's "Leigh Hunt: A Remonstrance," *All the Year Round* 2 (1859), 206–08. As for Boythorn, "Mr. Boythorn is (between ourselves) a most exact portrait of Walter Savage Landor": To the Hon. Mrs. Richard Watson, 6 May 1852, *Letters* 6:666. See also Shatto, *Companion to "Bleak House,"* 68–71, 93–94.
10. G. K. Chesterton commented on the crudity of this treatment of Skimpole, who is but "the dark side of Micawber": see his *Charles Dickens* (1906; rpt. New York: Schocken, 1965), 204.
11. Welsh, *City of Dickens*, 86–100; see also Norris Pope, *Dickens and Charity* (New York: Columbia University Press, 1978); and for an overview, David Owen, *English Philanthropy, 1660–1960* (Cambridge: Harvard University Press, 1964).
12. Matthew 20:1–16. Ruskin borrowed a phrase from the Authorized Version for the title of his tract on political economy, *Unto This Last* (1860).

13. For the connectedness associated with the mystery plot of *Bleak House*, see Peter K. Garrett, *The Victorian Multiplot Novel: Studies in Dialogical Form* (New Haven: Yale University Press, 1980), 59–71.

14. Cf. Dickens, "The Begging-Letter Writer," *Household Words* 1 (1850), 169–72.

CHAPTER 6
The Novel's Satire

1. *King Lear*, 3.4.28–36.

2. Ibid., 3.6.104.

3. For the contemporary opinion that Chancery suits brought about the ruin of property, see John Butt and Kathleen Tillotson, *Dickens at Work* (London: Methuen, 1957), 182–87.

4. Henry Mayhew, *London Labour and the London Poor*, 4 vols. (1861–62; rpt. New York: Dover, 1968). Most of Mayhew's essays first appeared in the *Morning Chronicle*.

5. Thomas Carlyle, *Sartor Resartus*, ed. Charles Frederick Harrold (New York: Odyssey, 1937), 272–87. See also James Eli Adams, *Dandies and Desert Saints: Styles of Victorian Masculinity* (Ithaca: Cornell University Press, 1995), esp. 21–25.

6. Thomas Carlyle, *Past and Present*, ed. A. M. D. Hughes (Oxford: Clarendon, 1918), 242–47. For a summary of Carlyle's impact on *Bleak House*, see Michael Goldberg, *Carlyle and Dickens* (Athens: University of Georgia Press, 1972), 59–77.

7. Garrett Stewart links Chadband to Pecksniff in *Dickens and the Trials of Imagination*, 114–36.

8. See above, chapter 1 and note 22.

9. See also Shatto, *Companion to "Bleak House,"* 208.

10. Cf. Moers, "*Bleak House:* The Agitating Women."

11. Shaileen Beyer called the repeated illnesses to my attention. For Ruskin, see above, chapter 1, note 21.

12. John Lucas, *The Melancholy Man: A Study of Dickens's Novels* (Brighton, England: Harvester, 1980), 204, 208.

13. *Little Dorrit*, chap. 2. For this aspect of the novel, see especially Ruth Bernard Yeazell, "Do It or Dorrit," *Novel* 25 (1991), 33–49.

CHAPTER 7

The Novel's Judgment

1. See above, chapter 1, note 12.
2. Wilt, "Confusion and Consciousness in Dickens's Esther" (chapter 2, note 3 above), 295, 285.
3. Ibid., 295–96.
4. For the relation of romance and wish fulfillment, see Frye, *Anatomy of Criticism*, 186.
5. See Butt and Tillotson, *Dickens at Work*, 182–87.
6. The grounds for locating the center of *David Copperfield* between numbers 10 and 11 are the separation of the hero from Steerforth, the courtship of Dora after the loss of Em'ly, and the independence forced upon David by his aunt. For an essay on the symmetry of a novel in weekly installments, see Jerome Meckier, "*Great Expectations:* Symmetry in (Com)motion," *Dickens Quarterly* 15 (1998), 28–49.
7. Shatto, *Companion to "Bleak House,"* 216–18. See also Daniel Hack, "'Sublimation Strange': Allegory and Authority in *Bleak House,*" *ELH* 66 (1999), 132–40.
8. See the textual note by Ford and Monod, eds., *Bleak House*, 851.
9. "He Do the Police in Different Voices," said of Sloppy by his mother in *Our Mutual Friend*, was the original title of *The Waste Land*. See *The Waste Land: A Facsimile and Transcript of the Original Drafts*, ed. Valerie Eliot (New York: Harcourt, 1971).
10. Cf. Alexander Welsh, *Strong Representations: Narrative and Circumstantial Evidence in England* (Baltimore: Johns Hopkins University Press, 1992), esp. chap. 2.
11. See Donald Fanger, *Dostoevsky and Romantic Realism: A Study of Dostoevsky in Relation to Balzac, Dickens, and Gogol* (Cambridge: Harvard University Press, 1965); Donald D. Stone, *The Romantic Impulse in Victorian Fiction* (Cambridge: Harvard University Press, 1980); and George Levine, *The Realistic Imagination: English Fiction from Frankenstein to Lady Chatterly* (Chicago: University of Chicago Press, 1981).
12. J. Hillis Miller, Introduction to *Bleak House* (chapter 4, note 6 above), 33. For an earlier argument that the two narratives are unresolved, see Joseph I. Fraden, "Will and Society in *Bleak House,*" *PMLA* 81 (1966), 95–101.
13. Miller, Introduction, 11.
14. Ibid., 22.

15. "Nobody, Somebody, and Everybody," 30 August 1856, in Charles Dickens, *Collected Papers,* 2 vols. (London: Nonesuch, 1957), 1:659–60.

16. Miller, Introduction, 27.

17. Ibid., 24, 29, 30.

18. D. A. Miller, *The Novel and the Police* (Berkeley: University of California Press, 1988), 67, 84–85n, 98–99n. The essay first appeared in *Representations* 1 (1983), 59–89.

19. Cf. Michel Foucault, *Discipline and Punish,* trans. Alan Sheridan (New York: Pantheon, 1977).

20. D. A. Miller, *Novel and the Police,* 69.

21. Ibid., 96.

22. Ibid., 97, 83.

23. Ibid., 98.

24. See Welsh, *City of Dickens,* 213–28.

25. Wilt, "Confusion and Consciousness in Dickens's Esther," 302–3.

26. See above, chapter 1, note 29.

27. See above, chapter 5, note 4.

CHAPTER 8
Dickens in Coketown

1. Stone, *Dickens' Working Notes for His Novels,* 250–51.

2. Quotations from the novel are cited by book, chapter, and page number from the Norton Critical Edition of *Hard Times,* ed. George Ford and Sylvère Monod, 2nd ed. (New York: Norton, 1990).

3. Cf. Joseph Butwin, "*Hard Times:* The News and the Novel," *Nineteenth-Century Fiction* 32 (1977), 175–77.

4. Forster, *Life of Charles Dickens,* 2:121–22; also, To Miss Burdett Coutts, 23 Nov. 1853, *Letters,* 7:213–14.

5. Lewis Mumford, *The City in History: Its Origins, Its Transformations, and Its Prospects* (New York: Harcourt, 1961), 446–81. In *The Culture of Cities* (New York: Harcourt, 1938), 144–45, Mumford used the name Coketown only in passing, but his chapter title, "The Insensate Industrial Town," reflected Dickens's themes. Since Mumford, it has sometimes been a point of honor among British urban historians to show how each industrial town differed from the others; but again, Dickens meant to generalize.

6. Ruskin, *Unto This Last,* in *Works,* 17:131n.

7. George Bernard Shaw, Introduction, *Hard Times* (London: Waverley, 1912), as reprinted by Ford and Monod, eds., *Hard Times,* 334, 336.

8. Mumford, *City in History*, 447.

9. F. R. Leavis, *The Great Tradition* (1948; rpt. New York: Anchor, 1954), quotations at 273, 295, 32, 273, 294. These opinions were radically revised by F. R. and Q. D. Leavis, *Dickens: The Novelist* (chapter 5, note 7 above).

10. Humphry House, *The Dickens World* (1941; rpt. London: Oxford University Press, 1960), 203–11.

11. Raymond Williams, *Culture and Society, 1780–1950* (1958; rpt. New York: Harper, 1966), 96.

12. Martha C. Nussbaum, *Poetic Justice: The Literary Imagination in Public Life* (Boston: Beacon, 1995), 1–78.

13. To Miss Burdett Coutts, 23 Jan. 1854, *Letters* 7:256. See Robert L. Patten, *Charles Dickens and His Publishers* (Oxford: Clarendon, 1978), 244–46.

14. Butwin, "*Hard Times:* The News and the Novel," 176.

15. Margaret Simpson, *The Companion to "Hard Times"* (Westport Conn.: Greenwood, 1997), 1–11 and Appendix D, 242–44, as well as Simpson's commentary throughout.

16. David Lodge, *Language of Fiction: Essays in Criticism and Verbal Analysis of the English Novel* (1966; rpt. New York: Columbia University Press, 1967), 159–63.

17. See Welsh, *From Copyright to Copperfield*, 16–28.

18. Quoted in Forster, *Life of Charles Dickens*, 1:25.

19. Ibid., 1:25.

20. Simpson, *Companion to "Hard Times,"* 130–31, 142.

21. See John D. Baird, "'Divorce and Matrimonial Causes': An Aspect of *Hard Times*," *Victorian Studies* 20 (1977), 401–12; also Simpson's *Companion to "Hard Times,"* 131–38.

22. In the manuscript of *Hard Times* (at 1.13.70 this edition), Stephen referred to a specific industrial accident, the mutilation of Rachel's younger sister by machinery, but the passage was not published. See Ford and Monod's textual note, 247; Butwin, "*Hard Times:* The News and the Novel," 177–85; and Simpson's *Companion to "Hard Times,"* 143–46.

23. Mayhew, *London Labour and the London Poor*, 2:173.

24. Robin Gilmour, *The Novel in the Victorian Age: A Modern Introduction* (London: Arnold, 1986), 98.

25. For Dickens's views in general, see Patrick Brantlinger, "Dickens and the Factories," *Nineteenth-Century Fiction* 26 (1971), 270–85; and Philip Collins, "Dickens and Industrialism," *Studies in English Literature* 20 (1980), 651–73.

CHAPTER 9
Louisa Gradgrind's Role

1. Charles Dickens, *Dombey and Son*, ed. Alan Horsman (Oxford: Clarendon, 1974), 8.93. Philip Collins, *Dickens and Education* (1963; rpt. London: Macmillan, 1965), 201–02, perceptively compares the dialogue to that between King Lear and the Fool.

2. The entire scene may also be read for the themes delineated by Dabney, *Love and Property in the Novels of Dickens* (chapter 4, note 1, above).

3. See Alexander Welsh, "The Allegory of Truth in English Fiction," *Victorian Studies* 9 (1965), 7–28.

4. Jerome Meckier, "Dickens and *King Lear:* A Myth for Victorian England," *South Atlantic Quarterly* 71 (1972), 89, suggests that there are "two Cordelias" in *Hard Times.*

5. Catherine Gallagher, *The Industrial Reformation of English Fiction: Social Discourse and Narrative Form, 1832–1867* (Chicago: University of Chicago Press, 1985), 149–66.

6. Two very minor exceptions are at 2.8.139 and 3.5.194. The narrator speculates about Louisa's thoughts at 2.7.125.

7. Stone, *Dickens' Working Notes for His Novels*, 252–53, 258–59.

8. See Introduction above, and Nussbaum, *Poetic Justice* (chapter 8, note 12, above).

9. Cf. Lodge, *Language of Fiction*, 163.

10. Stone, *Dickens' Working Notes for His Novels*, 254–59.

11. See Welsh, *City of Dickens*, 125–30.

12. See Daniel P. Deneau, "The Brother-Sister Relationship in *Hard Times*," *Dickensian* 60 (1964), 173–77.

13. Charles Dickens, *Little Dorrit*, ed. John Holloway (Harmondsworth: Penguin, 1967), 59.

CHAPTER 10
The Novel and the Circus

1. David Lodge, *Working with Structuralism: Essays and Reviews on Nineteenth- and Twentieth-Century Literature* (Boston: Routledge, 1981), 37–45.

2. Simpson, *Companion to "Hard Times,"* 33–35.

3. Joseph Butwin, "The Paradox of the Clowns in Dickens," *Dickens Studies Annual* 5 (1976), 131, notes this ambiguity.

4. Roger Fowler, "Polyphony and Problematic in *Hard Times*," in *The*

Changing World of Charles Dickens, ed. Robert Giddings (London: Vision, 1983), 99, shows that Sleary's speech is also working class.

5. [Charles Dickens], "A Preliminary Word," *Household Words* 1 (1850), 1.

6. Matthew 7:12.

7. Rosemarie Bodenheimer, *The Politics of Story in Victorian Social Fiction* (Ithaca: Cornell University Press, 1988), 189–207.

8. The classic essay is by Fritz Saxl, *"Veritas Filia Temporis,"* in *Philosophy and History: Essays Presented to Ernst Cassirer,* ed. Raymond Klibansky and H. J. Paton (Oxford: Clarendon, 1947).

9. Philip Collins, *Dickens and Education* (1963; rpt. London: Macmillan, 1965), 153–59; K. J. Fielding, *"Hard Times* and Common Things," in *Imagined Worlds: Essays on Some English Novels and Novelists in Honour of John Butt,* ed. Maynard Mack and Ian Gregor (London: Methuen, 1968), 182–203. See also John Manning, "Charles Dickens and the Oswego System," *Journal of the History of Ideas* 18 (1957), 580–86.

10. See letter to Charles Knight, 30 [Dec.] 1854, *Letters,* 7:492–93; also Welsh, *City of Dickens,* 16–19.

11. Bertrand Russell, *The Problems of Philosophy* (1912; rpt. New York: Oxford University Press, 1959), 46–59. For the aftermath of this discussion, see Saul Kripke, *Naming and Necessity* (Cambridge: Harvard University Press, 1980).

12. John Stuart Mill, *"Autobiography" and Other Writings,* ed. Jack Stillinger (Boston: Houghton Mifflin, 1969), 83. For *Hard Times* and Mill, see Timothy Peltason, "Imagination and Learning in George Eliot, Mill, and Dickens," *Essays in Criticism* 38 (1988), 49–54.

13. John Stuart Mill, *A System of Logic Ratiocinative and Inductive,* in *The Collected Works of John Stuart Mill,* ed. J. M. Robson et al., vols. 7 and 8 (Toronto: University of Toronto Press, 1974), 99, 136.

14. Ibid., 703–04.

15. Ibid., 89, 711.

16. Ibid., 943, 949.

17. John Stuart Mill, *Utilitarianism,* in *The Philosophy of John Stuart Mill,* ed. Marshall Cohen (New York: Modern Library, 1961), 342. Simpson also alludes to the passage in her *Companion to "Hard Times,"* 118.

18. Cf. David Holbrook, *Charles Dickens and the Image of Women* (New York: New York University Press, 1993), 44.

19. See Dabney, *Love and Property in the Novels of Dickens.*

20. *Little Dorrit,* 895.

21. William Makepeace Thackeray, *Vanity Fair,* ed. Geoffrey Tillotson and Kathleen Tillotson (Boston: Riverside, 1963), 666.

INDEX

Molière, 156, 178
Monod, Sylvère, 213n, 219n
Moynahan, Julian, 214n
Mumford, Lewis, 148–49, 219n

Newsom, Robert, 13–14, 26, 213n, 215n
Nussbaum, Martha C., xii–xiii, 151, 176

Orwell, George, 67
Owen, David, 216n

Patten, Robert L., 215n
Patterson, Annabel, 215n
Peltason, Timothy, 35, 40, 214n, 222n
Pope, Alexander: *The Dunciad,* 143–44

Rosso, Martha, 213n
Ruskin, John, 12–13, 149
Russell, Bertrand, 199

Saxl, Fritz, 222n
Scott, Walter, 77, 193
Shakespeare, William, 77, 193, 212n; *King Lear,* 13, 104–6, 169, 172–73, 185, 196; *Macbeth,* 13–15, 28, 145
Shatto, Susan, 213n, 215n, 216n, 217n, 218n

Shaw, George Bernard, 149
Simpson, Margaret, 152, 190, 220n
Slater, Michael, 23
Steig, Michael, 64, 214n
Stewart, Garrett, 27
Stoehr, Taylor, 214n, 215n
Stone, Donald D., 218n
Stone, Harry, 211n

Thackeray, William Makepeace, 5, 40; *Book of Snobs,* 156; *The Newcomes,* 208; *Pendennis,* 208; *Vanity Fair,* 208
Tillotson, Kathleen, 217n, 218n

Verdi, Giuseppe: *Rigoletto,* 172
Victoria, Queen, 6–7

Wagner, Richard: *Meistersinger,* 206
Watson, Lavinia Jane, 6–7
Watson, Richard, 16
Watson, Robert N., 212n
Weisberg, Richard, 215n
Williams, Raymond, 151–52
Wills, William, 5
Wilt, Judith, 20, 124–26, 144–45
Windsor, W. H. D., 215n

Yeazell, Ruth Bernard, 217n

Zwerdling, Alex, 214n